FOOTBALL
DONE
RIGHT

FOOTBALL DONE RIGHT

SETTING THE RECORD STRAIGHT ON THE COACHES, PLAYERS, AND HISTORY OF THE NFL

Michael Lombardi

RUNNING PRESS
PHILADELPHIA

For Millie, always the heart of the matter.
And for Dominic, Leo, Michael, Dean, and Sienna,
who supply trust and self-assurance with one smile.

Running Press
Hachette Book Group
1290 Avenue of the Americas, New York, NY 10104
www.runningpress.com
@Running_Press

Printed in the United States of America

First Edition: September 2023

Published by Running Press, an imprint of Hachette Book Group, Inc.
The Running Press name and logo are trademarks of Hachette Book Group, Inc.

The Hachette Speakers Bureau provides a wide range of authors
for speaking events. To find out more, go to hachettespeakersbureau.com
or email HachetteSpeakers@hbgusa.com.

Running Press books may be purchased in bulk for business, educational, or
promotional use. For more information, please contact your local bookseller or the
Hachette Book Group Special Markets Department at Special.Markets@hbgusa.com.

The publisher is not responsible for websites (or their content)
that are not owned by the publisher.

Print book cover and interior design by Sara Puppala

Library of Congress Control Number: 2023934517

ISBNs: 978-0-7624-7953-5 (hardcover), 978-0-7624-7954-2 (ebook)

LSC-C

Printing 1, 2023

CONTENTS

Foreword by Jim Nantz . . . . *vii*

Introduction *1*

CHAPTER ONE: The White Oaks. *3*

CHAPTER TWO: Situations Matter 22

CHAPTER THREE: The Lombardi Criteria for Coaches. 34

CHAPTER FOUR: Top Ten Coaches 39

CHAPTER FIVE: Television 57

CHAPTER SIX: The NFL Draft 68

CHAPTER SEVEN: Trades 81

CHAPTER EIGHT: Top 100 Players. 89

Acknowledgments *293*

FOREWORD

BY JIM NANTZ

TRAVEL MAGAZINE ONCE CALLED OCEAN CITY, New Jersey, "America's Greatest Family Beach Town." After reading this book, you'll agree that Ocean City should also be known as the hometown to one of the greatest minds in the NFL. Author Michael Lombardi embodies the American dream as much as anyone I've ever met.

Raised in Ocean City, with its boardwalk and beaches, Michael was the son of the town barber. His dad, Mike, was a friend to many in the seaside community of 11,000; he had time for everyone and they in turn trusted him. His customers were greeted with a warm smile at the Ideal Barber Shop on 8th and Central. There was a quality and consistency to his work and when fashion styles changed, Mr. Lombardi could adapt with the best of them to the trendy "plays" of the day.

All these traits left a mark on young Michael, who stopped by his father's shop after school and watched the kindness with which his father treated everyone. He witnessed the perfect execution and pride his dad put into every cut. When he wasn't serving as the shop's shoe-shine boy, Michael occasionally caught himself dreaming. Dreaming big.

The NFL always had his attention. And though Michael was a decent player— good enough to play college football at Hofstra—he was mesmerized by how the front offices of the NFL operated. You won't find many 14-year-olds who studied the league from the top down, but as a sophomore at Ocean City High School, there was Michael submitting a manifesto about Al Davis, the legendary owner of the Oakland Raiders, detailing how Davis built a winning football culture.

Blessedly for me, this year marks the 25th anniversary of calling Michael Lombardi a friend. He had just left the Eagles, where he served as General Manager, in the spring of 1998. CBS returned to the league and I was named the host of *The NFL Today*. Our producer, Eric Mann, was looking for a behind-the-scenes NFL insider and Michael was perfect for the job. By the end of his first month, all of us on the show realized that Michael had a warmth and personality—just like his dad—meritorious for bringing information to life on the set. Though my career has covered five decades, I've never seen anyone transition from a background information guy to a television star the way Michael Lombardi did overnight. The friendship we formed has never waned.

Though it was a sad loss for CBS when Al Davis came along the next season and brought Michael out west to run the Raiders, it was also one of the best examples of a boyhood dream becoming a reality. As General Manager, Michael built a football team that eventually won the AFC Championship and competed in the Super Bowl.

But Al Davis wasn't the only legend who saw Michael's talents and extended his trust. Michael has been a part of Bill Belichick's inner circle for 30 years, working together in both Cleveland and New England. Marty Schottenheimer and Bill Parcells are also among Michael's friends and mentors. The list is long, wide, and as impressive as any resume you can find.

Football Done Right is the latest example of Michael's skills and talent. It displays his encyclopedic knowledge of the NFL and its history. Michael makes compelling cases for how the Pro Football Hall of Fame should be restructured to honor the true greats, and he has convincing arguments for several deserving candidates that time has overlooked. And he informs us as to how everyone in the league needs to understand that you have to understand the past to excel in the present.

Consider yourself fortunate to be greeted with a warm smile, brilliant execution, and a heavy dose of pride as you turn each riveting page. I trust you will enjoy. This book is the ideal shop for all things NFL.

—Jim Nantz
November, 2022

INTRODUCTION

FORMER RAIDERS OWNER AL DAVIS ONCE told me: "You don't work in the NFL. You live in the NFL." For the past forty years of my professional life, I have lived, breathed, and exhaled the game of football, and I have suffered and occasionally rejoiced, all as a result of fulfilling my childhood dream of working in the NFL. Now is the perfect time for reflection—but not self-reflection. Rather, this is the moment to reflect on the journey the game of professional football has taken over the past one hundred years, from a Friday night in September 1920, when eleven teams united at Ralph Hay's car dealership in Canton, Ohio, to call themselves the American Professional Football Conference, to the present day, when football is indisputably the most popular sport in America. The formation of the NFL saw tremendous struggles; sacrifices had to be made and innovative people were needed to advance the game. *Football Done Right* will examine the many individuals who helped shaped the game we know today, both on and off the field.

Steve Jobs famously said, "You can't connect the dots looking forward; you must connect them looking backwards," and that's exactly what we'll do in this book. The NFL has countless dots, and *Football Done Right* will connect some of them from an insider perspective, providing a front-row seat to some of the greatest coaches and players who have transformed this sport. We'll begin with the five coaches who planted the roots of the game we now watch on Sunday. These men shaped the game with their ingenuity, divergent thought, and willingness to change the status quo. Each provided a step forward, and the work of each became impactful to all. They pushed, prodded, and developed the teachings required to advance football from a game once known for brute force to high-level chess played on grass.

Twenty-eight men who have coached along NFL sidelines now wear a gold jacket, representing their induction into the Hall of Fame, but there are no set criteria for entrance. Each coach has a different story, a different win-loss record. Some have won a championship; others have not. Some have coached fewer than one hundred games, and some have coached over three hundred. To truly understand the impact coaches have had on the game, we need to look past the simple notion that a championship title means entrance into the Hall. Championships are important, but so is the regular season. With robust and fair criteria in place, we will determine who is the best, regardless of the era.

Of course, we can't discuss football's journey without exploring how football became a made-for-television event because of three personalities off the field, men who brought us from our couches onto the field with their commentary. Thanks to them, televised games became family bonding events, bringing every-one together to watch hard-hitting action and to enjoy a few laughs. We'll also explore the personnel men—not just who they were, but how hard work affected the game. How these men made trades, the mechanics of trades, and the reasons teams initiate them will illuminate the way this chess-like game was established.

Last, but certainly not least, we will examine the great players of the game, starting with an important topic for the NFL: the race discrimination of the 1930s and '40s, which prevented great players like Kenny Washington from showcasing their talents. His vital story kicks off my list of the top one hundred players of all time. Once again, some are in the Hall; some are still playing, awaiting their turn; and sadly, some have been overlooked. By examining these players and their careers, this book will present an overview of the game—its developments and downfalls, its historical highlights and glaring omissions. Many of these I have evaluated firsthand, others through the power of video, and all have their place in NFL history. Each is its own dot, waiting for you to connect them to the others and see the full picture.

The game of football has provided everlasting memories for me and my wonderful family. With two sons now calling themselves NFL coaches, it is my hope that I can give something back to the game with a fuller understanding of how the NFL has gone from goal line to greatness. Let's begin.

CHAPTER 1
THE WHITE OAKS

"Innovation involves anticipation. It is having a broad base of knowledge on your subject and an ability to see where the end game is headed. Use all your knowledge to get there first. Set the trend and make the competition counter you."
—Bill Walsh

LOVE WATCHING OLD NFL GAMES AND seeing former Chicago Bears owner and coach George "Papa Bear" Halas in his overcoat, tie, and fedora, as if he's heading to a fancy dinner party. During the 1930s, head coaches dressed like most spectators in the stands. Their roles were limited during the week and even more so after kickoff. At that time, there were no electronic headsets or play sheets with more calls than you could ever imagine—just a coach wearing his Sunday best as he berated his players, the officials, or anyone else in his path. Coaches back then were equal parts fan, advisor, and promoter as they watched the single-wing formation operate. The ball rarely traveled in the air, and three- or four-yard gains seemed like explosive plays. Football was simply about toughness and muscle.

During the early stages of the NFL, most players were also coaches. Curly Lambeau and George Halas played on Sundays and coached during the week. They also lined the fields, made sure the uniforms were clean, and saw to it that the checks to the players never bounced. It was an all-consuming job with little financial reward.

Professional football wasn't the most popular sport in the late 1920s and '30s. As George Halas wrote in his memoir *Halas by Halas*, "Paid football was pretty much a catch-as-catch-can affair. Players came and went drawn by the pleasure of playing. Teams appeared one week and disappeared the next." College football, however, brought consistency, with teams and players that could be counted on to appear on the field week after week, and the fans flocked to watch the game. The enthusiasm toward the college game became infectious and created the migration toward coaching as a profession. The migration started slowly, with ex-players searching for their place in life after their time competing on the field expired. The game offered something more than money. It offered these men a chance to continue to compete—which fueled the fire of football's intellectual advancement.

In the movie *The Shawshank Redemption*, Red (played by Morgan Freeman) is sent by his friend Andy (Tim Robbins) to find the "Redemption Tree," or as it was known, the "tree of hope," upon his parole. The large white oak, with its powerful roots and large majestic branches, symbolizes gaining freedom through wisdom. The profession of coaching today owes its debt to five white oaks—noteworthy and formidable coaches—of yesterday, whose roots extend far and long, made it possible for many who came after them to benefit through their innovation and hope. Today's modern explosive offenses, dominated by star quarterbacks like Tom Brady (before he retired), Patrick Mahomes II, and Josh Allen, can thank these coaches for challenging the game's decades-old strategies and ultimately revolutionizing the sport. Even decades later, these oaks continue to influence every coach in football.

WHITE OAK NUMBER ONE

Colonel Blaik and the Lonely End

Colonel Earl "Red" Blaik caught the fever. After his graduation from West Point and the end of World War I, as a commissioned officer, he had no future in the rapidly downsizing military. Fulfilling his two-year obligation to his country, Blaik returned home to Dayton and picked up a hammer. Helping his father in the home construction business offered some stability, yet he longed for the gridiron. He yearned to become a leader, a teacher, and a coach, so he returned to the sidelines as an assistant coach—first to help Miami University in nearby Oxford and then to the University of Wisconsin before returning to coach at West Point.

One year at West Point became six. When the head coaching position at Army opened, Blaik was not considered because he wasn't an active member of the service. With no interest in staying longer as an assistant, Blaik accepted the head coaching position at Dartmouth. On the campus of this Ivy League school, Blaik developed his skills as a complete coach. Before Blaik's arrival, Dartmouth players wanted to play the game only for fun and to focus more on their academics. With Blaik, they ended up doing both. Blaik took the Dartmouth players' willingness to accept discipline, sacrifice, and subordination to the team effort and molded the team into a powerhouse. Everything he had learned from his days at Army became a staple of his teaching at Dartmouth. He perfected his coaching game with detailed fundamentals, demanding that the players rely on their ability to properly execute on every play. Blaik didn't invent new plays; he made the plays work more effectively. He dominated the league, ending Cornell's famous eighteen-game winning streak in 1940 and propelling this tiny little school into the national spotlight.

When Army called again—after they had removed its requirement that the head coach be on active duty—Blaik returned to the Black Knights as their head man, charged with restoring their football program. During the 1940s, the top floor of the gymnasium at West Point became the think tank of coaching. In the small, cramped rooms that looked out onto the beautiful Hudson River, coaches developed their craft under the direction of Colonel Red Blaik. With incredible attention to detail, a never-ending work ethic, and an obsession with studying game and practice film over and over again, Blaik showed that in order to achieve success, total dedication to the craft was required.

Years later, working for Al Davis at the Oakland Raiders, I was often told stories of how Davis loved to watch "The Great Army Knights," as he always referred to them. Davis's admiration of Blaik was obvious—he rarely spoke in glowing terms of other coaches. Though Davis never worked for Blaik, he learned this great oak's methods and philosophies by keenly observing him in action. Davis molded much of his approach to coaching on Blaik's, even using the color black, which was an identifying feature of the Army football uniforms, for the Raiders. Davis possessed the same passion and work ethic that Blaik instilled in every coach who had occupied a desk on the top floor at West Point.

Blaik moved the profession from yelling, screaming, and machoism into detailed teaching. He rarely raised his voice. His intelligence and understanding of the game conveyed the authority needed to command the players and coaches. Vince Lombardi discovered Blaik's method when he arrived at West Point in 1948. Lombardi, an emotional man with a fiery temper, would often be called into Blaik's office. Years later, Lombardi said of those meetings, "He toned down my temper, or tried to. He would twirl his 1920 West Point class ring and say, 'Vince, we don't do it that way here at West Point.'"

During his 1958 summer break, Blaik vacationed in the Florida Keys, where he could look out on the pristine ocean. As the waves came ashore, Blaik would watch them from his hotel room, consumed with finding a way to remove a defender from the "box." Every college defense Army faced was preoccupied with stopping the run, aligning as many defenders near the football as possible. As the boats sailed past his balcony, Blaik created a formation he called the "Far Flanker," which featured an extra end set wide, about twenty yards from the ball, creating an unbalanced line. A slight variation of the Bazooka formation Blaik had implemented the previous season, the Far Flanker was simple in reasoning and execution—someone had to go and cover the far flanker, removing a man from the box. If the defense didn't react or rotate their coverage, they became vulnerable to being attacked in the middle of the field. Blaik said later, "It did something that no other offense in my twenty-five years of coaching had accomplished: it forced a definite weakness in the secondary defense that could not be offset without removing an extra man from the line. And this man could not be spared, because we still had all our backs in close-attacking deploy." In the first game using this formation against a strong University of South Carolina team, Army racked up 529 yards of total offense (344 yards rushing, 185 yards passing) to win, 45–8. The hidden variation of the formation was that the far end never entered the huddle. He was always stationed away from the ball and relied on hand signals to relay the play, allowing the Cadets to play at a faster tempo and run more plays per minute. Before the second game of the '58 season, the formation was the talk of the nation. Stanley Woodward, sports editor of the *Newark Star-Ledger* and a great friend of Blaik, is credited with being the first to call him "The Lonely End."

Blaik's coaching influence far exceeded the college game. Murray Warmath (who won a National Championship at the University of Minnesota), and Bill

Yeoman (father of the veer offense at the University of Houston) learned their trade from working side by side with Blaik. Others, like Sid Gillman and Vince Lombardi, ventured off to the pro game. Blaik's teaching and methods also influenced others from afar, like Al Davis, who borrowed his attention to detail and his divergent thinking and incorporated both into their coaching playbooks. If you look closely at the game today—college or professional—with all the spread formations, hand signals, and manipulation of personnel, you can see a sprinkling of the innovative strategies Blaik eagerly introduced with The Army Knights.

WHITE OAK NUMBER TWO

Clark Shaughnessy and the T Formation

Clark Shaughnessy revolutionized football in the 1940s with the T formation, which made the quarterback the most important position in the sport. Before Shaughnessy, the quarterback was never even aligned under center. He was a blocker, not a passer, leading the back on sweeps or running the ball to the perimeter in the popular single-wing offense. The quarterback position had little value before the introduction of Shaughnessy's T formation. In the early days of football, all rules favored the defense. Offensive linemen were routinely slapped in the head even though they were not permitted to extend their hands, and wide receivers were regularly jammed without getting off the line. The wing style of blocking made pass protection just about impossible, and as a result, quarterbacks were frequently on their backs before even knowing if they had completed a pass. By simply adjusting where the quarterback was aligned, Shaughnessy dramatically changed the position, making it the centerpiece of modern football while incorporating the forward pass into offensive strategy. He also placed the flanker in motion, thus allowing him to escape the mauling of defensive backs, who were trained within the rules to grab, punch, and essentially treat the receivers as dummies standing in their way.

But Shaughnessy's revolutionary offense wasn't all passing. He built a running game off the T formation and devised the counterplay to pull linemen from one side of the ball to the other, creating better blocking angles. These counter concepts eventually became the foundation of the Joe Gibbs counter trey, a signature play of the three-time Super Bowl champion Washington Redskins. In his book, *The Modern T Formation*, Shaughnessy described his offensive philosophy:

The modern T formation affords a boxing type of offense. The quick opening plays can be compared to the left jab of a boxer, the man in motion and the faking of the backs to the feints, and the fullback plays to the real punch.

To make this type of offense go, a coach must have quick backs who are good fakers and dangerous in the open. The halfbacks should be good receivers. The fullback should be a fast, powerful runner and hard to bring down. The quarterback must be a good passer, and if he is fast, so much better.

Shaughnessy impacted both the college and pro games—at the same time. While leading Stanford to its undefeated 1940 season and an appearance in the Rose Bowl, he also helped George Halas of the Bears prepare Sid Luckman for the 1940 NFL championship game. (Can you imagine what the fanfare would be today if a coach were contributing to two teams at once?) Years earlier, Shaughnessy had convinced Halas to select Luckman and place him under center. Shaughnessy not only spoke glowingly of the quarterback, but told Halas how to install a passing game that would highlight Luckman's talents. Before that season, Luckman played left halfback and only attempted fifty-one passes during eleven games. But in 1940, the Bears—who were playing home games at Wrigley Field—had one of the most explosive aerial attacks of the era. Luckman threw 105 passes over a twelve-game season, completing forty-eight. He threw for four touchdowns and had nine interceptions. That season, the Bears had ten touchdown passes and fifteen interceptions. But this imbalance, which seems atrocious and unfathomable now, wasn't back then. Throwing the ball was dangerous, as no rules were in place to protect the passer or to allow a receiver to free release into his routes. Timing patterns and anticipating throws were next to impossible, but Shaughnessy knew they were the future of the game. Without Shaughnessy, Luckman might have remained a halfback, and Halas likely wouldn't have developed the passing game that defeated the Washington Redskins, 73–0, in the 1940 championship game.

Additionally, without Shaughnessy, the three-receiver set that's pervasive today might have taken decades longer to become customary. Shaughnessy developed this formation because he thought eventual Hall of Famer Elroy "Crazy Legs" Hirsch would be more successful as a flanker than as a running back. So he moved him to receiver, which best utilized his talents.

Shaughnessy was met with heavy skepticism over his forward-thinking ideas initially, but those ideas eventually paved the way for quarterbacks like Bob Waterfield and Norm Van Brocklin, who helped make the 1948 Rams offense the original version of the Greatest Show on Turf.

Shaughnessy defined each position clearly and succinctly, even by today's standards. He emphasized that running backs had to have the ability to catch the ball in space and gain yards after the catch—a philosophy that Bill Walsh carried with him when he was an assistant with the Cincinnati Bengals.

When I think of Shaughnessy's impact, I think of Ernest Hemingway. In *The Sun Also Rises*, Hemingway wrote that bankruptcy happens two ways—gradually and then all at once. Shaughnessy's influence was gradual during the 1940s and 1950s, but it slowly built momentum in the 1960s, when Sid Gillman showed coaches how to effectively throw the ball down the field, and continued into the 1970s, when Walsh introduced his West Coast offense. Then, "all at once" in the 1980s, most teams were running some variation of it. It would truly be impossible to break down any coaching tree without understanding Shaughnessy's impact, and it's fair to say that without him, there would be no Gillman. It's even fairer to proclaim that without Gillman, there would be no modern passing game. And without Paul Brown of the Cleveland Browns, there would be no organizational methods for coaches to copy. Every coach, scheme, play, or leadership style has deep and complicated roots.

WHITE OAK NUMBER THREE

Paul Brown and the Operating System

If Shaughnessy was the Steve Jobs of innovation in the 1940s, then Paul Brown was Bill Gates. Nicknamed "Precision Paul" for his close scrutiny of details, Brown developed a wide-ranging operating system for every aspect of football leadership—including authoring a teaching manual for how to build an organization. From theories about advanced game scouting to player procurement systems, Brown borrowed from other industries to learn how to calculate intelligence, competitive fire, and character, and was the first coach to organize information on every aspect of the football profession. Perhaps more than anyone else, Brown deserves credit for making professional football an actual job—and not merely a hobby—for coaches.

Brown, like Bill Walsh years later, always thought of himself as a teacher, and even began his career as an English instructor in his hometown of Massillon, Ohio. Brown wanted to lead with intelligence, not fear, and was determined to advance the game with his mind, not by simply degrading players with insults to motivate them. He respected his players as men first, and insisted that he be addressed by his first name, not "Coach."

Brown was also bullish about establishing sophisticated, research-driven methods of procuring and developing talent. He insisted that his players master the fundamentals of their respective positions and left absolutely nothing to chance. He frequently jotted down detailed notes and even forced his players to carry around three-ring binders, which he inspected for sloppiness. To Brown, discipline was a trait that needed to be ingrained in every aspect of their lives. It was not a faucet that could be turned on or off as needed—constant attention to the seemingly trivial was essential. Brown's consistent, stoic demeanor was a constant at Massillon High, at Ohio State, at Great Lakes, and with the Cleveland Browns, and he expected his players to look and act the part. He reinforced this in exhausting detail at each team meeting.

The Cleveland Browns were an awful collection of players when Paul Brown began his professional head coaching career in 1945; he sought to change that. Using his scouting notes from his time at Great Lakes and Ohio State, he built his culture on high-character players with whom he was familiar, either from observing them or having coached against them. In addition to his attention to off-the-field details, Brown wanted to advance his offense, replacing the single wing with the T formation. But he knew this would require finding a quarterback who could handle the new requirements of the position, which was far easier said than done. Quarterbacks then weren't just commodities you could pick up wherever. Hell, many of them just masqueraded as tailbacks who occasionally threw a pass. But Brown had an uncanny ability to see past a player's current production and project what his ability would be at another position, even if he'd never seen him play it.

Because Brown was so meticulous after each game, jotting detailed scouting notes of the players his team had faced, he didn't need to look far to find the perfect match for each position. He often reflected upon a 1941 game when his undefeated Ohio State team suffered its first loss, to Northwestern. One play from that game, in particular, stuck with him. Northwestern halfback Otto Graham started to his right with the score tied, preparing to run a single-wing sweep, and then stopped on a dime and launched a pass across the field for a touchdown. Right then, Brown knew Graham could be a T formation passer, a detail he noted after the game. So when the opportunity arose years later, Brown jumped at the chance to acquire Graham...and forever change his life in football.

The selection of Graham as quarterback for the Cleveland Browns was another example of how Brown's organizational methods revolutionized the off-the-field aspect of the NFL. Brown's ability to understand how a player's unique strengths improved when placed in the right system became a trademark of his talent procurement. It later became part of Bill Walsh's great Super Bowl–winning 49ers teams and carries on today. Players fitting perfectly into a unique system are still vital, as evidenced by former Browns quarterback Baker Mayfield. After Mayfield's first two seasons in the league, the Browns' front office learned what he did well and identified the source of some of his struggles. They hired Coach Kevin Stefanski to install an offense tailored to suit Mayfield's game. The results showed. Cleveland made the playoffs and won its first postseason game since 1994. Since then, the Browns have replaced Mayfield with Deshaun Watson. However, the salient point remains—identify the talent, then match the system to fit it.

Recognizing that the game was changing, Brown understood the need to teach his players specific skills. Because of his adamancy about teaching fundamentals, Brown developed relevant skills within his system. That also became another Walsh staple, learned while working for Brown. Walsh often told his assistant coaches, "The first year, we teach the system, and the second year, we develop those skills." This was vintage Brown.

Brown was an entrepreneur who saw an existing idea and made it better. Because Brown was a game student and then a teacher, he was a keen observer of other teams' methods. He was curious by nature, and thus willing to examine an idea and apply his methods to advance and improve it. He learned from George Halas the benefits of having his coaches sit above the field on game day for a better vantage point, and he also replicated Halas's scouting methods. He developed requirements for each position and modified his game plans each week. Halas had good ideas; Brown made them even better.

Working in the NFL was a part-time gig back in 1940, and coaches would take four to six months off from the game and find other jobs to supplement their income. While at Ohio State, Brown was fortunate to have full-time assistant coaches help with recruiting. Self-scouting became another Brown trademark. He'd break down each offensive and defensive play to understand why the play was successful or not, and then develop a strategy around it. That's how he wanted his coaches to spend their off-seasons, not selling cars. When Brown arrived in the NFL, he discovered the college game was ahead of the pro game and there wasn't money available for assistants to work full time.

STEADY BUT SLOW PROGRESS

In 1945, the league was dominated by George "Papa Bear" Halas's Chicago Bears. Halas was the driving force behind increasing the popularity of the sport, which had for years before him largely centered around violence rather than skill. From 1922 until 1967, Halas went 318–148–31 with the Bears.

While the thirty-one ties may raise some eyebrows today, they were a big part of the game back then, before the forward pass dramatically allowed teams to gain yards quickly. Teams in that era really struggled to move the ball up and down the field and frequently ran it, meaning the clock was regularly running. Accepting a tie wasn't viewed as negatively as it is today; it wasn't a loss, and it helped slightly in the standings.

Halas's teams were crowned NFL champions six times. But beyond the trophies, Papa Bear's most significant contribution to the game was his willingness to adapt and to understand that fans wanted more offense and less violence. By working with Shaughnessy to develop the T formation, Halas demonstrated his willingness to change his behavior for the good of his team and, ultimately, the entire NFL. Football likely never would've grown at the rate it did without Halas giving his blessing to the T formation. This is not to imply the 1940s became a passing era. Rather, Halas laid the groundwork for the evolution of the sport we all know today. And while drawing new ideas on the chalkboard was fun, it was harder to implement rule changes and convince fellow coaches to embrace an aggressive passing game. This evolution didn't just happen in a few years. The change took decades.

He immediately set aside money and added more coaches to his staff. Typically, in the NFL during this period, a staff had two or three coaches. But Brown raised that number to six and would always make sure that one of his assistants prepared the scouting report to illuminate the necessary strategy to beat a specific opponent. Brown's ability to prioritize self-scouting and advance scouting allowed him to take the guesswork out of play calling. He never wanted to run a bad play and felt strong preparation would eliminate this possibility. "We're making a science out of what is called in the game," he often said about his approach to scouting.

Brown used two rotating guards, called messengers, to deliver the plays he wanted from the sideline to the quarterback, heightening the coach's

Perhaps the best example of the shortcomings of the rules took place in the infamous Ice Bowl on New Year's Eve, 1967. In that game, Green Bay Packers quarterback Bart Starr was sacked eight times despite having two Hall of Fame linemen protecting him. He lost a total of seventy-six yards in that game, even though he attempted twenty-four passes. Today, had Starr been sacked that often in any game—let alone an NFC Championship game—his coach would have been under fire, which Packers coach Vince Lombardi managed to avoid.

Can you imagine what talk radio in Green Bay would've sounded like today after that game? "Lombardi has to go. He almost got Starr killed!" Or, "Lombardi's an idiot running a quarterback sneak on third down with fourteen seconds left in the game and no time-outs. What would have happened had Starr not scored?" But it was a different era, and a much different game.

Sacks and huge quarterback hits were part of the dangerous path teams had to navigate to attempt a forward pass. But in addition to the rule that allowed the defense to essentially assault receivers until the ball was in the air, there were no rules to preserve the health of the quarterback. If you look at clips from this era, you'll see defensive linemen take three, maybe four steps to hit the quarterback long after the ball is out of his hand. No part of the quarterback's body was spared from these violent hits, which, amazingly, they managed to survive. Had "Slinging" Sammy Baugh or Otto Graham been given the same protection rules as, say, Tom Brady or Patrick Mahomes today, the advancements in the game would have happened much quicker.

involvement. Under Brown's structure, quarterbacks didn't have the personal freedom to run the offense or deviate from the scripted game plan derived from the scouting report. Instead, Brown tied the sideline to on-the-field performance, making the coach move from a whistleblower to a high-level chess player and problem-solver. Because the coaches had more time to work on the tactical aspect of the game, along with the forward pass, football moved ever so slightly from a gladiator sport to a high-tech operation—or at least as high tech as the 1950s would allow—and interest in the sport grew as result.

Brown was the first coach to assess intelligence with psychological testing and determine a player's behavior patterns using physiological testing, hoping the information he gathered would allow him to assemble the most competitive roster. When Brown became the Browns' head coach, his number-one requirement for any player on the team was speed—regardless of position. Brown wanted the Browns to be the fastest team in the NFL. To determine and judge speed correctly, he introduced the forty-yard dash as the perfect distance for making this assessment. So many coaches in that era valued the one-hundred-yard dash, but Brown believed that was far too long. He viewed punts as a great indicator of speed, and because most traveled around forty yards during this time, that became his magic number.

Brown was clinical in his approach to everything, both on and off the field, and made sure to remove bias from his decision-making process. He designed specific tests to rule out potential players and believed firmly in standards for every position. Unless prospects met these, he would not even consider them. This method of procuring talent also became the genesis of the famed Dallas Cowboys system under Hall of Fame scout Gil Brandt, and was later modified by the New England Patriots under Bucko Kilroy and, ultimately, by Bill Belichick in Cleveland. Brown's circle of influence became powerful and everlasting, and many took his scouting ideas and organizational methods and conformed them to their own specific philosophies. Not a day goes by without someone working in an NFL office doing something that traces back to Paul Brown.

Brown became the number-one leader on the football clinic circuit, as coaches from every level wanted to learn and implement the wisdom of the "Brown Operating System." Brown's annual clinic in Cleveland was a harder ticket to acquire than *Springsteen on Broadway*. His influence spread near and far, and coaches coveted a chance to work for him. Many of those who did went on to find remarkable success in applying his methods with slight style tweaks. From Bill Walsh to Don Shula, Weeb Ewbank, Blanton Collier, and Chuck Noll, Hall of Fame coaches and NFL champions observed the master firsthand. While they may not have enjoyed some of his methods or stubborn, academic ways, they all took Brown's ideas and blended them into their beliefs. Walsh felt for years that Brown prevented him from becoming a head coach sooner, but he still knew that he was Brown's disciple and had learned a great deal from him over the years. Walsh was able to separate the business side of the sport from the football side and used Brown's organizational methods to build the San Francisco 49ers.

Even coaches who didn't directly work for Brown recognized his impact on the game. Sid Gillman told *Sports Magazine* in December 1986, "Before Paul Brown, pro football was a 'daisy chain.' He brought a system into pro football.

He brought a practice routine. He broke down practice into particular areas. He had position coaches. He was an organizational genius. Before Paul Brown, coaches just rolled the ball out on the practice field."

WHITE OAK NUMBER FOUR

Sid Gillman and the Long Ball

Sidney "Sid" Gillman's impact on coaching was similar to Brown's, namely in advancing the passing game. As a young boy in Minneapolis, Gillman worked as a movie theatre usher. Before the main movie attraction came on, the newsreels updated the audience on worldwide events, including entertainment and sports. Anytime there was football footage, Gillman would splice the football section, take home the reels, and repeatedly view them on his home projector. He loved to study the film instead of simply watching it. For Gillman, studying became a favorite pastime, something he would insist his future coaching staff do as well. Studying requires total concentration, which Gillman perfected early in life. This dedication to study separated Gillman from most coaches of that era. Before Gillman developed his obsession with sixteen-millimeter tape, no coaches watched or studied the footage. Gillman was the first to bring this element into the profession. He detailed the movements of all the players on the field, from their footwork to the reaction of the quarterback's shoulders to the depth of each player in the backfield—every nuance scribbled onto his pad for review. Gillman continuously moved the tape back and forth to draw the play design and the assignments of each player. Essentially, he was padding plays long before Bill Belichick made it famous. In addition, he kept an enormous library of each passing route from teams all over the NFL, college, and AFL, studying the most effective way to run all the routes on his passing tree. For Gillman, the details within the details made a huge difference.

In his home office later in life in La Jolla, California, Gillman had reel upon reel of tape stacked in perfect order and marked with the number associated with the route. Gillman's offense was all numbers—all based on his passing tree. Each one told the receiver what route he needed to run for the play. Any play in the Gillman offense consisted of three numbered digits: odds were for outside breaking routes; evens for the inside portion of the field. For example, if Gillman

LATE-NIGHT SCHEMING

As a player at Ohio State, Gillman served as team captain and was an All-Big Ten end. But more importantly, while working as a graduate assistant coach he found a mentor who would ignite his curiosity about the passing game. Francis Schmidt was an outlier in the coaching profession and the newly appointed head coach of the Buckeyes in 1934.

From his physical appearance and distinctive southern drawl, Schmidt sounded like Foghorn Leghorn with his penchant for beginning almost every sentence with "Lookee here." He not only pushed the envelope of expanding offensive football, but he frequently provided players and staff memorable soundbites before a game against a more talented opponent. Before the Michigan game, the Ohio State press asked Schmidt about his team's chances of pulling off the upset. Schmidt replied, "Lookee here, those fellows put their pants on one leg at a time, the same as everyone else."

Gillman established his freethinking football roots while serving Schmidt, who was a staunch believer in the forward—and even backward—pass. In-game sheets during this time had a section for backward passes (laterals), which Schmidt felt helped his offense. But these views were not the norm, which caused the media to label him Francis "Close the Gates of Mercy" Schmidt for his trickery, which often involved multiple laterals in a play. Schmidt once said:

called "Brown Flanker Right, 435," it meant the first digit was for the outside receiver to the left to run a quick "in cut"; the second digit was for the tight end who aligned on the left, meaning he was to run a shallow cross toward the sideline; and the third digit told the Z receiver (away from the tight end and off the ball) to run a deep out. The simplicity of his play calls, requiring players to know their alignment on the field and the passing tree, allowed Gillman the flexibility to alter his offense during a game with ease.

Gillman's career eventually took him to Denison University and then to Colonel Red Blaik's staff at West Point, where he learned discipline and how to better interact with players. While at Army, Gillman met with coaches from all over the Northeast who wanted to learn more about his passing game concepts. Vince Lombardi, then the head coach at St. Cecilia High School in New Jersey, would spend days learning from Gillman, and they forged a relationship

Every team must have a running attack, but you can't rely on that alone. The open style of offense, with passes being tossed on unorthodox downs and from unusual places, will gradually push the running attack into the background. I expect to see the time, before many years, when forward and lateral passes will make up the greatest part of the offense, with the running attack just something to fall back upon. The wide-open, chance-taking game is the style the fans want to see. The day of having a fullback plunge into the center of the line for a yard or two at a time is rapidly passing.

Schmidt was well ahead of his time. Using colored pencils—red, green, and blue—he would sit in his home office near the Ohio State campus, working all hours of the night designing new schemes like the I formation, which became a signature of Woody Hayes's Ohio State offense years later. Schmidt's playbook was over five hundred pages long and covered every detail imaginable.

"The light was always on in his room; I don't know if he ever slept," former player Nick Wasylik told the *Columbia Dispatch* in 1985. "It seemed like he lived, dreamed and ate football." Years later, many would say the same about Gillman, who was not only influenced by Schmidt's system, but who also sported his mentor's signature bow tie on the sideline.

so strong that when Gillman left Army, he suggested to Blaik that he hire Lombardi, a recommendation Blaik took. "The West Point players had credited [Gillman] with introducing practice films and game grades at the Military Academy, and Vince brought those ideas to the Green Bay Packers," guard Jerry Kramer wrote in his 1968 book, *Instant Replay*. Lombardi and Gillman remained close friends until Lombardi's death in 1970.

My story of Sid? Al Davis would often have me call Coach Gillman to make sure he had game tape to review. Each time we chatted, he reminded me how much he loved my "dad," as he thought Vince was my father. I didn't have the heart to tell him I wasn't.

Gillman loved offensive football from his playing career and early coaching days under Schmidt. He fought tirelessly throughout his entire career against the perceived notion that the pass was a gimmick and would fade away soon enough. He often told any young coach that the most important element of offensive strategy was to establish the deep ball. "Any coach that wanted to establish the run was full of shit, as he has to establish the pass if he wants to win," he once said. Without attacking the defense down the field, Gillman believed the other elements of offense simply couldn't generate points. Since the team with the most points won, and throwing helped score points, passing the ball was pivotal for success in the NFL. Gillman was a staunch believer in the passing game, even before the rules against receiver harassment were relaxed and offensive linemen were permitted to extend their hands. But he saw value in passing, despite the many obstacles in its way. To him, the deep ball required crisp route running, accurate throwing, and consistent execution. To throw deep, Gillman needed precise route runners who had both the speed to challenge defensive backs and the toughness to escape their mauling. Detailed coaching, preparation, and having an accurate, deep ball passer became the centerpiece of his offense.

Once the long pass became a potent threat, Gillman incorporated the draw play to keep the defensive line honest. He wanted the play to look like a pass, forcing the linebackers to drop into coverage. Then the quarterback would hand the ball off and allow the runner to pick and weave his way through a gap, finding daylight with the defensive linemen badly out of position. The complement to the draw became the trap play, which allowed the offensive linemen better angles to block a hard-charging defense desperate to get to the quarterback. The defensive linemen would run up the field, sensing a path to the quarterback, then get side-blocked from a pulling offensive line with an easy block to shield the back from potential tacklers.

In the 1963 AFL championship, Gillman's San Diego Chargers hosted the Boston Patriots in front of thirty thousand screaming fans at Balboa Stadium. Gillman used the trap to perfection, convincing the blitzing Patriots defense that the Chargers were throwing deep. Instead, they trapped their linemen, allowing running back Keith Lincoln to gain 206 yards on just thirteen carries en route to the AFL title.

Once the trap became an effective tool, Gillman used his expansive imagination to develop all types of screen passes—which NFL teams use successfully to this day. From the slip screen to the slow screen to the read screen, Gillman's arsenal became a staple of his offense and provided the offensive line different ways to confuse the hard-charging defense. With those staple plays, the Gillman offense became the most feared in football, independent of league.

WHITE OAK NUMBER FIVE

West Coast Bill Walsh

Bus One was always Bill Walsh's bus—and everyone knew it. If you decided to get on, you had to make direct eye contact with the main man. If that was a problem, the San Francisco 49ers provided four other buses for your non-eye-contact pleasure. Walsh was always pensive, reminiscent of Bobby Fischer contemplating his next chess move. His eyes would fixate on his lap but shift quickly anytime someone new walked on. He cherished his alone time in his reserved first-row seat, where he'd use small, white index cards to doodle the many thoughts that emanated from his racing mind. For Walsh, drawing was therapeutic. Much in the way that President John F. Kennedy would doodle sailboats with his pencil at meetings in the White House, Walsh would use his shortened golf shop pencil and etch football plays. These weren't the latest schemes from his current game plan, but patterns he was mulling over, such as those from a tape he might have recently viewed of Shaughnessy's T formation.

Walsh personified the definition of an entrepreneur. He didn't create motion in offensive football or the forward pass, but he made them much better, drawing on Shaughnessy's theories and subtly integrating these into his West Coast offense. Walsh would use his discerning eye to observe a simple move, step, or action, and then would incorporate these into the offensive designs that he sorted out through his doodles.

He never stole a specific play from Shaughnessy. In fact, Walsh prohibited his coaching staff from lifting plays from other teams. He despised being a copycat and considered it lazy, half-hearted coaching. Why? Because to him, if a stolen play broke down, repairing it relied on understanding the play's origins. But without that knowledge, the play was unfixable and led the coach to draw a simple conclusion: the players screwed up. And Walsh loathed blaming players. He once said, "I think the creative and innovative coaches are the ones who are introspective; ones who like to develop their ideas; ones who take a look at all the equations and want to find the right answers."

Walsh was always about two As—answers and accountability. If something failed, he'd put the onus on himself for not putting the players in the right situation. "We must first teach the system and develop their skills within the system," he often said. Walsh loved the early game of football and revered Shaughnessy's pragmatic mind.

Much like Shaughnessy, Sid Gillman served as inspiration for Walsh. While Walsh was on the Raiders' staff in 1966, he happened to catch *The Sid Gillman Show* on his hotel television the night before a game against the Chargers. He listened intently as Gillman, with Lance Alworth by his side, began describing the Chargers' passing game in great detail. Walsh was smitten and knew he needed to improve his knowledge and learn more about a systematic approach toward passing the football down the field. On the show, Gillman explained his overall beliefs regarding all eleven men on the offense. He detailed the level at which every route needed to be run, and explained the elite timing, balance, and accuracy the quarterback needed to possess. Philosophically, Gillman wanted to force the defense to defend literally every square centimeter. Gillman divided the field into sections, from the outside to the hash marks to the center, and wanted to flood each section with a potential receiver. This meant his running backs had to play a part in the offense beyond just carrying the ball. This strategy would then spread out the defense and allow the receivers more room to run, while also ensuring there were fewer tacklers to converge on the receivers after the catch.

When Walsh joined the Cincinnati Bengals in 1968, he implemented the team's new offense, which featured short passes with five potential receivers in the route, just one way in which Gillman's influence was felt. Walsh might not have made the defense defend the field's length, but he did design the horizontal passing game, using all 53½ yards across. He took elements of Gillman's coaching and molded them into his own system, using his own unique vocabulary and play designs. Walsh's system was built on words, not numbers. He would use descriptive phrases like "Bingo Cross," and the players would know what specific routes to run based on the coverage and concepts. Walsh relied on the quarterback's timing, which was tied to the depth of his drop, to throw the ball in rhythm and with anticipation.

Walsh's curiosity extended to both sides of the ball, and he often referred back to old games when preparing for an opponent. Walsh was on a mission to understand how each opponent's defense operated, how it adjusted, and—most important—what unconventional rules it had. He believed that with any organized team, the offense and defense had to have steadfast guidelines that instructed players on what to do when the unexpected occurred. Walsh insisted upon understanding these rules as if he were the defensive coach, and then he'd design plays to exploit them. To prepare for a 1985 playoff game against the Bears and their dominant 46 defense, Walsh began studying old variations of the double eagle, which involved defensive linemen covering the guards and centers. Walsh knew that the quarterback option was the Achilles' heel of this alignment, so he switched wide receiver Freddie Solomon with quarterback Joe Montana, thus allowing Solomon—who previously was a terrific option quarterback at the University of Tampa—to be the option quarterback. The choice to make this adjustment, one that few other coaches would have made, further exemplified Walsh's brilliance and was the exact reason he would turn to older tapes for new ideas. He would frequently credit his time as the Stanford defensive backfield coach from 1963 to 1965 as the master class he needed to become an adroit offensive teacher—and teacher was the title Walsh most coveted.

CHAPTER 2
SITUATIONS MATTER

"There is winning and there is misery."
—Bill Parcells

EVALUATING NFL HEAD COACHES IS LIKE evaluating former United States presidents. If a president was popular when leaving office, his presidency was viewed as a huge success based on the approval ratings. Conversely, if he had a low approval rating, then everything about his term was horrible. It's all perception based on numbers, essentially based on wins and losses, or on pleasing the voters.

Judging coaches should be easier than judging presidents—right? It's simple math: examine the win-loss column, determine how many playoff victories and Super Bowls accumulated, and—bingo—we have our ratings. However, we all know simple and the NFL never go hand in hand. There are layers upon layers to examine in order to understand the root causes of why teams win or lose, or

22

why a coach might be successful at one place and not another. The weird shape of the ball makes for some crazy bounces. When those bounces don't go in a coach's favor, does this make him a bad coach? In the eyes of some, maybe yes; for our ratings, no.

Packers Hall of Fame coach Vince Lombardi understood this better than most. In 1958, after waiting several years for his first head coaching offer, forty-four-year-old Lombardi received an offer for the Philadelphia Eagles' head coaching position. At the time, Lombardi served as the Giants' offensive coordinator and he felt he might never get a chance to become a head coach. So when the Eagles made an offer of $22,500 per year for their head coaching post, Lombardi was jumping to accept until Wellington Mara—his good friend and former Fordham teammate, as well as part owner of the New York Giants—interceded.

Word traveled quickly throughout the twelve-team league that Lombardi was planning to leave the Giants, which prompted Mara to call him. During their conversation, Mara told Lombardi that the Giants would match the financial offer and give him a $100,000 life insurance policy, and he promised Lombardi that when current Giants head coach Jim Lee Howell retired, Lombardi would be the next coach. All that sounded wonderful to Lombardi, yet he hesitated to accept the deal, in part because he was afraid he might miss his chance. He knew Howell was only fifty-three years old and planned on coaching for a few more years. When Mara sensed a hesitation in Lombardi's voice, he unleashed his best reason for Lombardi to reject the Eagles' offer. "They'll never let you run the team the way you want to," Mara said. He was well aware of the toxic situation within Philadelphia's ownership group. The Eagles' owners consisted of a conglomerate of local area businessmen and civic leaders who could never agree on anything. The local newspapers referred to them as the "Happy Hundred" due to their inability to have one leader or to ever reach a consensus. In fact, before offering Lombardi the job, they had made a strong run at Buck Shaw, who was coaching at Santa Clara College. Shaw would only accept the Eagles' offer if they allowed him to remain on the West Coast immediately following the NFL season. The Happy Hundred said no emphatically, and it was then that they had turned to Lombardi.

Mara knew Lombardi could never become a great coach in the wrong situation. If Lombardi had to deal with too many people interfering with his team, he would display that famous fiery temper, which would force the Happy Hundred to cut Lombardi loose. If that had happened, today there would be no legend in Green Bay and no Super Bowl trophy bearing Lombardi's name.

After listening to Mara, Lombardi turned down the Eagles and a year later became head coach of the Green Bay Packers. The Packers didn't have an owner.

Their board of directors—though meddlesome in the past—left Lombardi free to solely operate the team, allowing the coach to shine. As talented a coach Lombardi as proved to be, his talent might not have shined as brightly had the situation not been perfect.

Marv Levy, former coach of the Buffalo Bills and Kansas City Chiefs, also knows the value of being in the right situation. In 1978, fifty-three-year-old Levy became the head coach of the Kansas City Chiefs, taking over a 2–12 team from former coach Tom Bettis and interim coach Paul Wiggin. Levy slowly started to rebuild the Chiefs, going from 4–12 his first season to 9–7 in 1981, his second-to-last year with the team. In 1982, just one year after Levy's first winning season in Kansas City, the NFL players went on strike. The level of trust between management and players was nonexistent as players demanded more pay, more benefits, and the freedom to experience free agency. Levy got caught in the cross-fire and it cost him his job. He spent the next four years in coaching hell, trying to prove that the situation was bad and that he wasn't a bad coach. Fortunately for Levy, Buffalo Bills general manager Bill Polian ignored the false perceptions and made Levy the head coach of the Bills in 1986. Levy proved Polian's instincts correct. Once in the right situation, Levy demonstrated his talents. What appeared to be a failure in Kansas City become a marvelous success in Buffalo.

Through the years, some NFL head coaches have been victims of situations that have prevented them from gaining their rightful recognition. Their work has been Hall-worthy, but politics always play a major role. Deals are brokered between the voters and people vouching for candidates. At times, the voters allow their personal agendas to roadblock worthy candidates. For years, John Madden was convinced some writers who participated in the selection process were keeping him from the Hall. He never publicly gave names, but he confided to his friends that he felt some writers were jealous of his success. Everyone has an agenda, and rarely is it about doing the right thing. Too often, grudges and biases can be manifested in unexpected ways. Let's examine some situations that might have caused the voters to ignore worthy candidates.

SITUATION NUMBER ONE

Complexities of the Past Are Overlooked

Raymond Klein "Buddy" Parker of the Chicago Cardinals, Detroit Lions, and Pittsburgh Steelers was different from most players of his era. Yes, he was tough, willing to sacrifice his body for the team, and ready to play any role needed. What made Parker different was his curiosity about the technical aspect of the game, the strategy, the manner in which players were taught and asked to perform.

In 1935, his first year playing professional football with the Lions, Parker helped head coach Potsy Clark win the Western Division with a 7–3–2 record and earn their first NFL title by beating the New York Giants, 25–7, in the title game, held at the University of Detroit Stadium in front of fifteen thousand fans. In 1937, Parker was traded to the Chicago Cardinals, where he spent seven seasons playing for Coach Jimmy Conzelman. By 1943, his playing days were over, and he entered into the coaching ranks, first as part-time player and coach, and then in 1945 as a full-time coach. When Conzelman retired in 1949 to enter the real-estate business—clearly the NFL was not paying as well as it does now—the Cardinals named Phil Handler and Parker co-head coaches. But the co-head coach operation didn't work, and before the end of the season, Handler was in the front office and Parker was the full-time head coach. He led the Cardinals to four wins and a tie before losing to the Bears, 52–21, to close out the season. Parker resigned as head coach immediately after the game, claiming the job was "too damn demanding." But those closest to him felt he abruptly quit because of his uncertain job status.

The following season, he landed back in the Motor City, serving as the defensive backfield coach. Toward the end of the year, after head coach Bo McMillin resigned, the Lions management promoted Parker—and his career took off. With newfound freedom, Parker could run his program however he wanted, and he borrowed from the knowledge he obtained from watching and observing Paul Brown's methods in Cleveland and Clark Shaughnessy's offensive schemes. Parker was another in the long line of coaches who never worked with Brown or Shaughnessy but became part of their coaching trees from utilizing their teachings and then expanding them to fit his style and personality.

Parker, like Brown, shortened the Lions' practices in 1951, keeping the players fresh for games. He also subscribed to the Brown methodology of keeping things simple, relying on fewer plays and higher execution. Parker keenly observed that the last two minutes of each half were wasted during the game as teams didn't have a system in place to run plays quickly or efficiently or to utilize the sideline to stop the clock. "I've noticed how so many teams let down the two minutes before the half and the last two minutes of the game," he said. "It seemed you could get things done that you couldn't in the other fifty-six minutes of play. So, we drilled on it. Every day." This led to Parker inventing the two-minute offense we all know today.

It's frightening how advanced Parker's vision of the two-minute offense was at the time. In that era, every team huddled before every play; no one was ever in a hurry to get to the line of scrimmage, which is why so many games ended in low-scoring ties. But under the direction of Hall of Fame quarterback Bobby Lane, Parker had his offense use hand signals to instruct players about their next play, eliminating the need to huddle. Parker then coached up-tempo—similar to what we see today. He increased the pace of the game to run as many plays as possible and utilized the sideline to stop the clock, keeping the defense constantly exhausted. When you see Tom Brady, Aaron Rodgers, or Patrick Mahomes hand signal to their receivers, you can thank Buddy Parker for it.

Parker also designed a defense to handle the two-minute offenses that he knew other teams would employ. He created the nickel defense, which often is linked to former Washington Redskin and Los Angeles Rams head coach George Allen. Parker named the inside nickel corners "star" and "port," and today if you are on the practice field of the New England Patriots, you will hear Bill Belichick referring to his inside corner as the "star." Once again, what was old is now new.

From 1952 to 1954, for three years in a row, Parker also had the Lions playing in NFL championships against Cleveland, similar to what Buffalo Bills coach—and Hall of Famer—Marv Levy did from 1990 until 1993, except that Levy lost all four games, whereas Parker was 2–1 and a champion twice. Why is Levy's success valued more than Parker's? Probably because it was done during the modern era, and most of the voters on the Hall of Fame Selection Committee don't understand the challenge Parker faced.

Critics of Parker claim he left Detroit and was never able to get the Steelers to the playoffs. Fair enough, but—and this is a big but—before he arrived in Pittsburgh, the Steelers never had a winning record. Parker, however, was 51–47–6 with the organization. And after he left, following the 1964 season, the Steelers went an abysmal 25–70–3 over the next seven years. During this era, you had to win the division to qualify for the playoffs, so only two teams qualified. Had this rule been in place during the modern era, former New York Giants quarterback Eli Manning would never have been considered a potential Hall of Famer, because his two Super Bowl titles were earned in postseasons when his team was a wildcard entry. The expansion of playoff teams in 1967 and then again in 1970 allowed players and coaches to shine at the brightest moments, an opportunity Parker and others during the '50s and early '60s weren't afforded.

Parker has been up for the Hall several times but has never made it as a finalist. The Centennial Class of voters was established to shed light on the past, but in execution, the past is neglected in favor of more modern coaches like the

Steelers' Bill Cowher and the Cowboys' Jimmy Johnson. Parker has no sponsorship, no one with the clout to enlighten the voters on the challenges he needed to overcome in order to succeed. Voters act as if winning titles in the 1950s wasn't as a hard as winning or losing Super Bowls in the modern era—which is complete hogwash.

Because some coaches have not been able to break through the Hall's voting process, they have been pushed to the back burner and forgotten. As Marshall McLuhan once said, "Only the vanquished remember history."

SITUATION NUMBER TWO

Bad Owner, Great Coach

Sitting in his tiny, cramped office on the San Diego State campus, head football coach Don Coryell longed for something more challenging, something that might test his skills as a leader, an offensive mastermind, and a coach. The Aztecs' football program, under Coryell's watchful eye, was rolling. Coryell's team had lost ten games total in the last seven seasons. Even as they stepped up their competition level from the California Collegiate Athletic Association to the Pacific Coast Conference, their ability to continue to dominate remained. After a 10–1 season during which San Diego State was ranked twentieth overall in the Coaches poll, Coryell wondered: What could he do next? How could he break into the big leagues?

Coryell was an offensive genius, on the cutting edge of shifting from an all-running game into the world of drop-back passes. Because of his teachings, his quarterbacks—including Don Horn, Jesse Freitas, Dennis Shaw, and, most notably, NFL MVP Brian Sipe—exceled in the pros, which gave Coryell confidence that he could bring the San Diego State offense to pro football and change how offenses operated. Coryell's offense could move the ball at will, with a precise passing game that required the quarterback to play in rhythm, with touch and timing. In addition to developing quarterbacks, San Diego State became an NFL football factory under Coryell's guidance, sending receivers Isaac Curtis, Haven Moses, and Gary Garrison to play well at the next level.

Coryell expanded his success through his recruiting practices. He knew he was not getting the cream of the crop in the recruiting battles—bigger programs like UCLA and USC would have the pick of the Southern California high school football litter. So he adopted a different approach—being divergent in thought, Coryell recruited only from the Southern California junior college system, relying on players who were determined to prove those that passed over them wrong. But when it seemed the NFL wasn't noticing his passing game, his production on offensive, and his ability to win with less talent, Coryell decided to take matters into his own hands. After St. Louis Cardinals owner Bill Bidwell fired Bob Holloway, Coryell wrote Bidwell a long and detailed note explaining why he was the right coach for the organization, how he could bring a wide-open offense to pro football, and how he would make the Cardinals contenders in the NFC East. Coryell didn't know if the note would reach Bidwell in his St. Louis office or if Bidwell had any idea about Coryell and his college football accomplishments. But several weeks later, Coryell got a call from Bidwell, and on January 19, 1973, Coryell became the St. Louis Cardinals' head coach.

Coryell did amazing things during his five-year stint as the Cardinals' head man. The team made the playoffs twice, losing both times in the divisional round, and set numerous NFL records for offense football. Coryell had three double-digit winning seasons in his five years, but because of Bidwell's unwillingness to spend money to re-sign players, Coryell had a hard time keeping the players happy. Coryell was the poster child for working for bad owners and being a great coach. Had he worked for Eddie DeBartolo or Jack Kent Cooke, he might be one of the winningest coaches of all time instead of struggling to make the Hall of Fame selection list. His major contributions—implementing offensive football, advancing the forward pass, and instructing players on how to pass protect without having to keep seven blockers near the quarterback—are all utilized today in the pro game.

SITUATION NUMBER THREE
Two Hundred Wins Should Matter

After finishing at the University of South Carolina in 1965 as a quarterback and star baseball player, Dan Reeves had three options: play safety for the Dallas Cowboys, suit up for the Chargers of the AFL, or play baseball for the Pittsburgh Pirates. He ultimately chose the Cowboys under head coach Tom Landry, where he played safety and halfback, eventually becoming one of the league's best. Reeves was far ahead of his time in versatility. His soft hands made him an attractive pass catcher. His shiftiness as a runner allowed him to avoid big hits. His physical strength helped when he was called upon for pass protection. And he could throw the ball with great accuracy, a quality most running backs needed during that period.

During his remarkable 1966 rookie season, Reeves had sixteen touchdowns—eight receiving and eight rushing—amassing over 1,300 all-purpose yards while becoming a member of the *Sporting News* All-Pro Team, a monumental achievement during this era. But after a significant knee injury during the 1968 season, Reeves's career began to draw to a close. Coach Landry was always keenly aware that Reeves had long exhibited great leadership qualities, so he decided to convert him into a player-coach. This arrangement ultimately served as Reeves's apprenticeship, and he learned the game from an entirely new perspective. He remarkably won a Super Bowl as a player-coach in 1971, and when his eight-year playing career finally ended, he became a full-time assistant and won a second Super Bowl in 1977.

In 1981, Reeves took over as head coach of the Denver Broncos while also serving as the team's vice president. He was in complete control of football operations, playing a significant part in the team eventually trading for great Stanford quarterback John Elway in 1983. During his distinguished career in Denver, Reeves guided the Broncos to six postseasons, three AFC Championship games, and three Super Bowls. He was also the only coach to lead his team to back-to-back Super Bowl appearances during the 1980s. But the lopsided nature of these three Super Bowl losses hurt Reeves in his pursuit of the Hall of Fame's gold jacket. Losing repeatedly in the Super Bowl shouldn't be a barrier to entry to the Hall. Marv Levy of the Buffalo Bills lost four and got in. So did Bud Grant of the Minnesota Vikings. This isn't to say Levy and Grant don't belong, but voters can't hold these losses against Reeves. Critics might claim that John Elway carried Reeves to those three Super Bowls, but Reeves did it again with journeyman quarterback Chris Chandler when he coached the Atlanta Falcons.

These critics argue that Reeves was unable to win a title with the best quarterback in the game in Elway, but they naively overlook the teams he had to defeat just to get there—the New York Giants in 1986, the Washington Redskins in 1987, and the San Francisco 49ers in 1989. Beating them was a tall order for any coach, as they, too, were well coached and had excellent quarterbacks. Reeves may have had the best in Elway, but he didn't have the most complete team or one that matched the physical style or the explosiveness of his great opponents. Reeves was only the third coach in NFL history to lead three different teams to the playoffs (joining Bill Parcells and Chuck Knox). In total, he played and coached in six Super Bowls, won over two hundred games as a head coach, and yet when he passed away on New Year's Eve in 2021, he still was not a member of the Hall. Reeves is one of only ten coaches to have won over two hundred games during his NFL career. Shouldn't the fact that this is such a rarified group make simply belonging to it a main criterion for Hall of Fame selection? Let's not overthink this—win two hundred and you're in. Don't judge the margin of victories, the specific rosters, or whether the coach had a bad loss or two. Winning two hundred games is damn near impossible and requires longevity in a profession that is about anything but.

Besides longevity, the other obstacle to two hundred wins is that many NFL games are decided by three points or fewer. To be on the right side of the scoreboard that much isn't luck; it's skill. The league is designed for parity, and the system is rigged for most teams to hover around the .500 mark. With the margin of error so slim, it was obvious from the early days of the NFL that winning close games would be the hallmark of a great head coach—one who understands how to motivate his team each week and handle the details that are essential for winning. If only 2 percent of the men who have called themselves "head coach" have achieved this feat, it ought to be Hall of Fame–worthy.

SITUATION NUMBER FOUR

My Second Stint Is Killing My First

Former 49ers head coach George Seifert won 64 percent of his games, amassed 114 total wins, and made the playoffs seven times during his eleven-year career, winning two Super Bowls. He ranks thirty-eighth overall in wins, right behind former Rams and Washington Hall of Fame coach George Allen, who never won a title and appeared in only one Super Bowl. Yet Allen is in the Hall because of his 71.2 winning percentage over his twelve-year NFL head coaching career, while Seifert isn't.

Mike Holmgren won a title with the Packers and took Seattle to a Super Bowl; yet his name is rarely mentioned for the Hall. The same applies to Mike Shanahan, who won two Super Bowls with Denver and took Washington to the playoffs. All three men have something else in common—they left the game and later returned—and their critics claim their second stints as head coaches were not successful. When he returned with the Carolina Panthers, Seifert had a 16–32 record. Shanahan was 24–40 when he came back to coach Washington. But Holmgren was 86–74 with the Seahawks and won the NFC in 2005. He won more games with Seattle than with Green Bay because he coached longer—ten years as opposed to seven—but his winning percentage was not as good. In Green Bay, with Hall of Famer Brett Favre, Holmgren won 67 percent of his games, whereas with Seattle he won just 53 percent.

SITUATION NUMBER FIVE

Winning the Games That Count the Most

Another high-held criterion for the voters is winning a Super Bowl, which unde-niably should be a significant factor in determining who will earn a gold jacket. Weeb Ewbank of the Baltimore Colts and New York Jets, for example, ended his head coaching career one game above .500, but had a monumental win in Super Bowl III, leading the Jets to what is still their only title. That victory ultimately united the leagues, giving additional credibility to the old AFL while greatly advancing the sport's popularity. No one had given the Jets a chance in that game. Despite having Joe Namath, they were clearly the inferior team and were 19.5-point underdogs heading into the game, which remains the largest spread between two Super Bowl teams. But they controlled the game from start to fin-ish and conveyed to the 44 million people who watched the game at home that the AFL was a legitimate league and no longer just the NFL's stepsister.

Ewbank also served as head coach during the greatest game ever, when the Colts defeated the New York Giants in 1958 to win the NFL title. Ewbank coached for twenty seasons, had 130 wins, led his team to the playoffs four times, and won two NFL championships and a Super Bowl, which sealed his overall record for induction into the Hall. But he averaged 6.5 wins for every season he was a head coach. (The league played twelve games then.) Meanwhile, Marty Schottenheimer averaged 9.65 wins (during fourteen- and sixteen-game sea-sons). But because Ewbank won the biggest of games multiple times, he's the one with a gold jacket. Does that seem fair? This isn't to argue he shouldn't be in the Hall. He won the biggest of games and had a monumental impact on the sport by uniting the leagues with one of the greatest upsets ever. But regular-season and postseason success are too often neglected and titles too heavily weighed.

SITUATION NUMBER SIX

Sponsorship Matters

Since the Hall of Fame doesn't have set criteria for entrance, politics, political capital, and influence create candidates. When someone is willing to take up a cause for a friend, and then work the room for votes, the facts become irrelevant.

Using a persuasive voice to convince voters, as well as some quid pro quo, has led to many of the recent entries. Case in point: Carl Peterson and Dick Vermeil.

In 2002, former Kansas City Chiefs general manager Carl Peterson went to work for his good friend and former coach, Dick Vermeil. Vermeil had spent seven seasons with the Philadelphia Eagles after serving as a first-time head coach with UCLA in 1974–1975. He inherited a bad Eagles team that hadn't been in the playoffs since its 1960 title game appearance against the Green Bay Packers. (Interestingly enough, that game was Packers' head coach Vince Lombardi's only playoff loss.) Besides having a poor roster, Vermeil had no first-round picks until the 1979 season.

In 1976, after Vermeil's first three seasons as the Eagles' head coach, the Eagles finally made the playoffs. By 1980, Vermeil had his Eagles poised to be champions. The Birds finished the season in first place with a 12–4 record, losing three of their last four games only due to the fact they had already secured home-field advantage throughout the playoffs. The Eagles won both playoff games at Veterans Stadium and, for the first time in franchise history, were headed to the Super Bowl.

The Eagles were favored against the Oakland Raiders in Super Bowl XV by three points, but early in the game it was obvious that the bookmakers had it all wrong. The Eagles faced a far superior team and were soundly defeated, 27–10. The following season, the Eagles made the playoffs once again, this time as a wildcard team, before losing to their archrival, the Giants. But by 1981, when the players' strike ruined the NFL season, Vermeil would use the term "burnout" to describe how the previous seven years of overworking had affected him, and he ultimately opted to turn over head coaching duties to Marion Campbell, his defense coordinator. From 1983 until 1997, Vermeil stayed involved with the game by doing college color commentary on both CBS and ABC. Finally, in 1999, he came back to coach the St. Louis Rams.

The NFL to which Vermeil returned was vastly different from the one he had left in 1982. He struggled mightily his first two seasons, going 5–11 and 4–12, respectively, and was ordered by the front office to hire then-Washington assistant coach Mark Martz to run the offense. Vermeil was initially reluctant, but he knew that Rams president John Shaw was going to fire him if he didn't hire Martz, and that Shaw had already dismissed his old friend Jerry Rhome as coordinator. After much back and forth, Vermeil gave in to Shaw, and the following season the Rams went from twenty-fourth in points scored and twenty-seventh in yards gained to first in yards and points. Led by quarterback Kurt Warner and running back Marshall Faulk, they defeated the Tennessee Titans in one of the most famous Super Bowls ever.

The success following the addition of Martz raises a few questions: Would Vermeil have been as successful without him? How much credit should go to Martz for that Super Bowl, and how much should be bestowed on Vermeil? What we do know is that Martz ran the offense with respect to play design, game planning, and calling the game. He really had complete autonomy over it. This isn't to undermine the selection of Vermeil to the Hall of Fame. But you can't understate the role Shaw played in saving Vermeil's career by adding Martz. Immediately following the game, Vermeil retired for the second time in his coaching career, this time at the age of sixty-three.

After one year off, Vermeil chose to return for the third time, now reuniting with old pal Carl Peterson as head coach of the Kansas City Chiefs. Vermeil spent five seasons, earning one playoff win, and during the regular season winning a total of forty-four games and losing thirty-six. After the 2005 season, Vermeil finally called it quits for good. As an amazing friend and Vermeil loyalist, Peterson set out to get him into the Hall of Fame.

Over his fifteen years as a head coach, Vermeil won 120 games, ranking thirty-fifth overall in wins. He lost 109, giving him a 52.4-win percentage—only slightly behind former Vikings coach Brad Childress, Eagles coach and Super Bowl–winner Doug Pederson, and significantly behind Seifert, Shanahan, and Holmgren. Vermeil's teams made the playoffs six times in fifteen years, winning just 40 percent of their playoff games. So how is it that Vermeil gained access to the Hall before the others?

Vermeil is a beloved figure and one of the nicest men on the planet. He is adored by the city of Philadelphia, and his charming ways and sincere love of the game make him someone who is easy to support. Peterson worked relentlessly behind the scenes, doing his best Lyndon B. Johnson—the greatest vote counter of any President—to secure the votes needed to allow Vermeil to jump over others more deserving. Buddy Parker, Clark Shaughnessy, Mike Holmgren, Mike Shanahan, Dan Reeves, and Marty Schottenheimer all should have been selected for the Hall before Vermeil. But none of them had someone like Peterson working on their behalf. Sponsorship matters.

CHAPTER 3

THE LOMBARDI CRITERIA FOR COACHES

"Football is a game of errors. The team that makes the fewest errors in a game usually wins."
—Paul Brown

THE PROCESS OF SELECTION ALWAYS BEGINS with elimination. To properly find talent, select members for an organization, or give coaches a gold jacket, there needs to be a set a criteria of excellence. Once uniform criteria are agreed upon, then we can find the coaches who fit the criteria and debate their merits. Without precise criteria, everyone and anyone is eligible, and the loudest voice, rather than the most reasonable one, is heard. Determining talent and electing members to the Hall of Fame cannot be an arbitrary process; there needs to be a standard for admittance.

Without a standard of excellence, bias and politics can take hold instead of merit. It's never intentional or recognized. Voters will assure one another of their purity of intention, reminding everyone "they want what is best for the Hall." But we all have some form of bias in our own decision-making processes; it's unavoidable. If I were the NFL commissioner, I would immediately develop a standard of admittance excellence that coaches would need to meet in order to enter the Hall, replacing the sliding scales of the past with quantifiable merit. With that, I am proud to introduce...

CRITERION NUMBER ONE

Two Hundred Regular Season Wins— Automatic Hall of Fame Qualification

Let's end useless debate and stop examining playoff records. If you win two hundred games—either regular season games or regular season and playoff wins combined—you should get the gold jacket. This rule would allow Marty Schottenheimer and Dan Reeves to be welcomed into the Hall. Schottenheimer won two hundred regular seasons games in twenty-one seasons, yet only 2 percent of the coaching population has two hundred wins. If you're better than 98 percent of your peers, you belong in the Hall of Fame. How can this be debatable?

CRITERION NUMBER TWO

NFL/AFL Titles as Well as Super Bowl Wins Count

Don't distinguish between the two. Vince Lombardi won two Super Bowls and was the NFL champion three times; therefore, his title count should be five, not two. Hank Stram won two AFL titles and one Super Bowl, earning a total of three titles. Paul Brown won three NFL titles and four AAFC Championships. Curly Lambeau won six NFL titles. Titles are titles, no matter where they were earned.

CRITERION NUMBER THREE

Three or More NFL Titles or Super Bowl Wins

Vince Lombardi, Bill Walsh, Joe Gibbs, Hank Stram, Weeb Ewbank, Paul Brown, George Halas, Bill Belichick, Curly Lambeau, Guy Chamberlin, and Chuck Noll all meet the threshold. Only eleven men have won three or more titles. All of them wear a gold jacket.

CRITERION NUMBER FOUR

Two or More NFL Titles or Super Bowl Wins, Plus a 55 Percent or Higher Win Rate

Coaches in this category ideally would also have won over one hundred games. However, because of the reduced twelve-game schedule in the 1940s and '50s, the threshold would prove unfair to some. There are fourteen men with two titles: Don Shula, Tom Landry, Bill Parcells, Tom Coughlin, Mike Shanahan, Steve Owens, George Seifert, Buddy Parker, Tom Flores, Lou Saban, Jimmy Conzelman, Ray Flaherty, Jimmy Johnson, and Greasy Neale. Nine are already in the Hall. But introducing this standard would also allow for the addition of Parker, Coughlin, Seifert, and Shanahan. Flores gained entrance in 2021, but his win percentage was below the threshold, eliminating him under these standards. Jimmy Johnson would qualify because he had a 55 percent win rate, despite only winning eighty games. Johnson was an interesting case, as many of the voters on the Centennial Class Committee didn't feel he belonged due to his win total. It's low, but those who respected Johnson's career cited his role as general manager and team builder—selecting two Hall of Famers in quarterback Troy Aikman and running back Emmitt Smith—in addition to serving as the architect of the team that won three titles. Johnson would have qualified easily with three titles had he been allowed to coach in 1994, the year Barry Switzer took over. Greasy Neale also qualifies even though he only won sixtythree games during his Philadelphia head coaching career, since he had a 59 percent win rate.

CRITERION NUMBER FIVE

Either a 62 Percent Win Rate over Two Hundred or More Games, or a 60 Percent Rate Reaching the Playoffs

Most people believe winning a Super Bowl automatically qualifies a coach for the Hall, but there are currently thirty-four coaches with a title attached to their name who are not remotely worthy of the Hall of Fame. There has to be a higher threshold for onetime winners. Former Colts and Buccaneers head coach Tony Dungy would qualify under this rule, as he won one title, coached in 208 games with a 66 percent win rate, and made the playoffs eleven out of his thirteen seasons as a head coach—an astonishing 84 percent rate. Mike Holmgren would also qualify because of his Super Bowl win and because his teams reached the playoffs at the 60 percent threshold, as would current Pittsburgh Steelers coach Mike Tomlin, because of his one title and his 64 percent winning rate over two hundred games.

CRITERION NUMBER SIX

Game-Changing Impact

Did the coach, as either a head man or assistant, through his ingenuity and creative process deeply change the course of the game? If so, how? This criterion needs to be fully vetted, and only one member can be selected every five years, which will help voters do the proper research for potential candidates. Chargers head man Sid Gillman wouldn't qualify under criterion number five, but he would make it with this one, as someone who highly advanced the game and became a foundational mentor for present-day football. Without Gillman, the sophisticated passing game we all witness today might not even exist. Clark Shaughnessy qualifies under this criterion, with his forward thinking regarding the passing game and his development of defensive schemes. Had this criterion existed earlier, then-Redskins and Rams head man George Allen would need to prove he greatly advanced the game. Even though he held a 71 percent win rate, coaching in 168 games, he failed to win a title and failed to qualify for the playoffs 60 percent of the time. (He reached the postseason only 58 percent of the time.)

Former Cardinals and Chargers head man Don Coryell advanced the game enough to justify entry under this criterion. Coryell coached fourteen seasons, five with the St. Louis Cardinals and nine with the San Diego Chargers. He won 111 games over those fourteen years, finishing with a 57 percent win rate, which is higher than that of Vermeil, Flores, and Johnson. Coryell took his teams to the playoffs six times, for a 42.8 percent success rate, and lost two AFC Championship games. He expanded the passing game, first learning from Gillman, then implementing his own creative designs, which have influenced countless former and present-day coaches. Joe Gibbs learned from Coryell, and his methods highly impacted Bill Walsh, Tony Dungy, and John Madden. Coryell was ahead of his time and deserves to be identified as a game changer in coming years.

With these six criteria, the Hall would have a streamlined process of who actually qualifies and who does not. There would surely still be debates over who had been slighted, much as there are annually in the college football playoff system. But unlike in that opaque process, which baffles even the experts, the Hall's entry system would be known to all—and a purposeful debate could ensue over lowering the standards or making various exceptions. A gold jacket isn't meant for everyone who wins a title or for all who have a high win percentage. It's only meant to fit the truly elite. And taking serious measurements beforehand prevents some poor fits.

CHAPTER 4
TOP TEN COACHES

*"Things turn out best for those who make
the best of the way things turn out."*
—John Wooden

BEFORE CONSIDERING THE LIST OF THE all-time greatest coaches, it's important to understand that not all coaches have faced the same obstacles. Some had to deal with a salary cap, limiting spending on players. Some had owners who didn't care how much the team invested. Some coached during wars. Some coached in the turbulent 1960s during the United States' culture clash. Some had to deal with player strikes and the organization of the players' union, taking away the full authority of the team and coach. The common denominator, though, is that they all faced unique challenges related to their era. None had an obstacle-free path to the mountaintop.

The common thread that unites the following ten coaches isn't a scheme, team values, or a common leadership style. They each tremendously advanced the game in their own way. They took what they learned through observation and years of study under other head coaches, then applied this knowledge to their own coaching and teaching philosophies. All ten faced major challenges—from lack of money to lack of technology and even to lack of field space—but refused to ever settle for the status quo. They demanded more from themselves and their teams—and made the sport significantly better as a result. Today's highly sophisticated NFL still utilizes the methods devised by these coaches, and while football will undergo rule and strategy changes in the years and decades ahead, the fingerprints of these men can never be dusted away.

10
CURLY LAMBEAU

380 Games • 226 Wins • 132 Losses • 22 Ties • 6 Titles

An incredible athlete, Curly Lambeau enrolled at Notre Dame, where he played for the legendary Fighting Irish coach Knute Rockne. He fell in love with Rockne's aggressive offense, which emphasized throwing the ball down the field instead of just running. But after developing a severe case of tonsillitis, Lambeau was forced to return home to Wisconsin, where he took a job working for the Indian Packing Company. The following year, Lambeau organized a football team in which he played and coached, with money for uniforms provided by his employer, and later petitioned for his team's entry into the American Professional League.

Inspired by Rockne, Lambeau emphasized the forward pass, tossing twenty-four touchdowns and scoring 110 points over the course of his career, which are sensational numbers for the 1920s. In 1929, Lambeau won the first of his three consecutive titles. When left end Don Hutson arrived in Green Bay in 1935, Lambeau utilized his incredible skills in the passing game to secure three more titles—an astonishing six in total.

Lambeau was a screamer and a yeller, and would often fine his players their entire salary for not following his orders. Known as the "Belligerent Belgian," he frequently rubbed players the wrong way. In one instance, Lambeau went on a tirade about his team's passing attack—even inserting himself into the lineup to demonstrate what he wanted. But as the play began, the Packers' offensive line decided it would get a little revenge, getting out of the way on a rush to allow Lambeau to get run over. Would his leadership style and behavior work today? The simple answer is no. To build a team, an entire league, it's natural to ruffle feathers. Lambeau's style fit the time, and because of his persistence in demanding the best of his players and pushing everyone, the Packers and the NFL became a viable sports league.

There's a reason one of the world's preeminent athletic venues carries his name. It's easy to highlight Lambeau's weaknesses, of which there were many, but his impact on the sport at the time cannot be glossed over.

9
CHUCK NOLL

342 Games • 193 Wins • 148 Losses • 1 Tie • 4 Titles

As he watched Penn State score a touchdown and then execute a two-point conversion to lift the Nittany Lions over Kansas in the 1969 Orange Bowl, Pittsburgh Steelers owner Dan Rooney knew he had to hire the university's head coach, Joe Paterno. Rooney wanted him to take over for Bill Austin in 1970 and thought he had a deal lined up. But at the last minute, Paterno said no, forcing Rooney to continue his search. Seeking advice, he called Don Shula, who told Rooney in no uncertain terms that the man for the job was Chuck Noll. On January 13, in Miami Beach, Rooney and Noll met for the first time to exchange ideas and compare philosophies. Rooney learned about the depth of Noll's intellect and his philosophy on treating players equally. Noll didn't play favorites or ever let public perception sway his thoughts. He was all about the best man getting the job, regardless of race, draft position, or past history. Noll was not a screamer, but rather an instructor who shied away from brutal practices that were overly heavy on contact. He knew his team needed to be physical in its play, but not always in its preparation. He said that he believed too many teams overemphasized brute force and that full-scale contact ultimately wore down the players' minds and bodies. Noll had a knack for understanding personnel and each player's strengths and weaknesses, which certainly came across in his meeting with Rooney, who was impressed by Noll's existing knowledge of the Steelers' personnel. Two weeks later, Rooney offered Noll the head coaching position. The Steelers now had their fourth head coach in six years, but this one felt different.

Noll was a shining example of learning your craft and then applying your personality and beliefs with a humble confidence. He was well rounded in every aspect of the game, from his playing days along the offensive line to his coordination of the defense. Noll's coaching education allowed him to coach any position or player. He knew exactly the type of schemes that would prove beneficial to his players' talent level, because he understood players and plays. Noll took from his work in San Diego and Baltimore a love for scouting players, and he knew the exact characteristics he needed to assemble his roster. To him, talent evaluation was simple. During his Pittsburgh career, from 1969 to 1991, Noll played a vital role in assembling the incredible roster that became the Steel Curtain, which dominated the NFL during the 1970s.

Though he won four Super Bowls and his teams played in seven conference championship games, Noll never liked to be in the spotlight, nor did he want to take the glory away from his players. He remained in the background, working on his craft and teaching the game. He viewed himself as a teacher first and foremost. His poise and temperament distinguished him from so many of his peers. Former Giants general manager George Young, who worked with Noll in Baltimore, described Noll as "a head coach who has learned to control his ego better than anyone in the game. He's like a great Harvard professor who keeps turning out Rhodes scholars and yet doesn't want to do anything but teach, doesn't want to be a dean or a department head. He's happy where he is. I have seen less of a change in him as a person, since he was an assistant at Baltimore, than anyone else in such a high position."

8
DON SHULA

490 Games • 328 Wins • 156 Losses • 6 Ties • 2 Titles

Don Shula began his head coaching career with Baltimore when he was just thirty-three years old and worked a remarkable thirty-three seasons on the sidelines. His coaching longevity, his 328 career wins (the most in NFL history), and his undefeated season of 1972 will be difficult to ever surpass. In that undefeated 1972 season, Shula rarely had his Hall of Fame quarterback Bob Griese or his backup thirty-eight-year-old Earl Morrall throw a pass. (Morrall started nine games that season because Griese had been injured.) The Dolphins attempted just 18.5 passes per game on average and had the top-rated offense and defense in the league. When Shula's team returned to the Super Bowl in 1984, this time under the direction of second-year, future Hall of Fame quarterback Dan Marino, the Dolphins attempted 35.7 passes and had the top-rated offense in all of football. Shula was never old school and never pined for the "remember when" days as a coach. He stayed progressive and had his teams adapt to tweaks in the rules. Over his thirty-three years, Shula witnessed sweeping changes to the game and frequently adapted to keep his team relevant. Indeed, his adaptability and his willingness to change his methods and philosophy over the years might be his greatest virtue.

After losing to the 49ers in the 1985 Super Bowl, Shula's Dolphins failed to make the playoffs for four consecutive seasons—the longest drought of Shula's career—while Hall of Fame quarterback Dan Marino was in his prime. Over the next ten years, the Dolphins went to the playoffs only four times and played in only one AFC Conference Championship. Marino only played in eighteen playoff games during his remarkable career, which falls well short of the expectations for his career after his Super Bowl appearance in his second season. But despite the perceived failures, the Dolphins had just one losing season during this stretch, when they went 6–10 in 1988.

As Shula's son David said when presenting his father for the Hall of Fame, "Honesty is his credo. No team went into a game better prepared. Don Shula–coached teams were audible ready, so well prepared, they could adjust to any unusual circumstance. Being as good as everyone never entered his mind. Being better than everyone else is all he ever thought about."

7
TOM LANDRY

418 Games ● 250 Wins ● 162 Losses ● 6 Ties ● 2 Titles

In 1996, during the eighth season of *The Simpsons*, Homer purchases a fedora, hoping it will help his leadership skills at his new job. He was paying homage to the great head coach of the Dallas Cowboys, Tom Landry. Landry started wearing a fedora while he was an assistant coach with the New York Giants to protect his bald head from the brutal cold of the Northeast. By the time he arrived in Dallas as head coach in 1960, it was his trademark. When Cowboys scouts would travel the country visiting colleges in search of prospects, they would give away blue ballpoint pens with a fedora along the side. Everyone knew what the graphic represented.

Landry was an innovator, never afraid to try new, well-researched ideas. He developed the Flex to keep his middle linebacker from getting blocked. Prior to its use, defensive linemen were taught to control their gap of the defense and to penetrate, disrupting the offense. But Landry didn't want his linemen to be aggressive. He wanted them to control the offensive linemen, not allowing them to reach the second level of the defense, thus keeping the middle linebacker free to make a tackle. With the Giants, when Landry employed this method, he helped make his middle linebacker, Sam Huff, a Hall of Fame player. "Landry built the 4–3 defense around me," Huff said. "It revolutionized defense and opened the door for all the variations of zones and man-to-man coverage, which are used in conjunction with it today."

Landry was always tinkering with different ways to play, and as his success as a coach grew, so did his curious mind. He reintroduced the shotgun formation to football, which had disappeared in the early 1960s. He changed personnel groupings and made shifting and motioning a staple of his offense. Perhaps most of all, despite being trained as a defensive coach, he also called offensive plays. Landry was a meticulous coach who motivated his players through his knowledge and nuanced understanding of every aspect of the game. He also was always in control of his emotions. This self-discipline was ingrained in his teams, which almost always took on his personality and played at the highest levels. When asked why he was so stoic during the game, Landy replied, "Because I was concentrating on the next play."

During his twenty-nine-year head coaching career in Dallas, Landry had twenty consecutive winning seasons, from 1966 until 1985, won two Super Bowls, five NFC titles, and thirteen divisional titles. If there was an NFC Championship game being played from 1970 until 1982, the Cowboys were just about guaranteed to be in it. They reached ten of these during this stretch—dominating the NFC and making the conference's Eastern Division the most competitive in football. Because of Landry's style and his team's on-the-field success, the Cowboys became a ratings grabber for networks and were routinely featured each weekend. With their remarkable success and with broadcasting regulations allowing just one game on TV in most markets throughout the country at the time, the Cowboys earned the moniker "America's Team."

6
BILL WALSH

152 Games • 92 Wins • 59 Losses • 1 Tie • 3 Titles

What do Walt Disney, Andrew Carnegie, and Bill Walsh all have in common? They are all incredible entrepreneurs who took an existing idea and made it significantly better. Walsh didn't invent the forward pass, but he revolutionized the air with his theories and strategies. As outlined in Chapter 1 (see page 19), his West Coast offense has been utilized by countless coaches, and many former coaches would not have been nearly as successful over their careers without his influence. Had he actually been allowed to patent and sell his offense, he might have been as wealthy as the aforementioned entrepreneurs. He never saw himself as purely a coach. He viewed his role as chief strategy officer, problem-solver, culture creator, and most of all, shrewd and deliberative teacher.

Walsh had the rare quality, which most of the men on this list share, of understanding what the job was and what it wasn't. He could identify the critical problem, and then have the talent to find a solution. For example, after the 1985 season, our star pass rusher defensive end Fred Dean was no longer effective because of a knee injury, and Walsh knew he needed a replacement. One day in late March, a month before the NFL draft, Walsh called me into his office to give me an assignment. He wanted me to read every college report on defensive linemen or linebackers who were at least six feet, four inches tall and over 230 pounds. Walsh was specific in his instructions for me to not care about the grade of the player, or if the player was effective against the run. All he wanted to know from my reading of the report was if the player was athletic and effective at rushing the passer. Once I presented him with my findings of the players that fit his criteria, we watched the tape on every player. This search led us to finding Charles Haley, who not only replaced Dean but eventually joined him in the Hall of Fame.

Walsh was never on time for any staff or player meetings. It was one of the reasons Paul Brown bypassed him in favor of Bill "Tiger" Johnson to hire as the Bengals' coach. Brown loved punctuality, whereas Walsh favored taking his time on the project at hand. He was not going to leave an important meeting or conversation to be on time for *his* scheduled meeting. For Walsh, those in attendance would have to wait. What Brown misunderstood about Walsh's tardiness was that Walsh could juggle a thousand things at one time and each one would receive his full attention and intelligence. Walsh wasn't the absent-minded professor who forgot he had called a meeting, or was wasting time on some experiment. His day was engulfed with decisions, all of them needing his full attention and focus. Many of us cannot multitask. Walsh could.

Once the game began, Walsh saw what others couldn't. His mind worked quickly to anticipate the next move of the defense and always found an answer to solve the problem. He invented the technique of scripting the first fifteen plays to allow the entire offensive team to be prepared the night before for the plays, thus limiting the chances for a communication error or a mental mistake.

The script for instant success was ideally meant to score first, get the lead, and force the opponent to play from behind. For Walsh, having a set of offensive plays didn't make an offense. He wanted a philosophy tied directly to the plays, allowing the players to fully understand the intention of what he was trying to accomplish. He had a sense of urgency to play from in front, and this was the genesis of his scripting for success.

Football fans did not get to witness enough of Walsh's talents. Even he had second thoughts about his retiring. Sitting at the Sharon Heights Golf Club with *Sports Illustrated*'s Michael Silver in March of 2007 (Walsh would pass away in July of that year), Walsh reflected back on his coaching life and admitted he left too early. He told Silver, "I should have continued to coach. If I could have taken a month off, or something to get away, then maybe I would have stayed. But I had other jobs that required my attention." Walsh allowed his emotions to affect his decision to retire, which was uncharacteristic of his methodical, unemotional process. He spent his entire career not allowing his feelings to interfere with his work, and, in the end, in making the one decision that mattered most, he broke his own self-imposed rule.

During his ten years with the 49ers, Walsh amassed 102 wins, won a remarkable three Super Bowl titles, drafted multiple future Hall of Famers, and left the team in far better shape than when he inherited the organization in 1979. The 49ers under George Seifert would go on to win two more titles, with Walsh's fingerprints still on the franchise. Though those two Super Bowl don't appear on Walsh's record, it's undeniable that he played a major part in the formation of these teams.

5
GEORGE HALAS

497 Games • 318 Wins • 148 Losses • 31 Ties • 6 Titles

When George Halas was inducted into the Hall of Fame in 1963, his presenter, David Lawrence—the former governor of Pennsylvania and longtime mayor of

Pittsburgh—put it best: "Welcome to the Hall of Fame, George Halas. It's your player, coach, founder, come as you wish; we hail you as them all." No truer words could be spoken about a man who built the NFL with his sweat, tears, and wholehearted devotion. Despite wearing many hats, Halas is on this list for his ability to lead men, to dominate the era, to win championships, and to bring changes to the game that helped endear football fans all over America.

At just twenty-seven, Halas became owner of the newly named Chicago Bears. For the next seven seasons, his teams had winning records but no titles to show. After his team posted a 4–9–2 record in 1929, Halas decided to allow Ralph Jones to become the head coach. Just three years later, he won an NFL title. Halas served as the general manager/owner, bringing in Hall of Fame players like Bronko Nagurski and Red Grange to the Bears. Because he was the owner of the team and in complete control, he could shift between the front office and sidelines for years. But by 1958, Halas was once again back on the sidelines—this time permanently—and would go on to win another title in 1963. It was the franchise's eighth under his leadership/ownership. Halas retired as a coach for good in 1967.

Halas truly had a great eye for talent and built some incredible teams with players who would go on to become Hall of Famers. He was a demanding coach dedicated to the fundamentals, but he was also willing to adapt and alter his schemes as he saw fit. With a huge assist from Clark Shaughnessy, Halas made the T formation part of the NFL and embraced the forward pass, making the game more fan friendly. Halas was Mr. NFL for his entire career, one of the greats of any era.

4
JOE GIBBS

248 Games • 154 Wins • 94 Losses • 3 Titles

On September 27, 1987, the lights went dark on the NFL as tension between the players and owners led to a strike. Once the players walked out, the owners decided that if the current players didn't want to play, they would find some who did. Thus, replacement football was born, and for the first time in its history, the NFL held meaningful games with temporary fill-ins. Teams really scrambled to find players, but in less than two weeks, each had a roster.

The week before the strike occurred, the Redskins lost a heartbreaker in Atlanta, 21–20. Redskins head coach Joe Gibbs punted with over four minutes left in the fourth quarter on a 4th and 1 and never got the ball back again. (Twitter might've had a word to say about this had it been around then.) Entering the season, Washington had Super Bowl aspirations, and this loss stung. To make matters worse for Gibbs, the Redskins were a pro-union team. Having players cross their picket lines heightened the tensions between players and staff, casting major doubt on their season.

Gibbs never let the loss to Atlanta or the strike affect his coaching. He knew he had a championship-level team and wasn't about to let any obstacle stand in his way. Washington won the first two of the replacement games to set up a Monday night matchup against archrival Dallas. Cowboys star quarterback Danny White, running back Tony Dorsett, and defensive linemen Ed "Too Tall" Jones and Randy White all crossed the picket lines, giving Dallas a huge advantage in talent and making the Redskins an eight-point underdog. Gibbs didn't want any of his players to cross, so he took matters into his own hands.

The sixty thousand fans in Dallas Stadium and the huge national television audience watching at home witnessed one of the finest coaching performances of a lifetime. Gibbs was determined to run the ball effectively against the Cowboys' more dominating front. By using motion and shifts, Gibbs was able to create a half-man advantage in the run game, allowing running back Lionel Vital to gain 136 yards on twenty-six carries and Washington to gain 186 yards rushing on the ground. The key to any successful running game is to have a half blocker advantage, and with shifts and motion causing the defense to react late, Gibbs was able to control the ball for thirty-six minutes and come back to DC with the most impressive win of his illustrious career, even though undermanned and out-talented.

Over the course of his career, Gibbs won three Super Bowls, with three different "efficient" quarterbacks, a remarkable achievement. In his Super Bowl win in Dallas, Gibbs's play designs made Tony Robinson an effective thrower; Robinson only had eight incompletions, going 12–20 and throwing for 174 yards. Like all great offensive coaches, Gibbs made the game easy for the quarterback to perform. For all his remarkable achievements, it was this win in Dallas that was his finest act.

3
BILL BELICHICK

433 Games • 290 Wins • 143 Losses • 6 Titles (as of 2023)

Malcolm Gladwell writes in *Outliers*, "Extraordinary achievement is less about talent and more about special opportunity." Gladwell believes that had Bill Gates not grown up near the University of Washington with access to their computer lab, and thus valuable time on the computer, he might not have been the greatest code writer of all time. Time and place became his special opportunity. The same argument could be made regarding Bill Belichick. Belichick became fascinated by football at an early age while watching his father, also a coach, study the game each night. Being around the Navy football program, where his dad worked, and the Naval Academy in general was a special and transformative opportunity. Belichick began to understand the importance of team building, selflessness, and doing what is right for the team when it might not be right for the individual. By being on campus every day and getting to play catch with Heisman Trophy–winner Roger Staubach, Belichick gained valuable insight into the making of a leader when he was in just the fifth grade. Belichick may not hold a Naval Academy degree, but his methods are entirely Annapolis.

Critics might claim Tom Brady was the reason for Belichick's success. Brady undeniably played a huge role, but the combination of both men's talents formed a dynasty that will never be duplicated. Belichick's development of the Patriot Way, which Brady adhered to and promoted, allowed the culture in New England to manifest and grow stronger with each passing year. Belichick was never a bystander: if you watch clips of Brady playing during his first season, in 2001, and then in his last, in 2019, you can see how his game changed under Belichick. You can also see the differences in the Patriots' offensive football and how Belichick developed the team through those nineteen seasons by enhancing the skills of Brady and those around him. Likewise, the Patriots were never a one-man play with Brady in the lead role. The culture set enabled flexibility in the system and thrived on mental and physical toughness, all part of the Belichickian way.

The similarities between Bill Walsh and Belichick are staggering. Both men were in charge of all things organizationally and were involved in every decision. Nothing happened in San Francisco or in New England without both men granting their approval. Walsh built his organization around what he called "Standard of Excellence." Belichick crafted his as the "Patriot Way." They were different characterizations, yet both relating to the team culture so vital to their success. Both men had an incredible ability to stay focused in the moment, always giving their full attention to the matter at hand. As a result, both were always late for their meetings.

Belichick is truly an outlier, as he goes against most conventional NFL wisdom when crafting game plans or restoring his team from season to season. He often zigs when others zag. Again, like Walsh he can remain emotionless when making decisions, all wrapped around the code of conduct he repeats throughout the halls at Patriot place: "For the good of the team." These are not shallow words to justify his moves with the media. They are intertwined with his DNA as a coach. Each day, "the good of the team" dictates his every move.

In his twenty-two seasons with the New England Patriots, Belichick has had a 72 percent win rate and just two losing seasons. In nineteen of these years, he recorded double-digit wins and has only failed to make the playoffs three times. Belichick is also one of the three members of the exclusive three-hundred-win club, along with Halas and Shula. He has reached forty-four playoff games, outranking all other coaches, and his 72.1 percent win rate in these playoffs games far exceeds that of any other coach. With a solid foundation and a new quarterback, Mac Jones, Belichick is once again transcending the football world in his sixth decade in the NFL.

2
VINCE LOMBARDI

136 Games • 96 Wins • 34 Losses • 6 Ties • 5 Titles

When my mother informed me on September 3, 1970, that Vince Lombardi had succumbed to cancer, my world was shattered. I am not related to the legend, with whom I share a last name, but I was still devastated. Seeing him roam the sideline in his hat and coat each Sunday, when he was still a young man, provided me with a life dream. His death at just fifty-seven cheated all football fans. Lombardi was just entering the prime of his coaching career when he died.

There have been many books written about Lombardi, his leadership style, his quotes, and his methodology. Perhaps the greatest insight into this complicated, highly educated man comes from his own words—given to the Dayton Agonis Club on June 22, 1970, at Suttmiller's restaurant in Dayton, Ohio: "The difference between all is in energy, in the strong will, in a singleness of purpose, and an invincible determination. But the great difference is in sacrifice, in self-denial, in love and loyalty, in fearlessness and in humility, in the pursuit of excellence and in the perfectly disciplined will, because this is not only the difference between all, this is the difference between the great and not great." The last line of this speech offers the essence of how Lombardi lived his life and why he was so successful at coaching.

Like all the coaches on this list, Lombardi could have been successful in any profession. His core values, his work ethic, and—most of all—his understanding of what the job was and wasn't made him a powerful force. Some might believe understanding the job is the easy part, which is often not the case. Lombardi had the innate ability to totally focus on the one area that would make each player realize his full potential. When he arrived in Green Bay in 1959, the Packers had talent, yet they were not a talented team, nor were they disciplined, with mental toughness—all essential to the Lombardi way. The Packers became an extension of him as they pursued the excellence he so desperately wanted and needed in his life.

Unbeknownst to many, during his final years in Green Bay, Lombardi was battling ulcers and other various ailments. He resigned as head coach upon winning his third straight title and second Super Bowl after the 1967 season, and became the general manager of the Packers, hoping that the removal of the day-to-day pressure of running the team would improve his health. During his ten years in Green Bay, Lombardi won five titles—losing just once in the playoffs—and won 73.9 percent of his games.

When the itch to coach returned along with a lucrative offer from Washington Redskins owner Edward Bennett Williams, Lombardi decided to get back on the sidelines. His new team had a star quarterback, Sonny Jurgensen, and its future appeared bright. He went 7–5–2 in his first season in Washington and seemed destined once again for major success with the franchise before his sudden passing.

One of Lombardi's greatest strengths, like many others on this list, was his ability to adapt and remain curious about learning, using his Jesuit education to influence his zest for constant improvement. Like the other members of this list, Lombardi wanted to be viewed first and foremost as a teacher. His talent of being able to explain, demand, and understand the subject allowed him to be successful in any sport he coached when teaching at St. Cecilia High School. Not surprisingly, hanging on the wall of his Green Bay office was a teacher-of-the-year plaque from St. Cecilia. He was as proud of that honor as he was of any titles that he received coaching football.

Even though Lombardi has fewer than one hundred wins, his five titles in nine years made Green Bay into Titletown and the Packers one of the most famous franchises in all of sports. Like Curly Lambeau, Lombardi put Green Bay back on the NFL map and restored the reputation of this iconic franchise.

1
PAUL BROWN

326 Games ● 213 Wins ● 104 Losses ● 9 Ties ● 7 Titles

It is not a stretch to say that without Paul Brown's influence, the coaching methods and organizational practices of today would not exist. Almost every sentence describing how to build a winning team on and off the field starts with his name. Without Brown, there would be no Bill Walsh, Weeb Ewbank, Don Shula, Chuck Noll, or even Bill Belichick. This is not to imply these coaches were copycats, but rather to emphasize the significant influence Brown had on the entire sport. Without Brown, the coaching profession would not have reached the level of excellence it has today.

Brown dominated the coaching profession from high school to college, in the military, and eventually in the professional game. He never thought of himself as a coach—he was a teacher, a highly detailed, disciplined instructor who understood the essence of winning. He never screamed or yelled; he remained emotionless as he taught. The Roman emperor Marcus Aurelius once said, "The secret of all victory lies in the organization of the nonobvious." Brown understood how to find the nonobvious factors that determine winning and losing. For example, penalties in the kicking game would be a nonobvious detail. When a team receiving the ball in either a punt or kickoff is penalized, the penalty is enforced from the spot of the violation, which changes field position dramatically. Brown demanded no penalties in the kicking game, insisted on a clean exchange of the ball, and practiced to ensure that his team understood this nonobvious area was vital.

Brown also understood the difference between planning and strategy. Brown never planned to win; he was always strategizing to win the game—big difference. Planning is something you do when taking a vacation. Each day you plan your trip, aligning particular points of interest to view. Strategizing is asking yourself two key questions: How are we going to win the game? What will need to happen for the team to win the game? Once Brown found his answer through extensive film study, he would then practice to ensure the team understood what it would take to win.

His constant attention to the details of winning enabled him to create changes in the game, from inventing the draw play to developing the first face mask after his star quarterback Otto Graham suffered a severe cut in his chin that required twenty-three stitches. Brown had a curious mind, always wondering what he could do to make the game and his team better. He was never static—like all great teachers, he was always trying to find new ways to teach old subjects...and invent new ones.

Brown even had to overcome criticism and endure being fired. The criticism, directed at his interference with the game by using messenger guards, never bothered him. But the events of January 7, 1963, would linger in his soul until the day he died. In 1961, when Art Modell—a brash, young, handsome owner—took over the Browns, Brown had total control of the franchise, and this was written in his contract. Modell wanted to be involved, and Brown wasn't about to allow someone from the business world to affect his team. They were oil and water. After two years, Modell wanted to take back his team—hearing that Brown was too old and too set in his ways, and that the game had passed him by. So he made the change, causing Brown to say to his son Mike, "They took my team away from me." Devastated and slightly embarrassed, Brown retreated to La Jolla, California, and spent the next five years in exile.

Like all great men, Brown would rise again, making his return to Ohio, this time in Cincinnati, as the owner of the Cincinnati Bengals. Within three short years, he had the expansion Bengals winning the division title. In his last four seasons as a head coach, Brown's record was 36–20, for a 64.2 percent win rate. So much for the game passing him by.

Brown was a godlike figure during his day. Every coach—young or old—wanted to know his secrets, learn his new methods, and borrow his ideas. Brown would share very little, as he never wanted his competitors to learn his secrets. His coaching tree was extensive, and many of his disciples blossomed having learned the secrets from the master. Brown was calculating and secretive, and to protect the team's trade secrets he would prevent his assistants from divulging information at coaching clinics. Unless you worked alongside Brown, you could not understand the depth of the details in his coaching manual. No one has played as significant a role in the advancement of the sport. He remains the best coach of all time, and the Coach of the Year award ought to carry his name.

MISSING ART IN THE HALL

I worked for Art Modell for almost ten years, and he was incredibly generous, funny, and caring. His heart was always in the right place, though his actions were often misguided. He has been villainized for moving the team from Cleveland to Baltimore in 1996, and each time his name appears as a Hall of Fame candidate, the move seems to be the blockade. Yet, in reality, Modell is not a Hall of Fame owner—and the move isn't the reason. His supporters would say he made the league wealthy with his involvement of television deals and the introduction of Monday Night Football—which is true and important. He also fired three of the winningest coaches in professional football—Paul Brown, Bill Belichick, and Marty Schottenheimer. Those actions alone are the reason Modell is not a Hall of Fame owner.

Settling on the names in this list was not easy, as three other coaches merited consideration due to their work on the field. Marty Schottenheimer would have easily made the top ten had he won a Super Bowl, as this was the only deficit in his amazing career. Schottenheimer won games—he made the teams he worked for better and was consistent year after year. He valued all three phases of the game—offense, defense, and special teams—diligently choreographing the team's level of play to ensure they played complementary football. Bill Parcells, the former Giants, Patriots, Jets, and Cowboys coach, left an impact that was felt throughout each organization with which he worked. John Madden of the

Oakland Raiders still holds the highest win percentage of all NFL coaches, with over one hundred wins, and is often dismissed when discussing great coaches because of the Raiders' talent. For some, Madden didn't win enough championships, which is unfair.

What the game today misses more than anything is someone to train young coaches the art of being a complete head coach. Many of the men on this list served a long apprenticeship, learning the game from some of the greatest coaches in either college or pro football. They spent time learning each of the three phases of the game in detail, which then allowed them to understand the art of playing complementary football. They all understood how to avoid losing first, before being able to win. This sounds like an easy skill to learn, but in the NFL more games are lost than won.

Shula was young in age when he became a head coach, but not in experience or his training or development. His knowledge extended to three sides of the ball—which most of the coaches on this list understood. To any young aspiring head coach reading this list and wanting to become as successful as the men on it: spend time learning the entire game. If you coach offense, dedicate time during every off-season learning defense, from scheme to fundamentals to plays. Broaden your overall knowledge of the game through a growth mind-set.

CHAPTER 5
TELEVISION

"What's right isn't always popular.
What's popular isn't always right."
—Howard Cosell

METEOROLOGISTS DEFINE A PERFECT STORM AS a rare combination of circumstances coalescing into an unprecedented event, such as the storm that rocked the East Coast of the United States in 1991, causing over $200 million in damage. But perfect storms can occur outside the realm of meteorology, such as when three individuals working independently for the same cause generate a powerful force, creating an uncontrollable surge. In the case of the NFL, it was the efforts of three men working at different television networks that created the perfect storm causing football to usurp Major League Baseball as "America's Game."

STORM NUMBER ONE

Howard Cosell

Frank Sinatra stood in the tunnel next to his good friend Jilly Rizzo and the promoter Jerry Weintraub. A powerful voice boomed over the loudspeaker at Madison Square Garden, preparing the ABC live audience for what was ahead. The voice seemed familiar, and it was clear this introduction was not coming from any cue cards. But the words had flow, eloquence, timing, and accentuation:

> *Live, from New York, the city whose landmarks are familiar all over the world. The world's center for shipping, transportation, communications, finance, fashions, and above all, entertainment. A city that pulsates always because of the millions of people who live here, work here, visit here. And in the heart of the metropolis, the great arena, Madison Square Garden, which has created and housed so many champions. And which is why tonight from the Garden the most enduring champion of them all, Frank Sinatra, comes to the entire western hemisphere live with* The Main Event: Frank Sinatra in Concert!

After Sinatra doubled tapped the cheeks of Rizzo, his signature of affection, he stormed down the aisle like a prize fighter about to enter the ring. And as Sinatra stepped onto the square stage and launched into his first song, the man who had given him that famous introduction finally took a seat.

Howard Cosell was the voice everyone knew. His New York City tone, filled with a trial lawyer's vocabulary, made everyone feel like they were doing something important. Cosell's unfiltered opinions had made him a staple of America's living rooms since ABC launched *Monday Night Football* in 1970. He wasn't a natural football man; he was a former attorney who decided to enter into the world of broadcast at age forty. With his intelligence, expansive jargon, and willingness to tell it like it was, Cosell built a huge following. Many loved him, some detested him, but every Monday night, he and his partners—first Keith Jackson, then Frank Gifford and "Dandy" Don Meredith—created must-watch television.

In 1968, the NFL had two Monday night games, but they received little fanfare because they were local broadcasts. Commissioner Pete Rozelle had wanted more national telecasts to expand the league's footprint beyond just Sundays on NBC and CBS. He knew there was a major appetite for more football, but he faced networks wary of giving him the time slot, as so-called appointment television ruled the day during this era in America. Families frequently had the most current issue of *TV Guide* on display next to their favorite chair, as if it was the Bible. And if you missed your favorite program, there was no recourse unless you waited for the rerun season to begin. Viewers had to remain on schedule, and the television lineup often dictated their social calendar. With strong Monday night lineups, both NBC and CBS rejected Rozelle's idea to move football into that slot. With a horrible programming lineup that couldn't crack into the top thirty on any night, ABC was receptive to his idea. But there was still widespread apprehension among NFL owners about the effects on attendance that a nationally televised game would have. After a year of back-and-forth, the league and ABC agreed on a three-year contract for $18 million, starting in 1970. This amount equates to $137.89 million today, roughly $4 million per club, which is a truly incredible bargain.

On September 21, 1970, in Cleveland Municipal Stadium, the Browns hosted the Joe Namath–led New York Jets. Art Modell, the owner of the Browns and head of the powerful broadcast committee for the NFL, had been in contact with his ticket office throughout the day, as he knew any loss of gate revenue would sour his television deal. When the red light came on for Cosell to begin his opening, 85,703 fans were in the stands, the largest crowd in Browns history. But with Cosell's descriptions, hundreds of thousands of others felt like they were there as well. "It's a hot, sultry, almost windless night here in Cleveland," Cosell said. These words were the very start. With twelve cameras at each game and different angles of plays available beyond what viewers were accustomed to on a typical Sunday, fans gained intimate peeks into the finer details of the sport, and the NFL now had the perfect marriage of medium and message.

Cosell's mission was to bridge the gap between entertainment and journalism, and bring a rare sophistication to a world of machismo and testosterone. He became a lightning rod, pulling in those who loved him and drawing press from those who didn't. In the second half of that first broadcast, Cosell said, "Leroy Kelly [the star running back of the Browns] has not been a compelling factor tonight." The switchboards at ABC lit up, and for the new few days, Cosell was ridiculed by the press for being insensitive and callous in his treatment of Kelly. It was a microcosm of what was to come. From that night until he retired, one in every eight letters written to ABC had something to say about Cosell—good or bad. But Cosell never let the negative impact him. He never backed down from his signature phrase of "telling it like it is." And America, for the most part, loved it.

At halftime of that first *Monday Night* game, Cosell introduced his highlights of other games played throughout the weekend, provided by NFL Films.

A national audience was now going to see what occurred across the country for the first time, with Cosell doing the commentary. In retrospect, the highlights really made little sense. The games were not compelling, nor could the viewer capture the essence of what really happened. But Cosell's highlight package was really a monumental moment that added to the allure of watching *Monday Night Football*. The rundowns became as popular as the games themselves.

I can remember as a twelve-year-old pretending I was sleeping with my lights out and then sneaking downstairs, hoping to avoid my mother. I would watch these highlights, praying my favorite team, the Washington Redskins, would appear and I would be able to resolve the conundrum in my head of whether they had worn the dark burgundy or the white jerseys in their past game. The newspapers had no pictures of the games, meaning I had to just guess what they wore when reviewing the box score. There were many like me, young and old, who simply wanted to see their team. Cosell had no notes in front of him when presenting, just the shot sheet so he'd know what the viewers were seeing, along with an incredible memory, perfect timing, and voice inflection. These five minutes were truly must-see television for sports fans.

The chemistry between Cosell, Gifford, and Meredith in the booth was just about perfect, two ex-players and one antagonist playing off each other. The broadcast went against the traditional methods of the time and faced severe criticism from the print media, mostly directed at Cosell. He would often say, "If we see it, we have to say it," pushing both Gifford and Meredith to be more forthcoming. Neither ex-player wanted to spark debate, and they were less inclined to attack their former rivals and teammates regarding their play on the field. This didn't satisfy Cosell, though. He urged both to do so and would call them out if they didn't follow his lead.

The trio's popularity grew with each show, but Cosell had quickly become the face of the operation. Before long, he was an international star, and had developed a relationship with heavyweight boxing champion Muhammad Ali. Cosell's popularity soared to such unprecedented heights that he was given his own show, *Saturday Night Live with Howard Cosell*, which premiered in 1975 with guests Frank Sinatra, Siegfried and Roy, Paul Anka, and Shirley Bassey. At the same time, NBC introduced a live sketch comedy series program called *Saturday Night*, since Cosell's show already included the word "Live." But after one year, Cosell's show was canceled and *Saturday Night* became the new *Saturday Night Live*. One night ten years later Cosell hosted the comedy series, another tribute to his incredible fame and popularity. In his opening monologue, he walked on stage and said: "The applause of course is well taken, an extraordinary moment for all of you. And maybe in its own way a felicitous and even rewarding moment for me. But I must tell you, a fortuitus one. Yes, this is *Saturday Night Live with Howard Cosell*." It was classic Cosell.

No matter where he traveled, fans or foes came marching toward him for an autograph or just a hello. Al Michaels, his former partner on ABC's *Monday Night Baseball* (yes, Cosell did baseball because any time he was on a broadcast, the ratings soared), was riding in a car with Cosell after dinner in Kansas City one night in 1981 when they noticed two young men engaged in a vicious fight on a street corner. Cosell, according to Michaels, told the driver to stop the car and walked over to them. "I want you both to listen here," he told them. "It's quite apparent to this observer that the young southpaw does not have the jab requisite for the continuation of this fray. This confrontation is halted posthaste." The men knew who Cosell was and heeded his advice. He then signed autographs for them before returning to the car. The limo driver, Peggy, said, "Howard, I have never seen anything like that in all my years." Cosell leaned back, took another puff of his always present cigar and said, "Pegaroo, I know exactly who I am." So did all of America.

THE POWER OF THE BRAND

With the rise in popularity of *Monday Night Football*, the cost of ads soared along with ratings, as it seemed just about every company in America wanted to get its product aligned with the sport. John A. Murphy, the chairman of Miller Brewing Company in Milwaukee, was tired of playing second fiddle to powerful Anheuser-Busch. His goal was to take down the king of St. Louis and move his company from a regional brewery to a national icon. Murphy felt the best way to knock the giant off the block was to associate his brand with sports and felt *Monday Night Football* was the perfect way to achieve this. As opposed to selling his new product, Miller Lite, as a diet-type beer, his ad agency, McCann Erickson, chose once-popular jocks and comedians to remind the audience that Miller Lite was "Everything you ever wanted in a beer—and less." The ad campaign caught fire and so did sales for Miller Lite. Before long, *Monday Night Football* had viewers watching for more than just the game. Viewers wanted to hear the broadcast crew, take in the halftime highlights, and see the latest commercials. Instead of staying home on Monday nights, people flocked to bars all over the country to watch the game with other fans. The once-popular Monday night bowling leagues of the era began to fizzle as a result.

STORM NUMBER TWO

Brent Musburger

Brent Musburger uttered the famous words "You are looking live" from the CBS Broadcast Center on West 57th Street in New York City on September 21, 1975. From that day forward, *The NFL Today*, hosted by then thirty-six-year-old Musburger, became a crucial part of making the league explode. Before then, no pregame show had ever actually been live. Pat Summerall and Jack Whitaker had taped their CBS pregame show on Friday afternoons for a Sunday broadcast, which prevented fans from actually seeing the stadiums and learning the latest details leading up to a game. Robert Wussler, a senior executive at CBS Sports, decided that had to change, and wanted scores and highlights readily available to give fans a close examination of what was happening in real time. It was an enormously popular development. At 12:30 p.m. every Sunday, Musburger, former Miss America Phyllis George, and former NFL player Irv Cross would bring fans closer to the game, tearing down the barriers that had previously prevented viewers from learning about their favorite players, coaches, and teams.

Before Musburger welcomed the huge national audience, a perfectly crafted jingle, reminiscent of the Golf Masters theme song, would begin. From the first few notes, the viewers knew exactly what to expect. Musburger would take fans to every stadium on the CBS slate of games in the early window, then hand off to George, who would tell America whom she was profiling. Cross would then inform the viewers of his assignment for the day.

Musburger was much like a great point guard in basketball, controlling the flow, scoring at times, and taking the game over when needed. His charisma and charm were apparent through the screen. He could build excitement for the day with his timing, while throwing in interesting tidbits of background information that viewers previously didn't know. His ability to bring out the best in his cohosts was his greatest strength and established him as a pivotal component of the program. The three of them worked in perfect harmony, making viewers at home feel as though they were listening to their close friends discuss football on their couch in their living room.

One year later, Jimmy "the Greek" Snyder joined the show. Snyder had become famous for predicting Harry Truman would win the 1948 presidential election against huge favorite Thomas Dewey, the governor of New York, simply because Dewey had a mustache. With Snyder now on the desk, *The NFL*

Today had a legitimate gambling insider. Adding Jimmy was a brazen move at the time. The NFL usually disapproved of openly discussing gambling, but fans craved inside betting information. *The NFL Today* team decided it would skirt the issue by disguising the betting terms. Musburger would stand alongside of Jimmy with a giant board that listed the two teams in that night's broadcast, covering every aspect of the game. As the two hosts discussed the game, Musburger would apply checks to one side or the other. When the audience saw one side dominating the board, it would most likely be inclined to go with it as the favorite. During this segment, Musburger and Jimmy would go over every game, with Jimmy predicting the scores, knowing the audience at home was aware of the point spreads. No one kept score of Jimmy's predictions. Everyone simply trusted his judgment. Musburger played the perfect academic man, interjecting his knowledge of gambling into the conversation, while ribbing Jimmy for his love affair with Al Davis. In fact, most of the information Jimmy spewed came from his weekly conversations with the Raiders' owner.

In 1975, the federal government revised the Prime Time Access Rule, limiting the amount of time networks controlled local affiliates. Now on Sunday, the networks could use 7:00 to 11:00 p.m. eastern time to broadcast their programming, with the first hour (from 7:00 to 8:00) reserved exclusively for family-oriented programing or news. The window created by the new rule, along with the popularity of *The NFL Today*, allowed *60 Minutes* to find a permanent home on the network and build a huge following. Football games could extend past 7:00 p.m. and Musburger was going to dump a huge audience into *60 Minutes*, tremendously increasing their ratings. Before this move, *60 Minutes* was always on the move, looking for the best time slot. Now, the rescheduling of *60 Minutes*, with its fascinating news stories, directly following a live *The NFL Today* allowed a giant surge in popularity. Musburger talking football became pure gold for whatever followed.

We have to remind ourselves that during this era of television following sports in a comprehensive way was damn near impossible. Information was hard to obtain. Unless you had the Associated Press ticker in your living room you were in the dark until the morning papers arrived at your doorstep.

In 1964, Macy's department store introduced its Dial Santa line. Kids from all over the New York area who wanted to get in touch with Old St. Nick could call. Within a matter of two weeks, two million anxious New York area children dialed the North Pole, straining the telephone network system and causing it to break down. This prompted the telephone company to develop a system to handle the large volume of calls at one time. By 1972, Jack Goodfellow, a longtime New York Telephone employee, launched a permanent number strictly for sports scores using the idea from Santa, and Sports Phone was born. For a dime, fans and gamblers were able to keep up to date on the action. In only forty-six seconds callers heard up-to-the-minute scores—often over thirty scores—of every game in every league, and then a seven-second commercial. When games were not being played Sports Phone would air interviews of athletes from the games, a telephone version of what would later become ESPN's *SportsCenter*. By 1979, the service was averaging one hundred thousand calls per day. Andy Roth, who started as a Sports Phone announcer in 1979, has said, "The company could get upward of three hundred thousand calls on a good college football Saturday or an NFL Sunday, with the NCAA tournament also spurring heavy traffic." By 1981, that number grew to a total of 50 million calls per year, an indication of how fans were desperate to have up-to-the minute information. It was also an indication of how many people loved to gamble.

This incredible thirst for real-time data, as evidenced by the popularity of Sports Phone, was quenched by Musburger and *The NFL Today* on Sundays from 12:30 until 7:00 p.m. in between games. Fans trusted Musburger to get them the right information they needed, and he became the conduit to the game for fans. *The NFL Today* dominated the market share for its time slot, as people raced home from church to be in their living rooms to hear the iconic music. What is also important to understand is how gambling fueled the fire that made the NFL burn brightest, even though gambling remained underground, not discussed by the mainstream media. Gambling books were covert, never discussed yet widely available. Everyone knew a bookie, and much like when people recommend doctors, bookies got referrals.

Musburger understood what the betting man, sophisticated or not, wanted to know. He talked about key injuries, weather conditions, and late-breaking information from the coaches, and he wrapped them all around his commentary. He truly changed how NFL fans watched the game. Playing off what *Monday Night Football* did with Cosell, *The NFL Today* carried halftime highlights of the other CBS games. Musburger was magical with his voiceovers, and viewers remained glued to their televisions during the breaks in the action as he provided details about games they had not seen.

When *Monday Night Football* arrived, it provided a spark in the booth and also a way for bettors to watch live action. Those who won on Sundays came looking for more, while those who lost big sought retribution. What no one besides Wussler and Musburger seemed to understand was how many people in particular were betting. Sports gambling was much like prohibition—illegal, but still incredibly pervasive. Jimmy loved to joke that growing up in Steubenville he didn't realize gambling was illegal until he was twenty-five years old and away from his hometown. No one would think of *The NFL Today* as the first betting show of its time. But because of the information and discussions it provided of all of the games coast-to-coast, it was essential viewing for both the casual football fan and the high-level bettor.

STORM NUMBER THREE

John Madden

The 1978 season for the Oakland Raiders offered tremendous hope and promise. Bookmakers set their odds to win the Super Bowl at 4–1 after the team had fallen just short to the Denver Broncos in the AFC Championship game, 20–17, a season before. Head coach John Madden was no stranger to expectations, as he was entering into his tenth season at the franchise's helm. Madden had made the playoffs in all but one year of his reign, but ten years can wear on anyone, particularly when you're working for owner Al Davis. Madden was the head coach, but Davis was the owner/general manager and had the only opinion that mattered. His incredible will to win, his insatiable appetite for studying the game, and his relentless approach would bring anyone around him to the brink of total exhaustion. And by the end of the '78 season, when Madden's team was plagued by turnovers and the poor performance of their star players, he needed a respite.

Madden didn't leave the sidelines with any specific plans. He was not overly intrigued by television, but knew he wanted to stay close to the game in some capacity. While coaching the Raiders, he would frequently call in to *The Emperor Gene Nelson Show* on KYA, and fans in the Bay Area were enlightened by his intimate knowledge of the game and easy communication style. He was seemingly a natural. He never divulged too much about the Raiders as they prepared for their next game, but he always said enough to intrigue listeners. Even a year out of football, he continued doing his radio appearances, as he was still in demand. It seemed only natural he'd be a good TV fit.

Madden was reluctant upon receiving his first television offer. He didn't want to rush into anything, as ten years in football created medical problems that Maalox never seemed to cure. The decade on the sidelines took a major toll on his body, as his weight would balloon during the season because of the stress. However, Madden sensed this was his opportunity and long thought that if you let your moment pass, you might never get another. He accepted an offer from CBS.

Once in the booth, it became clear Madden had two strengths that few other announcers possessed. First, he was an excellent teacher of the game. "I'm a coach and a teacher, period," he frequently said, never believing he was a television star. His second strength was his infectious personality, which didn't need the lights of a television camera to shine. He was witty and intelligent, and never relied on football technique talk that bored the audience. He always analyzed both sides of the game while giving critical opinions as well. Madden was truly just being himself—and America fell in love with him.

Pat Summerall and Tommy Brookshier had been the number-one team at CBS in 1979, but besides being partners in the booth, they were best friends and drinking buddies. When it was announced that Madden would replace Brookshier, Summerall was asked if he would miss his old partner. He replied, "I will miss him like crazy on Saturday night." Summerall was the perfect play-by-play man to pair with Madden. His voice was smooth and silky, and he brought out the best in Madden. All great duos know their roles. Dean Martin played well off of Jerry Lewis. Bud Abbott worked around the zany Lou Costello. The partnership between Summerall and Madden was no different. Madden said of their working relationship: "Well, you know, I tend to be a rambler, as you know, and Pat could punctuate anything I said. And that gave me a real confidence that I could go anywhere, any way, and sometimes, I mean, a play would start up and you wouldn't be finished and he could, in two or three words, sum up what I'd been saying in five minutes or whatever."

Madden became famous for a single word he would frequently utter: "Boom." But that's also what happened to his career. His infectious personality made him a fan favorite and an endorsement king, someone America trusted like an old friend. He came across as a simple, common man, easily identifiable with the audience, and made everyone at home feel like they knew him in some respect.

Even food benefited from the Madden touch. During a Rams-Saints game in New Orleans, Glenn Mistich's catering company brought a turducken to the booth, which Madden sampled. Turducken is the combination of three birds—chicken, duck, and turkey—into one and was mainly a Louisiana dish before Madden put the first bite in his mouth. Herbert's Specialty Meats from Maurice, Louisiana, lays claim (though debated) to inventing the concept in 1985. When Mistich and his wife, Leah, a daughter of the Herbert family, opened Gourmet Butcher Block, they had turducken as one of their holiday items. Madden remembers the first time he sampled the specialty item: "One of the guys on the Saints' staff was a friend of Glenn's, and we were talking about turducken," Madden said in a telephone interview. A turducken was subsequently sent to the booth, and Madden dug in. "I'm there eating this turducken with my fingers,"

Madden recalled. "[Saints owner] Tom Benson comes in and I have all this stuff on my fingers and I'm doing that thing in my head where I'm wondering, 'Do I shake his hand?'" Madden did shake Benson's hand, grease and all.

After that game, America wanted turducken at Thanksgiving and Christmas. Everyone was calling the Gourmet Butcher Block to place their holiday orders. "I'm very grateful," Mistich said of Madden's promotion of the turducken. "I can't say enough about what he's done for our business. He's definitely put it on a national level. Turducken is even in the dictionary now." That Madden magic even turned food to gold.

He was intelligent and authentic, but never attempted to be the smartest person in the room—and he often said what most at home were thinking when it came to food and other nonfootball subjects. Like Cosell, he entertained without lecturing. His popularity spawned one of the best-selling video game franchises of all time, and when the fledgling Fox network bid on the NFL package, they made sure to go to Madden directly.

WHEN THE STORMS MERGED

Over 113 million people watched Super Bowl LVII on February 12, 2023. But to give credit to just the teams, the players, the coaches, or even the advertisers would be shortsighted. This monumental growth in viewership really stemmed from the groundwork laid decades prior by Cosell, Musburger, and Madden. The combination of these three men increased the NFL's popularity by leaps and bounds, and the league will continue to feel their impact for the rest of its existence. Madden is in the Hall of Fame for his coaching, but the others are not. Why the Hall has yet to create a television wing is beyond me.

It's often asked, "If a tree falls in the forest, and no one is around to hear it, does it make a sound?" Well, I'll ask, "If an NFL safety swoops in to make a game-saving interception to lead his team to the playoffs, but virtually no one sees it and everyone instead just has to read about it in a newspaper article, is it really that impactful?" To me, the answer is an obvious no, but that was essentially the case prior to the work of Cosell, Musburger, and Madden. These three were journalists, marketers, entertainers, and essentially public relations professionals for the league at a time when it needed all the help it could get.

CHAPTER 6
THE NFL DRAFT

"When forming a team, seek character, not characters."
—Bill Walsh

THE BIRTH OF THE DRAFT

DE BENNEVILLE "BERT" BELL NEVER LIKED to fly. The owner of the Philadelphia Eagles would rather take a Pullman coach train, even though one particular trip to Minneapolis was time sensitive. Bell was in hot pursuit of the best player in the country, Stan "King Kong" Kostka, a fullback and linebacker from the University of Minnesota. Before he got on the train, Bell had called Kostka and point-blank asked him if he would sign a contract with the Eagles if Bell offered him a contract for more money than any other NFL team. Kostka told him he would, and once he heard that rousing yes through the phone, Bell excitedly booked his trip.

During the 1930s, college football players were available to all teams, though a completely open market with no rules gave the Packers, Bears, and Giants some financial advantages. Bell's franchise was at a crucial crossroads for survival. When Bell met Kostka in the lobby of a downtown Minneapolis hotel to make his sales pitch, Kostka informed him he had an offer of $3,500 from an unnamed team. Bell immediately told him that his offer was $4,000. Even without representation, Kostka knew that wasn't Bell's final offer and told him he needed an hour to mull things over. By the time Kostka returned to the lobby, Bell had upped his offer to $6,000 per year, and even then Kostka was uninterested. Kostka was playing Bell—and the owner knew it. Even with the best offer, Bell knew his team was at a huge disadvantage, and he recognized that things needed to change.

When he arrived back at his suburban Philadelphia home, Bell began working on a proposal to his fellow owners. "I made up my mind that this league would never survive unless we had some system whereby each team had an even chance to bid for talent against each other," he later said.

A year later, at the 1935 May league meeting at the Fort Pitt Hotel in Pittsburgh, Bell addressed the eight other owners while revealing his proposal to create a more competitive league: "Gentlemen, I've always had the theory that pro football is like a chain," he said. "The league is no stronger than its weakest link, and I've been a weak link for so long that I should know. Every year, the rich get richer and the poor get poorer. Here's what I propose. At the end of every college football season, I suggest that we pool the names of all eligible seniors. Then, we make our selections in inverse order of the standings, with the lowest team picking first until we reach the top-ranking team, which picks last. We do this for round after round until we've exhausted the supply."

Bell's idea solicited a rousing debate among the men in the room. Papa Bear Halas liked the idea, in part because it would eliminate a bidding war and help to control costs. He wasn't in favor of relinquishing his dominance in the player acquisition market, nor was Giants owner Tim Mara, but Halas understood the need for competitive balance to engage fans. If the league were to ever fully blossom, the benefits of one had to be sacrificed for the needs of all. Halas, always a dominant voice, was able to persuade Mara and the other owners. Bell's proposal was unanimously accepted.

It's hard to believe Bell could have ever imagined the popularity the draft would garner. Bell's vision was to simply address the league's weakest link— not to create what's presently a full-scale business and the sport's second-most popular event behind the Super Bowl. Currently, cities bid to host the draft, and tens of thousands of people attend just to hear some names called. Former commissioner Pete Rozelle would be astonished by the level of engagement in the days and weeks leading up to the event. I saw this firsthand when I went to the 1980 draft in New York at the Sheraton Hotel, waiting in line at three o'clock in the morning to get one of the five hundred seats available for the public. Bell's creation really gained major momentum in 1980 when the president of what was at the time a fledgling TV network in desperate need of programming asked if it could televise the draft: Rozelle agreed to allow ESPN to broadcast it, but didn't exactly believe hearing names called would make for great television.

THE WAR ROOM

The white walls immediately capture your attention upon entering the room. Their shiny glow is like the sun peering through the window in the early morning, almost forcing your hands to block the streaming of light. A large conference table sits in the center of the room, surrounded by television screens, like the White House's situation room. Welcome to an NFL draft room, a sacred and secretive place where NFL teams enrich their bloodlines.

The process of building a draft board begins with thousands of name cards aligned by position on a side board, each featuring each player's height, weight, and speed. Across the room is the main board. At the start, it's all white, except for position names in dark bold letters placed horizontally along the top. Running vertically on the left are numbers from 9.0 to 5.6, set high to low.

Over the next month the empty board will be filled with the cards of draftable players. It's a long and grueling process. The thousand names on one board will be reduced to one hundred on the other. Scouts make their case for each player they have evaluated. All grades are attached to brief descriptions predicting each player's future in the NFL. The harmony and rhythm between the words and numbers make a draft board come alive. The grades are the lifeline, as they signify the round in which the player can be eligible for selection. If the grade is too low, the player won't be available at the right time. A grade too high causes a player to be overdrafted, creating false expectations. Each player at his position must be stacked vertically, from top to bottom, with the highest to the lowest acceptable grade. Any player who makes the draft board is a worthy consideration, with significant expectations.

What most fans and draftniks don't understand is that each team's draft board is essentially two boards in one. The vertical board, aligned by position, is the easiest one to formulate. You ask one simple question when players have the same grade: who is better? The board is then stacked accordingly. The horizontal board offers the biggest challenge because there are fewer experts available to make the decision. For example: there are two players, both graded a 6.2, which means both will be potential starters in the league by their second season. One plays cornerback; the other plays offensive guard. Who is better? Who will make the most impact? Some might say to take the player at the position of need. True. What happens if both positions are needed? Who can make the right call? Only a few members of the organization have evaluated and compared the prospects; therefore, they must make the call. And this is the hardest call to make.

Another problem occurs when a player—regardless of position—is wrongly aligned. During the 1992 draft meetings in Cleveland, when I worked as the personnel director for the Browns, our main focus was always on defensive lineman, offensive lineman, and Bill Belichick mandated we control the middle of the field in every game, which required domination in both lines. Therefore, we started at our core positions. The first player discussed was Chester McGlockton, an enormously talented defensive tackle from Clemson. He dominated the game...when he felt like it. He would dwarf the offensive linemen attempting to block him and they would bounce off him much like bullets off Superman. His talent was clear, but his lack of passion was clearer. Big Chester only played when he wanted to play, which was not all the time. It was easy to proclaim McGlockton as the best defensive lineman in the draft, and stacking him vertically wasn't a challenge. The main issue occurred when we compared him horizontally to other players.

In the Browns' grading system, there was a specific category for players deemed underachievers, limiting the scouts from grading the player too high. All our scouts hated the restrictions. With McGlockton, limiting his grade meant we would never select him, which to most of the scouts meant we were hurting ourselves, not Chester. After we debated the talents, commitment, and passion of McGlockton, enough people in the room argued he wasn't an underachiever. We reluctantly moved him into the elite area on the board, as one of the best players. Without the underachiever grade attached to McGlockton, our board was wrong and poorly aligned from a horizontal perspective, creating chaos. I often told the room that our biggest problem wasn't the player we were discussing; rather, it was our grade on Chester. As Bill Parcells would often say, "One wrong, all wrong." With the wrong placement of McGlockton, the entire board became wrong.

EVERYONE'S A GENERAL MANAGER; SOME ARE CALLED DRAFTNIKS

The introduction of the draft gave way to a new term in the English language: *draftnik*. A draftnik is a die-hard fan dedicated to following and studying the NFL draft, and acting as the general manager of all NFL teams, publishing highly popular mock drafts, giving fans a hint of their favorite teams' potential selection. In the years following the implementation of the draft, draftniks didn't go unnoticed. They became a valuable part of the draft. The first draftniks weren't reporters or former football executives, but two seemingly ordinary brothers—Pete Marasco, an insurance salesman from Philadelphia, and Carl Marasco, a title agent from White Plains, New York. The Marascos combined their work using newspaper clippings, college football brochures, and observations from games they would watch on television to compile their own list of potential picks. Their projections caught the eye of Chicago newsman Hub Arkush, and before long, the Marascos were writing a column for *Pro Football Weekly*.

Being a draftnik took on added significance when Jerry Jones (no, not *that* one, but a pharmacist from Mariemont, Ohio) started following the draft as a hobby. Soon he was publishing a typewritten, thirty-page pamphlet aptly named *The Drugstore List*. Jones became a cultlike figure to draft enthusiasts all over the country. In my days as an executive, I often called Joel Buchsbaum, a reclusive Brooklyn native who had a photographic memory and would analyze over eight hundred prospects annually. Buchsbaum would never have to look at his notes to tell you a player's background or statistics, and I certainly wasn't the only one calling him. Former Giants and Browns general manager Ernie Accorsi once said about Buchsbaum, "There weren't a lot of people who influenced all these top people in the league like Joel did." One of the reasons he was so influential was that he understood how the draft process was linked to organizational construction. He knew one draft couldn't build a champion and that it instead took repeated good selections to generate long-term success.

THE ART OF TEAM BUILDING

Team building requires coordination between coaching and scouting, and an integration of scheme into ability. Most often, that coordination falls to the head coach, who has the most control of what the on-field product looks like. Bill Parcells always wanted to do the shopping for players because he knew best the ingredients needed for the feast he cooked. Being a successful head coach requires being a leader who can cultivate talent while serving as a technician and schemer, and taking pride in making everyone better. Great team building can result in a dynasty.

Green Bay Packers

Ask any casual fan about who created Titletown, and Vince Lombardi is almost guaranteed to be the answer. While Lombardi deserves much of the credit for the success of the Packers, he wasn't alone. In the 1950s, head scout Jack Vainisi, a Chicago native and Notre Dame graduate, worked quietly behind the scenes to allow the head coach to be the main attraction. But the coaches he served prior to Lombardi weren't any good. Before Lombardi arrived in 1959, the Packers won thirty-two games, lost seventy-four, and tied two. They were horrible in just about every aspect, except picking talent. Vainisi had an eye for seeing beyond a player's surface-level talent and for projecting him onto an NFL roster. He was a hard and meticulous worker who relied on information from coaches and film to compile his reports, all written in perfect Catholic school penmanship. These papers gave anyone reading them a critical means of visualizing a prospect, as Vainisi's descriptive adjectives brought the lesser known to light.

Vainisi's work speaks volumes. He played a crucial behind-the-scenes role in bringing Lombardi to Green Bay. He knew the next coach of the Packers had to be the board's idea, not his, which made him work the back channels so he could essentially be free of involvement. In Vainisi's first phone call to Lombardi, documented by David Maraniss in his riveting book *When Pride Still Mattered*, he informed him that he was "not authorized" to make the call. Vainisi had to make the board believe Lombardi was their idea all along, and he did so by having powerful friends—Paul Brown of Cleveland, George Halas of the Bears, and Red Blaik of West Point—call the board directly to recommend Lombardi.

Vainisi knew Lombardi was the only choice, but he never wanted credit for the board's decision; he only wanted to win and help those he drafted improve.

By the time Lombardi unpacked and moved into his office at Lambeau Field in January of 1959, the talent was already in place, including quarterback Bart Starr, offensive tackle Forrest Gregg, running back Paul "Golden Boy" Hornung, tight end Ron Kramer, running back Jimmy Taylor, middle linebacker Ray Nitschke, offensive guard Jerry Kramer, wide receiver Boyd Dowler, and linebacker Dan Currie—all found during what could be considered otherwise unsuccessful drafts. Now this talent just needed to be molded. Lombardi, with a major assist from Vainisi, made a few shrewd trades, acquiring defensive tackle Henry Jordan, defensive end Willie Davis from Cleveland, and guard Fuzzy Thurston from Baltimore.

Lombardi's brilliance as a coach was most evident in his player development, his ability to bring out the best in individual team members, and his skill at building a cohesive team, all geared toward one specific goal: winning a title. In addition, his ability to recognize talent and to understand whom to develop and whom not to was another huge strength. Frequently, coaches inheriting a losing team believe there is zero talent on the roster. Once Lombardi gave these players a chance, he saw that the foundation of actual talent was strong. Vainisi knew when to take a more measured approach and trusted Lombardi to develop talent, even when some of his draft picks didn't fit the style or demeanor of players that Lombardi valued. Lombardi and Vainisi had formed an unparalleled partnership, operating independently while masterfully coexisting.

No one in the Hall of Fame from the personnel side had as much success in such a short time as Vainisi. Though he died at the tender age of thirty-three from a heart attack, he achieved much in such a short time span that he merits Hall of Fame recognition. He handpicked Lombardi to be the head coach of the Packers. He drafted or signed as college free agents nine Hall of Fame players, all part of the Packers' championship run. And when you consider the fact that he played a crucial role in trading for Willie Davis and Henry Jordan, he really sent eleven men to the Hall, winning two Super Bowls and five NFL championships in the process.

Vainisi deserves to have his name etched in Packers lore alongside Lambeau's and Lombardi's. When the team returned from Los Angeles the evening after defeating the Rams and clinching the 1960 Western title, fans stormed Austin Straubel Airport to welcome their team home. Lombardi addressed the cheering crowd and ended his talk by saying, "I want to leave one thought with you. A great part of this team was due to one man who is no longer with us: Jack Vainisi. May God rest his soul." Lombardi knew. We all should as well.

Pittsburgh Steelers

The dynasty of the Pittsburgh Steelers can largely be attributed to one draft in particular. The seeds of the 1974 draft were essentially sown the day head coach Chuck Noll began working with owner Art Rooney Jr., director of player personnel Dick Haley, and head scout Bill Nunn. Noll had a sharp eye for talent and a rare ability to teach and develop. He was strong in his opinions and never yielded to media pressure, as evidenced by his decision to pass up drafting Terry Hanratty in the first round and instead picking Joe Greene, a lesser-known defensive tackle from North Texas State. Noll understood the needs of his scheme and recognized the types of players he needed. Nunn, with his sharp and candid evaluations, assisted Noll in giving the team a distinctive edge as well as in gathering more information about players from historically Black schools—including L. C. Greenwood, Mel Blount, and Mike Wagner, whom Pittsburgh selected in later rounds—instead of traditional blueblood colleges that had been favored in the past.

Unlike other teams at the time, who were willing to part with draft picks in order to acquire proven talent, Chuck Noll placed extreme value on his draft picks. When he took over, he eliminated the philosophy of trading away picks, trusting that his great eye for available talent was far a more reliable approach than executives trading dozens of phone calls to haggle over fledgling players.

In the ensuing NFL draft, the Steelers held the twenty-first overall pick and were debating whether to take wide receiver Lynn Swann of USC or John Stallworth of Alabama A&M. Noll liked both players but favored Stallworth. The clock was ticking, and the Cowboys, with the twenty-second pick, were ready to snap up Swann. Noll was ultimately convinced by Dick Haley, Nunn, and the rest of the personnel people to go with Swann because they believed Stallworth would still be there later in the draft. Had Noll not been convinced, the decision would have dramatically changed history, a thought that undoubtedly ran through the heads of Cowboys coach Tom Landry, president Tex Schramm, and personnel director Gil Brandt when they later watched Swann make incredible plays in Super Bowl X.

When Steelers scout and part owner Art Rooney Jr. took a scouting trip to Kent State the previous fall, he was looking for a middle linebacker who didn't fit the traditional mold. He found it in Jack Lambert, a tall and skinny kid who was diving headfirst all over the gravel practice field to make tackles. Rooney wanted someone who could run backward and defend the pass while still playing with enough toughness in the run game, and Lambert fit that description to a tee. By defining what he wanted at the middle backer position (scouting inside out), then searching for players who fit those characteristics, Rooney helped the Steelers find their perfect defensive fit. Many had believed the team would select Matt Blair, a linebacker from Iowa State, who fit the established profile of a middle backer, and even many in the Steelers draft room and scouting department were in favor of selecting Blair. But Noll listened to all the pros and cons on each prospect, and once again, with little time to spare on the clock, informed everyone Lambert was their second-round pick, the forty-sixth selection overall.

Without a third-round pick, there were thirty-five names that needed to be called before the Steelers selected again. They prayed that Stallworth would still be available. The Steelers had reliable information on Stallworth that no one else had, having seen him play at A&M, and used that to secure him when it was their turn.

In the fifth round, Noll needed to bring a player on board he could develop to ultimately replace starting center Ray Mansfield. In watching University of Wisconsin film, Noll noticed Mike Webster, a short but powerful center who demonstrated incredible balance and strength. "Mike wasn't tall enough, he didn't weigh enough, but the thing he had that made the difference was he had great playing strength," Noll later said. "You could see it on the field. He would come off the ball with great quickness. I can remember having some films of him against I think it was UCLA, which had these huge, huge tackles. He just destroyed him. Wisconsin moved the ball up and down the field. He not only blocked well on the run, but he also pass protected well."

Before the drafted ended the next day, Nunn was on the campus of South Carolina State signing safety Donnie Shell. In total, this draft produced five Hall of Famers, Lynn Swann, Jack Lambert, John Stallworth, Mike Webster, and Donnie Shell, four of whom were Steelers.

With this collection of young talent, combined with the 1974 players' strike, Noll and his coaching staff were able to spend more time teaching and developing their rookies. This made a pivotal difference. Accumulating this level of talent in one draft is amazing, but actually cultivating it is what separates Noll from most coaches. He is in the Hall because of his ability to coach, teach, and win. But his selection to the Hall could also be due to his incredible eye for talent and his willingness to evaluate the pros and cons of each player. Noll's motto was always "Whatever it takes," an adage he brought to the Steelers while establishing the organization as one of the league's truly elite.

The Houston Oilers

Bill Belichick once said, "We are building a team, not collecting talent." Collection of talent looks great when draftniks issue their draft grades, yet it doesn't always translate to wins and championships on the field. Teams and fans get enamored with the success of the draft, who made the team who didn't, and so forth. Yet winning is all that matters. The story of the Houston Oilers during the early 1990s is a lesson in an organization being compartmentalized and having too many cooks in the kitchen. There is the old saying "They never dedicated a monument to a committee," and the Oilers had many committee members but not a single one who could tie everything together.

COMMITTEE MEMBER
NUMBER ONE

Ladd Herzeg knew numbers. Give him a spreadsheet and financial statements, and the young whiz kid was in his element. His intellectual brilliance shined so brightly handling the Cleveland Browns' accounting that Browns owner Art Modell told Houston Oilers owner Bud Adams to hire him as CFO. Adams did. When Herzeg arrived in Houston in 1979, he wasn't involved in any football decisions, but he essentially served as Adams's bean counter—and Adams loved his beans. Herzeg observed head coach Bum Phillips following other NFL teams' patterns by trading away first-round picks for aging veterans, thus mortgaging the future. Phillips had become head coach and general manager in 1975, taking over for Sid Gillman. During his five years running the Oilers, he made a total of three first-round picks.

With Herzeg whispering in his ear about the impending doom created by the shortsighted Phillips, Adams fired Phillips on New Year's Eve and named Herzeg general manager. Herzeg recognized his shortcomings and knew that despite his financial skills, he needed a football person alongside him.

COMMITTEE MEMBER
NUMBER TWO

Herzeg hired Mike Holovak, the former Boston College and New England Patriots head coach, as his executive vice president. Holovak was a seasoned pro in all aspects of football. He loved watching tape and was disciplined in his life, sticking to his daily routine, which included jogging about five miles every day regardless of the weather. Holovak knew the coaching side of the game and understood the art of team building—and would follow the chain of command with fierce loyalty.

With Holovak making the draft picks, the Oilers' talent continued to elevate. They restocked their offensive line in three consecutive seasons, acquiring Hall of Fame guards Mike Munchak in the first round in 1982, Bruce Matthews in 1983, and finally tackle Dean Steinkuhler (who started in one hundred games) in 1984. Holovak found talent all over, from the USFL allocation draft, which produced running back Mike Rozier, to dipping into the CFL and signing star free agent Warren Moon. Herzeg had dispatched Holovak to Canada to evaluate Moon, as he was certain there would be a bidding war for his services. Moon had been a highly successful college player from the University of Washington who had been overlooked during the 1978 NFL draft and had chosen to sign with the CFL. He absolutely dominated the league, allowing his coach, Hugh Campbell, to secure a lucrative contract with the USFL's Los Angeles Express.

COMMITTEE MEMBER
NUMBER THREE

Once the USFL folded, Herzeg hired Campbell as head coach of the Oilers, which seemed to give the team a crucial edge in the Moon sweepstakes. The Oilers, in turn, gave Moon the richest contract in the NFL for any player at the time. By adding him and continuing to accumulate other talent to surround him, the team assembled a formidable roster, capped off by a brilliant draft choice. The 1986 draft had plenty of quarterbacks available, but only one had the "can't-miss" label—Purdue's Jim Everett had a power arm and could make any throw with ease. He was a natural thrower with a high IQ and the instincts to play the position for years to come. Holding the number-three pick, Holovak thought teams across the league would be desperate to make a trade. After all, the Oilers already had Moon. But they instead deliberately held on to both quarterbacks.

In week one of the 1986 season, 49ers quarterback Joe Montana severely hurt his back, and head coach Bill Walsh feared the injury might be career ending. When the team learned of Everett's availability, they moved quickly, knowing that the rival Rams had a strong relationship with Everett's agent. The 49ers were right in fearing the involvement of Los Angeles. The Rams agreed to a four-year deal totaling $3 million that netted Houston starting Pro Bowl guard Kent Hill, emerging defensive end William Fuller, and two first-round picks, along with a fifth for Everett. It was a true bonanza for the Oilers. With Holovak and his staff making the picks, the Oilers were set up for the future.

COMMITTEE MEMBER
NUMBER FOUR

Campbell was eventually fired, and defensive coordinator Jerry Glanville took over as head coach, launching the franchise to previously unimaginable heights, which included a seven-year playoff run. By 1988, Herzeg had run into trouble with Adams for his behavior off the field and was offered a contract without a raise. Herzeg tried to call Adams's bluff. He viewed himself as irreplaceable, a sentiment Adams didn't share. He instead turned to Holovak and made him general manager. The pair had long had a strong bond, dating back to their old AFL days. Based on the talent the franchise had accumulated, it was an easy decision for Adams. But when Glanville lost four of their last six games (one 61–7) and the team was eliminated in the wildcard round, Adams fired Glanville and hired veteran coach Jack Pardee.

COMMITTEE MEMBER
NUMBER FIVE

Pardee turned the Oilers into a run-and-shoot offense, highlighting their incredible talent at wide receiver, quarterback, and offensive line to become one of the most potent attacks in football. Houston's ability to throw the ball in the ideal conditions of the Astrodome made it just about impossible to defend.

COMMITTEE MEMBER
NUMBER SIX

When Buddy Ryan took over as defensive coordinator, all hell broke loose. The win-it-all or break-it-down mandate, along with several looming free agencies, created widespread chaos throughout the organization. Ryan essentially operated independently and relished the opportunity to be subversive. He made it clear that he hated the run-and-shoot offense, openly creating conflict among the staff. Neither Pardee nor Adams could control this hired-for-gun coach. The 1993 team started slowly and then won its last eleven games before falling to the Chiefs at home in the divisional round. Always a man of his word, Adams decided to tear the team apart.

BREAKDOWN OF THE COMMITTEE

In many respects, Adams had been cheated as owner, as his team was never able to realize its full potential despite its immense collection of talent (three Hall of Fame players and several Pro Bowlers). Holovak was cheated as well, having given the organization years of truly incredible work. He was the only committee member willing to forsake his ego for the good of the team. He became a victim of not having a great coach and leader to mold the talent. Much like Jack Vainisi in Green Bay, Holovak is lost in history because of the lack of leadership. But for all the talent the organization had assembled, a lack of cohesiveness and a unified team culture never allowed the Oilers to reach their full potential. Because Holovak was a former coach himself, he never wanted to meddle in the coaching side and instead allowed it to operate with complete autonomy. But Holovak's labor of love truly depended on the coach, and since the organization could never seem to find the right one, Holovak will never gain the recognition he deserves. Bill Belichick called the '93 Oilers "the most talented team I ever faced in my career." It was deservedly high praise, but the Oilers' results highlight the point that no matter how much talent is acquired, unless the right man is commanding it, it will almost always fall short.

CHAPTER 7
TRADES

*"Identical information can lead to opposite conclusions
based on relative perceptions of its receivers."*
—Naved Abdali

"TWO CHAIRS, NO WAITING," READ THE bright red sign that greeted customers as they walked into the Ideal Barbershop. But waiting is what most of the men loved. With seven seats scattered around five large vertical ashtrays, the sizeable waiting area was surrounded by dark wood paneling, providing customers with a comfortable club-type setting. But sometimes people came for the debate, not the haircuts.

My father acquired Ideal from a man I only knew as "Freddie the Freeloader," back in the mid-1960s. And once my dad became owner, Freddie continued to work in the shop. What Freddie loved most was not cutting hair but debating sports. So instead of retiring to Florida, he stayed to cut a few heads and make his opinions known.

Freddie was adept at cutting and talking simultaneously. Two clips, five opinions, two more clips, and another dissertation, making sure the customer and those waiting heard his points and took note. A bald man wanting a slight trim around the ears might be in the chair for a half hour under Freddie's style of clip. Freddie particularly liked trades—and former Eagles coach and general manager Joe Kuharich bore the brunt of his—and the shop's—daily displeasure. Before Kuharich was fired by the Eagles' new owner, Leonard Tose, his tenure had been full of dubious moves. He traded quarterback Sonny Jurgensen to Washington for Norman Snead and cornerback Claude Crabb—a surprising exchange between bitter rivals that would almost be unheard of today. But back then, without the internet and reporters tweeting at a moment's notice, NFL executives were brazen and willing to tempt fate. Everyone in the barbershop hated the trade because Jurgensen, a Hall of Fame inductee in 1983, went to the Pro Bowl in 1964, 1967, and 1969 under Vince Lombardi. For the record, Jurgensen was the only Hall of Fame quarterback to never win a playoff game, which was never mentioned in the shop, as debaters were never keen on letting the facts get in the way of the argument. Although the anger toward Kuharich for ruining the Eagles was unanimous, the debate over the best quarterbacks in the NFL during the 1969 season still raged.

I didn't realize it then, but the Ideal Barbershop became the 1969 version of ESPN's highly acclaimed *First Take*—and nothing made debates more compelling than breaking down trades. Fans love evaluating, predicting, and speculating over controversy. And at ten years old, I learned that trades mattered and that the construction of the team meant just about everything. It made me want to one day sit in a general manager's chair. Flash forward some fifty years and I still love trades, both making and debating them. What sports fan doesn't think he or she could lead a franchise better than the people currently doing so? But trades that look bad to fans (and the media) often are misunderstand. Too often, the trade is made for three, often intertwined, reasons.

REASON NUMBER ONE

Desperate Times Call for a Desperate Trade

In 1974, a lopsided deal between the Green Bay Packers and the Los Angeles Rams rocked the NFL. The trade was dubbed "The Lawrence Welk Trade" after the famous bandleader and TV show host who yelled to his orchestra before each song, "A one, and a two, and a three." In this deal, the Packers gave up two number-one picks, two number-two picks, and a third in exchange for aging quarterback John Hadl.

In 1974, the Packers were nothing like what they are today. Yes, they still had a great fan base, but they were not winning championships. Just three years removed from their second Super Bowl title, the Packers had lost many of the hallmarks of the Vince Lombardi era. New head coach Dan Devine needed a solution for the team's offensive woes.

He witnessed Hadl playing for the Rams against the Packers in week five of the season, a game Green Bay won, 16–6; Hadl's arm looked tired and dead. So ten days later, how could Devine possibly be willing to pay a huge price for him? The answer lies in pressure and desperation, which are so frequently the factors that spark trades—one team is desperate, while another is thinking long term. When a player is traded for a draft pick, the trade cannot be fully valued until the selections are actually made, which—to Rams general manager Don Klosterman—made his team the deal's winner. He would go on to select defensive tackle Mike Fanning, who played eight solid seasons for the franchise, and then defensive backs Monte Jackson and Pat Thomas. Then he drafted guard Dennis Harrah and tackles Doug France and Jackie Slater with the remaining picks. This nucleus of players would propel the Rams to their Super Bowl XIV appearance.

Devine left town after the season to become the head coach of Notre Dame, leaving legendary quarterback Bart Starr to clean up the mess he created. Devine never explained the rationale behind the trade or the logic, or lack thereof, of overpaying for a player he saw with his own eyes was declining. It was a colossal mistake. Sure, the team needed a quarterback, but Hadl was not the right man for the position. After this disastrous trade, the Packers only had two winning seasons and just one playoff appearance. It wasn't until Ron Wolf arrived in 1992 as general manager that the Pack actually returned to its past glory.

REASON NUMBER TWO

One Player Away

In the 1989 season, Jimmy Johnson, the newly appointed head coach of the Dallas Cowboys, had inherited a poorly constructed team with one star: Herschel Walker. Though Johnson did have Michael Irvin, the wide receiver had yet to showcase the talent that would eventually earn him a spot in the Hall of Fame. Johnson realized immediately that he would have to acquire more picks to fill the gaping holes on his roster—and relied on his college scouting connections and eagle eye to find talent. One day, while on his usual afternoon jog with his coaching staff, he came up with the idea to trade Walker. He never saw his running back as a building block or the kind of talent who was a seamless fit for his offense. Walker was a point-of-entry back, meaning he needed to enter a gap without restriction, then allow his speed and power to take over. Johnson wanted a shifty back, one who could make a tackler miss instantly and then gain yards. So as much as the media and even his fellow coaches loved Walker, Johnson only saw his faults. Walker wanted to be spoiled. Throughout his whole professional career, he had gotten what he wanted. But Johnson had too much work and too little time to spend kissing his ass.

Once he informed his staff of his decision, which was much to the dismay of offensive coaches David Shula and Jerry Rhome, Johnson contacted several teams to gauge their interest levels. The New York Giants, Atlanta Falcons, and Cleveland Browns seemed the most intrigued. The Browns were an aging team with Bud Carson, a new, but also aging, coach who was hired for one reason: to stop John Elway and the Denver Broncos. Carson, a longtime NFL assistant and brilliant defensive mind, was faced with a narrow window of opportunity in which to lead the Browns to the Super Bowl. After losing a heartbreaking overtime game in Miami, bringing their record to 3–2, he knew the team desperately needed a difference maker. With Browns general manager Ernie Accorsi handling the trade conversations, and with Johnson's willingness to take draft picks, the Browns seemed to be the favorite to land Walker. So Accorsi made his move, offering two nonconsecutive number-one picks and several second-rounders. Johnson had sensed the Browns were serious, but he also knew there could be more meat on the trade bones across the league. He placed a call to Vikings vice president and general manager Mike Lynn, another suitor with strong interest. Johnson was blunt with Lynn, telling him he already had a huge offer from the Browns. Nothing makes another team work harder or faster than competition. Lynn became fearful that Johnson would move Walker to Cleveland and knew he needed to act quickly. As was the case with the Browns, the sting of narrowly losing out on two Super Bowls made Lynn act in desperation and overreach to get closer to the title. The prior two seasons, the Vikings had lost on the last play of the game to the Washington Redskins in the NFC Conference Championship, and in the divisional round to the San Francisco 49ers. The similarities between the Browns and Vikings made each desperate, and organizational brass convinced themselves their teams were just one player away from clutching their first Lombardi trophy.

Lynn decided to wow Johnson with five players, all of whom were either aging or having no impact on the current Vikings team. The players included in the offer were linebackers Jesse Solomon and David Howard, cornerback Issiac Holt, defensive end Alex Stewart, and running back Darrin Nelson.

Along with the five players, Lynn also offered a first- and second-round pick for the following year, 1990. Lynn was counting on Johnson being the typical impatient head coach who was simply worried about today, not tomorrow. By using the players, Johnson would void the conditional picks, thus allowing Lynn to trade nonassets for a huge asset. And he'd preserve his draft picks. With these five players, the Cowboys would improve in all areas. And who could turn down a seven-for-one deal? For Lynn, none of the players really mattered. From his perspective, he was trading two high picks for a Pro Bowl player in his prime, one who could do everything at an elite level.

Johnson was then going to send Walker to Minnesota. The only condition in the deal was that he had to make a decision on the players before February 1, 1990, to trigger exercising the conditional draft picks. When the players from Minnesota arrived, the Cowboys' coaches were elated, as they finally improved their talent base for the remainder of the season and appeared poised to make a run. Defensive coordinator Dave Wannstedt said, "I told him, 'Jimmy, these guys are better than what we've got.'" Johnson's response was telling: "I know, but I've got something else in mind." The picks gave him flexibility and the opportunity to move up and down in the draft. Johnson went on to make fifty-one total trades during his five years in Dallas, with the Walker deal setting the stage for many of them.

After the season, Johnson attempted to reengage Lynn on a revised deal so he could keep the players along with the conditional picks. By this point, though, Lynn was angry, realizing he was on the losing end of the deal. But he was forced into modifying the deal—Johnson would send back a third-round pick in 1990, along with a tenth-rounder and a third-rounder in 1991. This revised deal allowed Johnson to keep three of the players and their conditions. For Lynn, the deal became an embarrassment of a once bright career. The Vikings acquired a talented receiver in Jake Reed but never went to the Super Bowl. They weren't one player away. They were several.

When the deal was all said and done, Walker played two seasons in Minnesota, never fitting into their offense. Johnson suspected this would be the case all along. He went on to use the Minnesota first-round pick, along with other draft assets, to move up in the draft and select Emmitt Smith. Then, through various trades, he added Russell Maryland and defensive backs Clayton Holmes, Kevin Smith, and Darren Woodson.

"The Great Train Robbery," as Johnson called the Walker deal, might have been the start, but had he not traded for pass-rushing Hall of Fame player Charles Haley from the 49ers, his dynasty in Dallas might never have gotten off the ground. Johnson's finest trade was sending a 1993 second-round pick and 1994 third-round pick to San Francisco for Haley, a deal that shifted the balance of power in the entire NFC.

REASON NUMBER THREE
Get Him Out of the Building

Trades such as the one discussed above often backfire for the team insistent on removing a player from its locker room. Players who are exiled frequently come back with a vengeance. Charles Haley was the missing link to the Dallas defense. He made a monumental difference in the team's defense—playing a pivotal part in the Cowboys winning their first Super Bowl in 1992, while going on to add two more. The 49ers would only win just one more. As much as they tried to replace Haley's ability to create pressure on the passer, they truly could never replicate his production.

If Haley was a top talent, why did the 49ers trade him for second- and third-round picks? Gossip. The NFL is much like a social club. Scouts, coaches, and executives willingly exchange information from team to team, some of it false, which becomes the foundation of an evaluation of a player's character. In the case of Haley, everyone in the NFL knew he carried some baggage with him, in part because he suffered from bipolar disorder, which wasn't diagnosed until after he retired. Haley had numerous altercations with his teammates over the years.

The combination of Haley going after megastar receiver Jerry Rice and his constant attacks on George Seifert gave the 49ers no choice but to exile him to Dallas. But why Dallas? Because word was out on Haley and few other teams felt they could manage him. Every team wanted to watch him play on Sunday, but no one wanted to deal with him in their locker room from Monday to Saturday.

In August of 1992, I was sitting at my desk in Berea, Ohio, working as the director of player personnel for the Cleveland Browns. My phone rang, and it was John McVay, the general manager of the San Francisco 49ers, on the other end. McVay was a father figure to me. He took me under his wing in 1984 and helped develop my NFL career. He was always so upbeat and positive, the perfect balance of charm and toughness, so when he started the call with "Michael, my boy," I knew he had something up his sleeve. McVay kindly informed me that he was going to make me executive of the year if I was willing to give him two second-rounders for Haley. McVay knew I was a sucker for Haley. He knew I loved him as a player from the day I first saw him hunting down Georgia Southern quarterback Tracy Ham. My first reaction was "Coach, we are rebuilding the team with a bunch of young players—not sure he fits for us right now." At this point, McVay gave me fatherly advice and said, "If you want to get good faster, make the deal." We regrettably didn't. Had we had Haley as a part of those Cleveland teams, particularly the one in 1994, when we allowed only 204 points the entire season, we might have advanced further in the playoffs. To this day, I regret not pushing hard to bring Haley to Cleveland.

There are different reasons the "Get him out of the building" trades occur— and it's not always a player's behavior. Sometimes, teams need to part with a player when his stock is high, even though his talent is low. This happened when I returned to Cleveland in 2013 as general manager.

In the 2012 draft, the Browns set their sights on Alabama running back Trent Richardson. Richardson had that "can't-miss" label, as he was a unique mixture of size and brute strength. Picking Richardson at number three made him the highest-selected running back since Reggie Bush in 2006. But the Browns didn't feel they were just acquiring a running back. They felt they were getting a true playmaker, one who was capable of scoring whenever he touched the ball.

Because there is so much time between the end of the NFL season and the NFL draft, various campaigns around certain players can gain momentum, creating enormous interest in their draft stock. And once a player gains a favorable label, as Richardson did, the aura around him continues to grow bigger and brighter as groupthink takes over. All this adoration can create a false narrative in the mind of fans, media members, and even NFL executives, which lingers through the early part of the player's NFL career. It's almost as if people heard Richardson was great and fit the prototype of a successful NFL player—great high school, Alabama, two-time national champion—so no need wasting time watching him. Then, even if they struggle initially, can't-miss players get a long rope in proving that the original label was correct. In his first year, Richardson had a minor knee surgery, which limited his effectiveness early in the season. He ended up starting fifteen games in 2012, carrying the ball 267 times for 950 yards. His 3.6 yards-per-attempt average ranked him thirty-seventh out of forty-four running backs. For a can't-miss player, he looked average, nonexplosive, nothing like the best player in any draft. If you had removed his name from the back of his jersey and said he was a college free agent from Mt. Union College, no one would have thought otherwise.

When I joined Cleveland in January of 2013, everyone, including the new coaching staff, offered a thousand excuses as to why Richardson looked so slow and nonexplosive—his weight gain, his lack of an off-season program, and his lack of familiarity with the offense. It was never his lack of talent or the possibility of being a blown pick. It was all based on the circumstances of the past season.

Once the off-season was over and the team reported to training camp, strength coach Brad Rolle told me Richardson was in the best shape of his life— a lean, mean, fighting machine ready to take over the NFL. But when the practices started and the preseason games began, nothing looked different, nothing changed, and still the perception somehow was that he was a can't-miss player. My thoughts were a little different. If Richardson was in the best shape of his life and if this was all he could do, then we had to trade him before others could see what I was seeing. And we did.

After two games in the regular season, we contacted the Colts, who were desperate for a running back to help their star second-year quarterback, Andrew Luck. Had we called other teams, then Richardson's value would've declined. We needed a team that relied on its old college scouts and shared the same enthusiasm as the media and draftniks about Richardson. And the Colts were the perfect team, desperate to make a deal and believing they were just one player away from making a major leap. Capitalizing on perception can go a long way toward making a good trade. Especially when you know that "get him out of the building" is a major driving factor.

CHAPTER 8
TOP 100 PLAYERS

"Great men are not born great, they grow great. . ."
—Mario Puzo

THE OTHER DAY, I WAS LISTENING to the great Deion Sanders talking about the Hall of Fame and how his gold jacket should be different from others. Setting aside his false sense of modesty, the man known as "Prime Time" is 1,000 percent correct: not everyone in the Hall has the same talents. Yes, they all wear the same color of gold, but there should be a separation of players into different levels, honoring their talents and contributions to the game. In every exclusive club there must be levels of importance, as no two players are the same, let alone the three hundred members in the Hall of Fame. In this chapter, I present my own top 100 list, specifically designed to recognize different levels of talent.

My top 100 board will mirror an NFL college draft board, which is organized based on the value of the player. A first-round pick is worth more than a fourth-rounder, so a draft board must take into account the difference, and thus have distinct levels. On most NFL college draft boards there are four to five levels of players. Each level signals a different impact the player is projected to have on the team—as starter, potential starter, developmental player, backup, and so forth. In a similar fashion, my board is divided into five sections, each of which represents a different level of achievement for the outstanding players included in it: The Everlasting, The Excellent, The Exceptional, The Extraordinary, and The Elite. These designations will not only address Prime Time's complaint, but will provide a clearcut breakdown of the players' contributions to professional football.

LEVEL ONE: THE EVERLASTING

All players at this level have left their mark on the game, both when they played and for generations to come. The sheer mention of their name brings an instant highlight to mind, a remembrance that automatically brings a smile to all fans, regardless of the years gone by.

100
KENNY WASHINGTON

3-Year Career • 27 Games Played; 5 Started

140 Rushing Attempts • 859 Rushing Yards
Gained • 8 Rushing Touchdowns

First All-American in UCLA History

Led the Nation in Total Offense with 1,370 yards (1939)

We were all cheated. By the time Kenny Washington enrolled at UCLA, he was chiseled at six feet, three inches and 235 pounds, and blessed with great speed, superior hand-eye coordination, and a powerful, stiff arm. During his two seasons of varsity baseball at UCLA, Washington hit an astonishing .450 compared to Robinson's .350. To many who observed both, Washington had more natural talent and speed, and the better arm. Washington could easily throw a football over sixty yards with one flick of the wrist. Though he was pigeon-toed and ran awkwardly, as if he had two broken legs, he always delivered a forceful hit upon contact. Washington loved contact, demonstrated remarkable athletic skills in the open field, and because of his height, ran the ball much like Raiders Hall of Famer Marcus Allen, but with even more breakaway speed. When any player from the conference was asked who the best player was, Washington was always the answer. After the final game of his senior season, as Washington walked off the Coliseum field for the last time, the fans gave him a standing ovation. Washington's best friend, Woody Strode, called it "the most soul-stirring event I have ever seen in sports. Someone told me that [future Oscar-winning actress] Jane Wyman was crying in the stands. And as Kenny left the field and headed to the tunnel, the ovation followed him in huge waves. It was like the pope of Rome had come out."

After finishing his college career, Washington went to the 1940 College All-Star Game at the invitation of George Halas. Halas wanted to sign him as an undrafted player, but the league refused to break away from its practice of segregation. After Washington scored a touchdown in that All-Star Game—leaving no doubt as to who the best player on the field was—Halas intensely pursued him and even had him remain in Chicago for several days in hopes that he could sign with the Bears and upgrade the team. But fellow owners still refused to allow integration.

By the time Washington was finally allowed to play in the NFL in 1946, the knee injuries he sustained playing in a semipro league had diminished his talents. In total, Washington played twenty-seven games during his pro career, carried the ball 140 times, and gained 859 yards, a 6.1 yards-per-attempt average. He scored eight career touchdowns and held the record for the Rams' longest run from scrimmage record, a ninety-two-yard gallop against the Chicago Cardinals in Comiskey Park.

Washington was cheated out of his career, plain and simple. We were cheated from watching him play. The one hundred thousand fans that made him take a bow with their thunderous cheers after his final college game thought they would see him again, but sadly, they never did. When you watch his tape from his UCLA days, it's easy to understand why everyone thought he was the best player in college football.

Was it Washington's fault he wasn't allowed to compete? Nope. I have zero doubts that Washington would have been a top player in the NFL and would have been a top 100 player. The UCLA tape is good enough for me to say with conviction: Washington belongs on the list.

99
MEL HEIN

2x NFL Champion • 5x First Team All-Pro • 4x Pro Bowl

All-Decade Team: 1930s

15-Year Career • 170 Games Played; 153 Started

10 Interceptions

College Football Hall of Fame, Class of 1954

Hein played for the New York Giants from 1931 until 1945. Like most players from his era, he went both ways, playing offensive center and linebacker. He was not a big man, standing slightly over six feet tall and weighing 225 pounds—light for an offensive lineman. What Hein lacked in size, he made up for with toughness and athletic talent. Hein had outstanding speed for an offensive lineman, which served him well when he switched over to defense. He was truly a sixty-minute man. He rarely came off the field and loved playing both ways. He only asked out of a game one time, to tend to his broken nose. (Remember, there were no face masks when Hein played.)

Hein's ability to run and play with great toughness is something to admire. His athletic talent would have allowed him to play the game today—perhaps not at center, but as a roaming coverage middle backer who loved contact.

Winning the Joe F. Carr Award in 1938 for the NFL MVP was a great honor for Hein, considering the award for the MVP often goes to the skill players, not centers or linebackers. Former NFL commissioner Carr, for whom the MVP award was named, was also responsible for preventing college players from playing in the pro game under assumed names. Don't laugh: it happened all the time, as players would play two games on weekends, one for their college team and another for the pro team in their area. The college game was more popular than the pros during the 1920s and '30s. As commissioner, Carr didn't want to alienate colleges against his growing league, which was desperate for fans. Therefore, he passed a rule to limit college players from playing until they graduated college courses. Tragically, after Hein accepted his award for the 1938 season, Carr died of a heart attack in May of 1939.

98
RON KRAMER

2x NFL Champion

1x First Team All-Pro • 1x Pro Bowl

10-Year Career • 128 Games Played; 99 Started

229 Receptions • 3,272 Receiving Yards Gained •
16 Receiving Touchdowns

After three seasons of working with the personnel department in Cleveland, Belichick wanted to grade the scouts' performance, not to direct blame, but rather to learn in which areas we needed to improve our evaluation process. From our research, we found that most scouts had trouble evaluating positions requiring proficiency in two or more areas. One example was the tight end position. Tight ends must be able to control the end of the line in the run game, have the power to handle big defensive ends, and then be fast and dynamic to make plays in the passing game down the field. Their position requires unique skills. And if they are only good in one area, then the defense can adjust their call and personnel groupings to remove the tight end's area of strength. When a team has a dominating blocker and a down-the-field threat in the passing game, all wrapped up in one player, it's nirvana. The Packers had the perfect tight end for their power sweep with Ron Kramer.

From 1961 to 1964, Kramer set the edge in the run game, allowing the sweep to become the play most identified with the Packers. In addition, he also had 138 receptions for 2,202 yards and fifteen touchdowns. During those four years, Kramer was the best player at his position in the league and easily could have been the best player on the Packers' offense. The tape doesn't lie. Kramer had size, speed, power, and toughness. He was a down-the-field threat in the passing game and hard to tackle once the ball arrived in his soft hands. He exceled at things that are not noticeable, but played a huge factor towards winning championships, which the Packers did in 1961 and 1962. Lombardi once said of his tight end, "Having Ron Kramer on the team is like having a twelfth man."

Had Kramer played today, his career would be viewed differently. As it stands now, he is not close to getting a gold jacket, in part because—like scouts—the Hall of Fame voters have a hard time evaluating the dual-role performer. Kramer's statistics don't jump off the page. Yet every time you watched Paul Hornung or Jimmy Taylor run the famous Green Bay power sweep, Kramer was the man making it all happen.

When he played from 1957 to 1967, the game was trench warfare, and the importance of a multitalented player like Kramer was ignored. Kramer was also overlooked because he played on a team with thirteen other Hall of Fame players. Six were on the offensive side. How could his talent be fully recognized when surrounded by so many good players?

In 1965, wanting to be closer to his family, Kramer asked Lombardi to trade him to Detroit. The trade prevented him from accumulating the statistics needed for entrance into the Hall. In Detroit for three seasons, Kramer won fifteen games and never was able to showcase his incredible talents. If he had continued in Green Bay, he would easily been a first-ballot Hall of Fame player. He chose his family, which is admirable. But those of us who watched him play understood his talents and contributions to the Packers, as indicated by his selection to the Fiftieth Anniversary All-Time Team as an honorable mention. Had Kramer played today, he would look like a smaller Rob Gronkowski in terms of height. He would still be able to win on third down with his quickness, attack the seams with his speed, and be a force in the run game. Though he dominated the game without stats, Kramer for me is a top 100 player. The tape never lies.

HOLDING COURT

Kramer was an elite athlete in every sport he played. In basketball, he was all–Big Ten at Michigan, starting at center for three seasons. He served as team captain, averaged 20.4 points his junior season, and held the Michigan scoring record for a brief period. The Washington Generals, opponents of the Harlem Globetrotters, offered him a professional basketball contract, and he was also selected in the fifth round of the 1957 NBA draft, thirty-fourth overall by his hometown team, the Detroit Pistons. Kramer turned down both offers to focus on football.

97
ADAM VINATIERI

4x Super Bowl Champion

3x First Team All-Pro • 3x Pro Bowl

All-Decade Team: 2000s

24-Year Career • 365 Games Played; 0 Started

97.3 Extra Point Percentage • 83.8 Field Goal Percentage •
Game-Winning Field Goals in Super Bowls XXXVI and XXXVII

During the 1996 preseason, New England Patriots coach Bill Parcells was willing to forgo his incredibly reliable kicker, Matt Bahr, and take his chances with a former World League kicker from South Dakota State, Adam Vinatieri. Parcells was extremely fond of Bahr, because, in the words of Parcells, "he knew what he was getting." What Parcells got was reliability; he could count on Bahr to make pressure kicks, as long as he was inside of forty yards. But Vinatieri could do everything Bahr could do, and then some. His powerful and deadly accurate leg offered more range than Bahr did and allowed Parcells to forgo his constant fourth-down decisions in the opponent's territory. Vinatieri also helped Parcells's kickoff coverage by booming the ball through the end zone. Additionally, Vinatieri could produce in any kind of severe weather, which is a critical trait for teams playing in a cold-weather climate. And most important, he could make tough kicks under extreme pressure. Outside of his two game-winning Super Bowl kicks—one against the Rams, the other against the Panthers—Vinatieri makes my top 100 list for his tying and winning kicks on a snowy night in January in 2001.

The famous "Tuck Game" against the Raiders—on a Saturday night in Foxborough, Massachusetts—established Vinatieri's reign as the top kicker in the NFL. After the Patriots retained the ball from the "Tuck" ruling (I still don't agree with the call), their offense ran four more plays and sent Vinatieri out to attempt a forty-five-yard kick to send the game into overtime. The field was covered with snow and the footing was horrible for everyone, especially Vinatieri, who needed to drive the ball through the whiteness created by the wind and snow.

That kick, from my view in the press box, looked like a Tiger Woods 2-iron off the grass at the Masters—low, powerful, and accurate. Then, minutes later, as the snow continued to fall in overtime, Vinatieri did it again. Another Tiger Woods special—this time like a 7-iron—launched off his foot. The kick was high, powerful, and accurate. It not only won the game for the Patriots, but also started their dynasty.

I had given top 100 consideration for Baltimore kicker Justin Tucker, with his incredible consistency and deadly accuracy. However, winning big games with one kick, along with longevity, made Vinatieri the choice. Tucker might get there, just not right now.

96
LARRY LITTLE

2x Super Bowl Champion

5x First Team All-Pro • 2x Second Team All-Pro • 5x Pro Bowl

All-Decade Team: 1970s

14-Year Career • 183 Games Played; 155 Started

During the late 1960s and much of the '70s, the running game dominated the offense in professional football. And since it was so impactful, defensive tackles were at a premium. To defuse the running game, teams needed big tackles who could anchor the line, stop all penetration, and create movement. And since tackles were so talented, the guards assigned to block them needed to be exceptional. In this era, football was a middle-of-the-field game; controlling the inside meant control of the game. And no team dominated the middle of the field like the Miami Dolphins, with offensive guard Larry Little leading the way.

The game eventually changed as the players became bigger and faster. It became harder to control the middle of the field. Now the defense had to defend both the width and length of the field, making it a space game. Football shifted its focus from run to pass, becoming entertaining in the process.

Little was over six feet, one inch tall and weighed 255 pounds, which was average for that era. He often gave away thirty pounds to the tackle he faced, relying on his foot quickness to drive a defender off the ball. Playing offensive line requires quick feet, which is why the forty-yard-dash time is relevant to the evaluation process. Little was extremely quick and powerful. When a lineman like Little got his second step off the ball onto the ground quickly, it allowed him to secure the necessary position. Had Little played today, his lack of height would not hinder his play. His athletic talent, along with his lower-body strength, would have enabled him to compete at a high level.

Even though the Dolphins didn't throw the ball often, Little was still an excellent pass protector against the opposing defensive tackles. The offensive linemen were always in a three-point stance, no matter the down and distance, with their stance tilted toward the run, which made pass protection even harder. If a current defensive lineman played against the Dolphins, or any team back then, they would scream, "Run, run, run" before the snap because of the heavy run stances of the offensive line. Before every play, an offensive lineman stance is referred to as a "bird or rabbit," which then tells the defensive line to play accordingly. If a current defensive lineman played against the Dolphins (or any team back then), there would have been nothing but rabbit calls. With Little's quickness, he was able to get in position, slide his feet, and control the rush. His superb athletic skills initially went unnoticed by scouts during his college career at Bethune–Cookman; Little is one of fifteen players in the Hall of Fame who went undrafted. Yet his run blocking allowed the Dolphins' offense to control the game on the ground and become the only undefeated team to win a title in NFL history.

95
STERLING SHARPE

3x NFL Reception Leader • 2x NFL Touchdown Leader •
1x NFL Receiving Yards Leader

3x First Team All-Pro • 5x Pro Bowl

8-Year Career • 112 Games Played; 112 Started

595 Receptions • 8,134 Receiving Yards Gained •
65 Receiving Touchdowns

Awarded Triple Crown for Receivers, 1992 • 1 of 7 players to Lead
the League in Receptions, Yards, and Touchdowns • First Player
in NFL History with 2 100-Reception Seasons Back-to-Back

Imagine being the finest athlete in your family and your little brother is in the Hall of Fame, but you're not. Sterling Sharpe deals with it every day of his life. Sharpe has been neglected by the Hall voters for far too many years. They claim his seven-year career is too short to be worthy of wearing a gold jacket, an excuse they use whenever it fits their agenda. They ignore what he accomplished before a neck injury forced him to retire and what could have been had he stayed healthy. Only Jerry Rice and Randy Moss have eclipsed his eighteen touchdown receptions in a single season, which demonstrates his incredible skill set. What makes it even more impressive is that Sharpe—with the neck injury and discomfort in his arm—scored thirteen touchdowns in the final six games of his career. In his last three seasons in Green Bay, with Hall of Fame quarterback Brett Favre, Sharpe scored forty-two touchdowns and a 7.46 ratio of catches to touchdowns, dominating the game.

When head coach Mike Holmgren arrived in Green Bay in 1992 along with Favre, their partnership created the perfect setting for Sharpe to highlight his skill set. Sharpe was the ideal receiver for the West Coast offense. He had great power in his lower body, could run every route, and was able to make yards after the catch. Sharpe was never viewed as the fastest receiver in the game, yet he always seemed to get behind the defender. His powerful running style was deceiving to defenders. His soft hands, combined with his incredible toughness, made him hard to tackle. When a great talent is featured in the right scheme, amazing production occurs. Sharpe became the first receiver in NFL history to have two consecutive seasons with over one hundred catches. Not even Jerry Rice, Steve Largent, nor any other Hall of Fame receiver had that consistent production.

Sharpe dominated the game in the prime of his career until a stinger caused by blocking Atlanta safety Brad Edwards sent him to the sideline. The injury forced him to have multiple surgeries to fuse two vertebrae in his neck. Once the procedures were completed, so was Sharpe's playing career.

Sharpe is overlooked by the Hall voters because he was never media friendly. He constantly ignored the press, refusing to engage in any conversation with any media member. As a result, no one supports his career for consideration into the Hall. No one stands on the table to discuss how Sharpe impacted the Packers' offense. Every team knew Sharpe would get the ball. Being great means playing great when the other team attempts to neutralize your impact. No defense could touch Sharpe. It is a shame the voters don't understand his greatness. It's a bigger shame his incredible career was shortened. Judging the film from his seven-year career, it's safe to say he was a top 100 player of all time.

94
JACK CHRISTIANSEN

3x NFL Champion • 2x NFL Interception leader

6x First Team All-Pro • 5x Pro Bowl

All-Decade Team: 1950s

8-Year Career • 89 Games Played; 88 Started

17 Interceptions; 3 Returned for Touchdowns

Each time you review a box score from a football game on any level, always examine the number of incompletions the quarterback has thrown, and then examine the number of balls deflected by the defense. Those two numbers tell an important story. For example, during the 2019 season, former Browns quarterback Baker Mayfield attempted 534 passes, and 217 fell incomplete. Of those 217, ninety-six were touched by the defense, for an average of six passes per game. Alternatively, the Packers' Aaron Rodgers averaged less than one that season. The more times the quarterback allows the defense to touch the ball, either batted at the line or down the field by someone in the secondary, the higher the chances for turnovers. Because, let's face it, the defense cannot create turnovers unless they get their hands on the ball. Pretty simple, right? When a secondary player is always around the ball, making plays in the passing game, then his value to the team is significant. Which is why Jack Christiansen is one of the top 100 players ever to have played in the NFL.

Christiansen played for the Lions from 1950 to 1958, approximately the same time that Buddy Parker was head coach. And under the direction of Parker, the Lions were one of the best teams in the NFL. It's true, the Lions and winning at one time went hand in hand. Lions fans flocked to 2121 Trumbull Avenue in Detroit, the site of Briggs Stadium, to watch "Chris's Crew" make life rough on opposing quarterbacks. Christiansen had a knack for being around the ball, and his instincts and great hands allowed him to collect forty-six interceptions during his eight-year career. Christiansen's ability once the ball was in his hands made him elite. He was a defensive player who became offensive, impacting the game on all four downs with his return ability. Christiansen took the NFL by storm his rookie season, putting the fear of God into every punter in the league when he averaged 19.1 per return and scored four touchdowns. The next season, he averaged 21.5 and scored two touchdowns. After his first two seasons, the opposing coaches smartened up and tried to kick the ball away from him, which worked to a degree.

Christiansen averaged 12.1 per return and scored eight touchdowns in his career. As a comparison, Devin Hester, of the Bears and Falcons, averaged 11.7 per return during his twelve-year, 156-game career and scored fourteen touchdowns on punt returns. Hester was dynamic, but Christiansen was more so.

Christiansen's abilities helped the Lions win championships in 1952, 1953, and 1957. During the 1952 championship run, in the final two games of the season against the Dallas Texans and Chicago Bears, Christiansen also played offense, carrying the ball nineteen times for 148 yards and scoring two touchdowns. The Lions reached the playoffs and eventually won the title.

On every draft board I have been lucky to build, players having a significant impact on the kicking game would get a black dot next to their name, which signaled their four-down ability. If they were elite in the return game, they would receive two black dots. Christiansen has two black dots.

93
BRONISLAU "BRONKO" NAGURSKI

3x NFL Champion • 1x NFL Rushing leader

4x First Team All-Pro

All-Decade Team: 1930 • All-Time Team: 75th Anniversary

8-Year Career • 97 Games Played; 75 Started

633 Rushing Attempts • 2,778 Rushing Yards Gained •
25 Rushing Touchdowns

International Falls, Minnesota, is nicknamed the Icebox of the Nation because of its incredibly harsh winters; it averages over one hundred days of sub-thirty-two-degree weather. Besides being the coldest place in America, two other things make International Falls famous. The first is Frostbite Falls, the fictional town that Rocky and Bullwinkle called home, which was modeled after International Falls. The second thing that makes the city famous is that it's where the legend of Bronislau "Bronko" Nagurksi began.

Far and away the toughest, meanest, and most talented player of his era, it's only fitting that Nagurski came from this faraway place. Standing over six feet two and weighing more than 230 pounds, Bronko looked out of place on the field. He was bigger than most, faster than many, and tougher than the rest. The stories of his brute strength are endless, because he was freakishly strong without the benefits of any weight-lifting training. Nagurski acquired his strength naturally from farming and working in the fields. His size and athletic talent made him the Bo Jackson of his era.

Nagurski played offense and defense, never leaving the field. One man could never get him on the ground, as he would bulldoze his way to yards. Nagurski wasn't fancy: he attacked the entire game, relishing in the physicality of the sport. To visualize Nagurski today, think of Derrick Henry of the Titans and how he looks like a man among boys against smaller defenders. Like Henry, Bronko would initiate contact, then watch men bounce off him. He might not have had Henry's stiff arm, but defenders paid a huge price attempting to get him on the ground.

Head coach George Halas always wanted to keep Bronko fresh for defense, which is why he averaged fewer than ten carries a game throughout his career. Halas always kept talented runners on his roster. What he didn't have were many dominating tough guys like Nagurski, who played with a reckless physical style. If Bronko were playing today, he might be a linebacker, an edge rusher, or a tight end, or perhaps he would remain at tailback, and continue to run people over. With training and nutrition, Nagurski easily could carry 250 pounds, maintain his speed and quickness, and carry the ball more than ten times a game. Had he attempted more rushes during his career, we might be comparing Henry to him (minus the ponytail).

One thing is for certain: Nagurski dominated then, so much so that Halas retired his number, 3. And most important, he would dominate now no matter where he played.

92
JACK YOUNGBLOOD

1x Defensive Player of the Year • 2x Sack Leader

7x First Team All-Pro • 5x Pro Bowl

All-Decade Team: 1970s

14-Year Career • 202 Games played (201 consecutive); 187 Started

151.5 Sacks (unofficial; sacks were not officially recorded until 1982)

7 Straight Division Titles • 1 Super Bowl Appearance

Whenever Rams defensive end Jack Youngblood is discussed, we usually hear about him playing two playoff games—a Super Bowl and then a Pro Bowl—with a fractured fibula. Playing with the injury, and playing well, certainly deserves high praise. However, Youngblood's legendary toughness tends to steal the spotlight from his incredible pass-rushing career. He was more than tough; he was a factor in every game, accumulating 151.5 sacks during the 1970s, when passing the ball wasn't as popular as today.

The Rams' starting end, Deacon Jones, was near the end of his career when they drafted Youngblood in 1971. At thirty-three years old, Jones was having a hard time fighting off Father Time, as were others on the famous "Fearsome Four," the vaulted Rams front. They still had Merlin Olsen at defensive tackle, who was effective even at age thirty-one, but the Rams needed fresh blood to rebuild their front. With Youngblood's arrival, taking over for Jones in his second season, the Rams' front was fearsome again.

During the 1970s, the Rams were a great team without a great quarterback. They could never find a player capable of getting them over the top—not even Roman Gabriel, John Hadl, Shack Harris, Ron Jaworski, Pat Haden, Joe Namath (at the bitter end of his career), or Vince Ferragamo. They would make the playoffs and then vanish immediately. They relied on their run game and defense to win games, which worked well during the regular season and fell flat in the playoffs. How good were they on defense? From 1973 until their Super Bowl season in 1977, the Rams allowed 11.86 points per game during the fourteen-game regular season. The NFL didn't begin playing sixteen games until after the 1977 season. In 1975, they only allowed 135 points for the season, an average of 9.64 per game. Remarkable, right? During this time, Youngblood dominated. He recorded 70.5 sacks over those seventy games. In 1979, Youngblood recorded eighteen unofficial sacks and won the defensive player of the year.

Youngblood was a force in both run and pass. He was a problem, from any offensive tackle to block, in part because of his athletic talent, but also because of his relentless drive and effort. Just ask former St. Louis Cardinal Hall of Fame offensive tackle Dan Dierdorf, who said, "Youngblood is by far the best defensive end I've ever faced and may be the best all-around end in football." Roger Staubach, the quarterback of the Cowboys, offered further praise for Youngblood: "I'd have to give Youngblood the vote as the best defensive player I ever competed against." And finally, the great John Madden eloquently described Youngblood, saying, "If a Martian landed in my backyard, knocked on my door, and asked me, 'What's a football player?' I'd go get Jack Youngblood." Had he played today, Youngblood would dominate like he did during the 1970s. And what if he ever played on a team whose offense could get the lead early, allowing him to spend most of his time only rushing? When I answer that question, I realize Youngblood is a top 100 player who belongs on my board.

91
DOUG ATKINS

2x NFL Champion

1x First Team All-Pro • 6x Second Team All-Pro • 8x Pro Bowl

All-Decade Team: 1960s • All-Time Team: 100th Anniversary

17-Year Career • 205 Games Played; 176 Started

Al Davis, the former owner of the Raiders, loved watching defensive linemen. He studied their techniques, fundamentals, and, most important, how they were able to get into their stance. Bad stances turned him off as much as slow forty times. Davis wanted his ends, right or left, to have their right hand in the ground. Davis believed a right-handed stance allowed the lineman to gain a half step forward with his right foot, which allowed a slight advantage on the way to the passer. When watching the mammoth Doug Atkins get into his stance at left defensive end, with his right hand down, my mind instantly shifts to Davis.

Atkins was the quintessential Raiders player, even though he never wore the silver and black. Davis loved size and speed, and he really loved the great size and great speed Atkins displayed over his seventeen-year career. Much like fellow Tennessee native and University of Tennessee alumnus Reggie White, Atkins could make any offensive lineman look inadequate. He would toss tackles with his powerful club move inside and they would fly in the air as if they weighed only a hundred pounds. When you watch Atkins play, he moves like White and plays with the same power, dominating the game.

Atkins was over six feet, eight inches tall, which sounds great in theory for any defensive lineman, yet can present a problem. Sometimes being too tall forces the player to play too high, allowing the offensive line to win the pad-level game. Atkins was a giant in height and his pad level was always perfect. He was able to bend well and could generate power from his lower body. His natural athletic skills were rare. Atkins was a great high jumper, finishing second in the SEC championship track and field event with a mark of six feet, six inches. He initially enrolled at Tennessee to play basketball, until legendary Tennessee football coach Robert Neyland watched him move on the court and convinced him to join the football team. Once on the gridiron, the big man took over. When discussing top pass rushers in NFL history, legendary NFL Films announcer John Facenda perfectly described how Atkins played: "He was like a storm rolling over a Kansas farmhouse. He came from all directions, and all there was to do was to tie down what you could, and hope he didn't take the roof."

Because sacks or tackles were not recorded during Atkins's playing career, it's hard to quantify his production, but the game film sheds insight into his incredible talents. Had he played today, he would be compared to White or the other great physical marvels at the position. Atkins was thirty-seven when he began playing for the newly formed New Orleans Saints and retired after three seasons, at the tender age of thirty-nine. During his time with New Orleans, Atkins played in thirty-nine games and totaled thirty sacks. His contributions were evident by the fact that the Saints honored him by retiring his number, 81.

90
MIKE WEBSTER

4x Super Bowl Champion

7x First Team All-Pro ● 9x Pro Bowl

All-Decade Team: 1970s & 1980s ●
All-Time Team: 75th & 100th Anniversaries

17-Year Career ● 245 Games Played; 217 Started

From his first day lining up across from Steeler defensive tackle Ernie Holmes, Mike Webster knew he needed to improve his overall strength, especially in his upper body. He had the quickness to block Holmes, but lacked the strength to maintain the block. Webster was never a naturally big man, but working on the farm in his home state of Wisconsin provided him with discipline and toughness, which became the fabric of his NFL career.

For his first two years in Pittsburgh, during the off-season, Webster would leave his home in Lindenvale, Pennsylvania, and head over to the Red Bull Steakhouse. Webster wasn't heading to a lunch meeting or to consume red meat, but rather to improve his strength. Below the restaurant, an old boiler room had been converted into an underground powerlifting gym. Not many NFL players were pumping iron back then; some used weight resistance bands to slightly improve their core strength. Most believed strength came naturally—if you had it, great; if you didn't, your career wasn't going to last long. The Steelers understood how weight training could improve football skills, and players like Steve Courson, Tunch Ilkin, and Craig Wolfley joined Webster on a quest to improve their power. The dynasty of the 1970s Steelers was in part a result of the work done in that boiler room, along with the porterhouses and filet-mignon being cooked one floor above. By his third season, Webster was blocking Holmes and everyone else who lined up across from him.

Webster became a workout warrior able to translate his new and improved power to the field. He needed all the power he could muster with the shift in defensive philosophy occurring in the NFL. The 5–2 defense invented by University of Oklahoma's Bud Wilkinson was reconfigured into a 3–4 defense, with a big tackle aligned directly over the center's head. This defense required the center to do two things simultaneously: snap the ball and engage the nose tackle, knocking him back. It was like sumo wrestling. The center needed to be athletic enough to stay on his feet and quick enough to get into position to maintain the block. Because Webster had great balance and natural hip roll, the improvement in his upper- and lower-body strength allowed him to handle the assignment. Webster knew his career depended on maintaining his strength, so he became a fanatic about pumping iron to compensate for his lack of natural size. It's no surprise he was nicknamed Iron Mike. With added strength, an incredible passion to play the game, and both mental and physical toughness, Webster was the glue that held the Steelers' offense together.

When you watch Webster play, his bend—the ability to lower his butt as far to the ground as possible with incredible toddler-like flexibility—supplied him with transitional power from pumping all that iron. The spring from that stance enabled the power to manifest itself. This made Webster a great center. Had Webster not gotten stronger, he would have never blocked Holmes. And when he did, he blocked everyone.

89
RON MIX

1x AFL Champion

8x AFL All-Star • 9x All-AFL

11-Year Career • 142 Games Played; 130 Started

One of the hazards of having two competing leagues is that some of the players from the supposed lesser league are not held in the highest esteem, in part due to a preconceived gap regarding the level of competition. In the NFL's eyes, the AFL was the lesser league. This narrative is completely unfair, as many AFL players were as good as, if not better than, some playing in the NFL. What many do not realize is that the AFL only had eight teams, which allowed them to strengthen their rosters, whereas the NFL had between twelve and fourteen teams, watering down the talent. Even though the Packers defeated their AFL opponents in the first two Super Bowls, the AFL was always for real and never the lesser league.

Ron Mix was could have played in any league, on any field, at any time. His talent at USC was obvious to any scout, regardless of league. As a senior, he became the first pick of the Baltimore Colts, with every intention of playing in the NFL. The Colts offered him $8,000 per year, plus a $1,000 signing bonus, but then the upstart Los Angeles Chargers offered $12,000 per year and a $5,000 bonus. Instead of jumping on the deal with the Chargers, Mix countered the Colts' offer with one he hoped they wouldn't refuse: $10,000 per year and a $2,000 signing bonus. In an unpleasant manner, the Colts gave Mix a firm no and informed him that he would be begging to come back to them in a year, when the AFL folded, and the salary would be lower. Mix wasn't intimidated, and he went with the Chargers.

Mix was highly intellectual and took a cerebral approach to the game, including being one of the first players to incorporate a systematic method of weightlifting into his in- and out-of-season training. He had sensational athletic talent, running effortlessly and leading the back on the Chargers' signature toss sweep. Because the Chargers threw the ball often, Mix was equally effective with pass protection, using his long arms and quick feet to stay inside out on the rusher and prevent the quarterback from being hit.

Finally, I regard Mix as one of the best tackles in the game because he passes my dirty uniform test. During his career with the Chargers, Mix wore white pants until the team changed to yellow pants in 1966. When an offensive lineman wears white, it's much easier to spot grass stains on his pants, which means he is spending too much time on the ground—the worst place for an offensive lineman. After the game, the lineman with the cleanest pants is often the best. Mix's pants appeared fresh after each game, which is why he is one of the best tackles ever to play.

88
GENE UPSHAW

2x Super Bowl Champion • 1x AFL Champion

3x First Team All-Pro • 5x Second Team All-Pro •
6x Pro Bowl • 2x First Team All-AFL

All-Decade Team: 1970s •
All-Time Team: 75th & 100th Anniversaries

15-Year Career • 217 Games Played; 207 Started (202 consecutive)

I grew up in an area of New Jersey that didn't know whether Philadelphia or New York served as the main television market. Normally, this sort of confusion creates problems; however, it was the greatest gift ever. Instead of getting only New York or Philadelphia stations, we got both. For a football-hungry kid like me, it meant I could watch games at one o'clock and four o'clock every Sunday afternoon in the fall. Doubleheaders deluxe! The Eagles and Giants dominated the earlier time. When they played the Redskins, I was euphoric.

At four o'clock, the AFL games began, with Curt Gowdy on the mic and Al DeRogatis commenting alongside him. Most of the time, the games featured the Western Conference teams, including the Chargers, the Broncos, the Chiefs, and—closest to my heart—the Raiders. I loved seeing that Raiders shield and the metal barrier fences around the field at Oakland Alameda Coliseum. My excitement was off the charts as John Facenda narrated the poem "The Autumn Wind," written by former NFL Films president and son of NFL Films founder Ed Sabol, Steve Sabol, signaling the battle I was about to witness.

I really loved seeing the Raiders' offensive linemen walk onto the field, especially Gene Upshaw. In his signature white neck collar and with his arms covered with pads, Upshaw looked like a Roman warrior about to enter the Coliseum. Upshaw initially played offensive tackle in college at Texas A&M University-Kingsville. Al Davis moved him to guard, even though he was taller than most guards. Davis wanted someone who could match the physicality and size of the Chiefs' Buck Buchanan and the Chargers' Ernie Ladd, both physical players who dominated inside.

Moving Upshaw to guard was classic Davis, who always focused on the individual matchups within the game. With Upshaw, he found a player who could match the size of Buchanan and Ladd, but who also had the speed to get around the edge. (During this period, guards had to run to the edges and be capable of blocking in space to free the back on the outside.) Upshaw was the perfect Raider. His athletic talent and balance in the open field allowed him to cut down supporting defenders, thus freeing the runner.

Always the trendsetter, Davis understood the need for arm length and height inside to match with tackles, who were becoming bigger, faster, and harder to block. A "size war" was happening in the AFL, and Upshaw's play served as the model for future NFL guards and for any guard Davis selected in the draft. Upshaw would be the perfect Raider today. With his frame, he could have easily added more bulk and still remained explosive and quick. Upshaw was also tough and durable, starting in 202 games straight over his fifteen-year career, only missing games during his last season. In 1981, when he turned thirty-six, Upshaw perfectly could be summed up perfectly by the final lines of the poem, "The Autumn Wind":

The Autumn Wind is a Raider,
Pillaging just for fun.
He'll knock you 'round and upside down,
And laugh when he's conquered and won.

87
JOHN RANDLE

2x Defensive Player of the Year ● 1x NFL Sack Leader

6x First Team All-Pro ● 7x Pro Bowl

All-Decade Team: 1990s ● All-Time Team: 100th Anniversary

14-Year Career ● 219 Games Played; 185 Started

137.5 Sacks

Sometimes in scouting, you can recognize a college player's talent and wonder where he would play in the pro game. A player's talent on the screen works, but the measurables for any position might not. You project the player into other positions, hoping and praying he can make the transition, but knowing it probably will never happen. Once you watched the tape from Texas A&M, it was obvious. Randle was what scouts refer to as a "wife pick," meaning he was so talented that my wife could recognize him as a player. Randle literally jumped off the screen with his lightning quickness, dominating anyone in his path. Randle displayed it all on the tape—quickness, power, relentless effort, and incredible lower-body strength. Buccaneers personnel director Jerry Angelo, one of the best evaluators in the NFL, knew John Randle had elite talent for a defensive line. He was working for Bucs head coach Ray Perkins, and both men were indoctrinated with the Giants' size-and-speed grading system. For an undersized player like Randle—he was a shade under six feet, one inch tall and weighed 244 pounds—there wasn't a viable grade. Angelo couldn't figure out what position was right for Randle, and not even a brief tryout in Tampa proved helpful. Losing out on Randle bothered Angelo for the rest of his successful career.

Under the direction of defensive coordinator Floyd Peters, the Minnesota Vikings favored a smaller, quicker defensive line, but Peters also wasn't in love with the idea of signing Randle. Peters knew Randle would get bounced around inside by the bigger guards. Eventually, after Randle trained using a heavy metal chain and lock secured around his waist to increase his weight to 251, Peters let him in the Vikings organization, and the rest is history.

Minnesota was the perfect place for Randle. Playing in the Dome with extraordinary crowd noise allowed Randle, with his mind-boggling quickness, to win the line of scrimmage because his opponent could not hear the snap count. As fans, we rarely discuss the importance of the snap count, yet it's the one thing that gives the offense an advantage. When the home crowd dulls the quarterback's cadence and everyone is waiting for the center to move the ball, the advantage swings to the defense. And with someone like Randle on the other side, that advantage becomes substantial.

Randle arrived in Minnesota in 1990, when the Vikings needed fresh talent after giving away all their picks to the Cowboys. Coach Monte Kiffin arrived a year later and began utilizing Randle for the 3-technique (lining up on the outside shoulder of either guard) in his 4–3 defense. Randle soon became a dominating force inside. His job was to get off the ball, penetrate, and raise hell, much as he did at A&M. By this time, he had gained weight and understood how to play with great leverage. Randle was impossible to block, run, or pass on.

Randle's quickness, his explosive "get off," and the way he controlled the line of scrimmage fit perfectly into the Kiffin scheme. Kiffin knew Randle needed to be on the move, like a boxer jabbing and dancing before landing the big punch. Sometimes we make scouting too hard. Sometimes players don't need a change of position—they only need a change of how we evaluate them.

86
LARRY FITZGERALD JR.

1x First Team All-Pro • 11x Pro Bowl

All-Decade Team: 2010s

17-Year Career • 263 Games Played; 261 Started

1,432 Receptions • 121 Receiving Touchdowns

1 Super Bowl Appearance

When Bill Belichick stands in front of his team and discusses playing receiver, he makes it real simple. He will declare with authority that it "isn't that hard. First you have to catch the goddamn ball; second, get open." He never mentions being the fastest or scoring points; he breaks the position down to the most basic level. And Larry Fitzgerald does both at an elite level, and then some.

I have been watching Fitzgerald play since high school, as we both graduated from Valley Forge Military Academy in Wayne, Pennsylvania. Like all elite players, Fitzgerald dominated at VFMA, dominated at the University of Pittsburgh, and dominated at the professional level.

Fitzgerald had the best hand-eye coordination I've ever seen in any player over my career, including the great Jerry Rice. He had a strong wrist, which allowed him to stop the ball immediately as it reached his soft hands. He might not have been the fastest of the receivers, but his size, body control, and superior balance allowed him to make plays in traffic, and every 50/50 ball seemed to always end up in his hands. Fitzgerald's play supported the theory that even when he was covered, he was open. Quarterbacks knew that Fitzgerald would make the tough catch. He was fearless going inside, willing to take the big hit to make the catch. And he always bounced up quickly, throwing the ball to the nearest official.

Drafted in the first round by Denny Green in 2004, Fitzgerald has caught passes from a long list of quarterbacks—some good, some bad, some really bad, and one Hall of Famer—including Josh McCown, Shaun King, John Navarre, Kurt Warner, Matt Leinart, Derek Anderson, John Skelton, Kevin Kolb, Ryan Lindley, Carson Palmer, Drew Stanton, Blaine Gabbert, Josh Rosen, Sam Bradford, Mike Glennon, Kyler Murray, Chris Streveler, and Colt McCoy. With his 61.3 percent catch rate, imagine the receiving numbers and touchdowns Fitzgerald would have accumulated had he been in Indianapolis with Peyton Manning, or New England with Tom Brady.

Fitzgerald played the game, in the immortal words of Hall of Fame basketball coach Larry Brown, "the right way." He was unselfish, a great teammate, and willing to work hard off the field, which enabled him to play seventeen seasons. During his NFL career, Fitzgerald is the only player since 1950 to have a streak of four playoff games with one hundred-plus yards and a touchdown catch. He played big in big games.

85
MARSHALL FAULK

1x Super Bowl Champion • 1x NFL MVP •
3x NFL Offensive Player of the Year • 1x NFL Rushing Leader •
2x NFL Scoring Leader

3x First Team All-Pro • 3x Second Team All-Pro • 7x Pro Bowl

12-Year Career • 176 Games Played; 156 Started

2,836 Rushing Attempts • 12,279 Rushing Yards Gained •
100 Rushing Touchdowns

767 Receptions • 36 Receiving Touchdowns

When NFL offenses broke away from the traditional two running backs in the backfield and spread the field with their personnel groupings, the game became more open, but also more complex. Offensive football became a vertical and horizontal game, with the need for spacing, and the defense had to worry about the passing game on first down. Now someone from the defensive staff had to alert the play caller about which personnel group was on the field. Dynamic receivers were now more important than running backs...unless the running back was like Marshall Faulk. Faulk wasn't really a running back at all; he was a playmaker. He didn't need a lead blocker to make him effective and he didn't need a running play to take over the game. He ran routes like a wide receiver and was a nightmare for any opposing defense once he was displaced from the formation. Faulk essentially was two players in one. When he was behind the quarterback, he became the point guard for the offense and made those around him better.

Because of the devaluation of the running back position in the NFL today, we tend to lose sight that it's the running back, not the receiver, who makes the spread more effective. When the running back is dynamic, like Faulk, the defense has a tough question to answer: do they load the box—the area from the tight end to the opposite tackle—with enough run support, or do they spread out their pass coverage? In the 2019 Super Bowl between the Rams and the Patriots, Rams defensive coordinator Wade Phillips called his defense by whichever running back the Patriots had in the game, not the personnel group. This stifled the Patriots' offensive attack until the fourth quarter, when offensive coordinator Josh McDaniels placed two backs in the backfield with two tight ends, forcing Phillips to keep his big players on the field. Once that occurred, McDaniels spread the backs away from the formation as receivers and turned the tide of the game. This adjustment allowed the Patriots to produce their only touchdown of the game. The way this game unfolded serves as the perfect example of why a player with the skill set of Faulk was so valuable.

Faulk's talent entered the league at the right time. His 767 receptions dwarfed those of outstanding receivers like Paul Warfield, who totaled 427 receptions over his thirteen-year career. Lance Alworth played in a highly sophisticated passing game with the Chargers and only had 542 career receptions. If Faulk had played in the 1940s or '50s, his impact would not have been fully felt. Certainly, he would have been a great runner from the backfield, with speed, lateral change of direction, and—most important for any runner—the ability to make yards after contact. Swing pass routes highlighted this time period for running backs, as their main job was to run the ball with power, not dance around in space. Time and place matter, and Faulk's incredible pass-receiving skill set enlightened others as to what made the spread formation most effective.

84
ART SHELL

2x Super Bowl Champion

2x First Team All-Pro • 2x Second Team All-Pro • 8x Pro Bowl

All-Decade Team: 1970s • All-Time Team: 100th Anniversary

15-Year Career • 207 Games Played; 169 Started

Like all Raiders players, Art Shell was big and fast. With Upshaw at left guard and Shell at tackle, the Raiders were a mammoth line for the time, and they'd still be mammoth today. Shell was like a dancing bear, light on his feet and able to redirect in space with excellent body control. Listed at 265 pounds, which was big for the time, Shell looked bigger on game film. With incredible balance, he could handle power easily and was rarely off his feet. His punch was like a heavyweight boxer's, with snap velocity and power. Once Shell got his hands on you, it was over.

The 1968 AFL/NFL draft was the second time the leagues worked together in selecting players. The first pick overall in the draft was Ron Yary, an offensive tackle from USC and future Hall of Fame player for the Vikings. And seventy-nine picks later, the Raiders selected Shell, which provided them with a player of equal talent to Yary, after Raiders scout Ron Wolf loved what he witnessed while watching Shell play at Maryland Eastern Shore. Reflecting back on the organization's decision to take Shell in the third round, former Raiders coach John Madden commented, "The primary thing we saw in Art was his great size...but we were also excited that he was an accomplished basketball player. With that size, combined with his ability to move his feet and the agility he showed on the basketball court, we knew we had a quality prospect." Willing to take the time to develop Shell's skills, the Raiders had a legitimate starting tackle, capable of neutralizing the best pass rushers by Shell's third season.

The Raiders' passing game was about the deep ball. They wanted the quarterback to take a seven-step drop, hold the ball, and make plays down the field. This required talented tackles who could pass protect effectively for an extended time, thus allowing the receivers to get open. Shell was perfect for the scheme. Had he played today, he'd be an effective road grader, knocking defenders off the ball, and he'd benefit greatly from the short, quick passing game, which doesn't require pass blocking for extended time.

In addition to having a great NFL career as a player, Shell became the first African-American head coach in the NFL, serving two stints with the Raiders and posting a 56–52 record, with three playoff appearances.

83
JUNIOR SEAU

4x Defensive Player of the Year

6x First Team All-Pro • 3x Second Team All-Pro • 12x Pro Bowl

All-Decade Team: 1990s • All-Time Team: 100th Anniversary

20-Year Career • 268 Games Played; 243 Started

56.5 Sacks • 18 Interceptions •
43 Passes Defended • 80 Tackles for Loss

Junior Seau often talked to himself, repeating, "Run and hit. Run and hit, baby." The phrase was the perfect description of his job and performance in the NFL. Seau ran fast and hit hard. One of my many beliefs regarding defense is summed up in these words: "When your 'Mike' linebacker (i.e., middle linebacker) is slow, your defense is slow." Defending the width and the length of the field requires a special player to handle the inside linebacker position, particularly when the ball is in the red zone. Without a Mike who can run, the red zone defense becomes vulnerable.

Seau could run fast in any direction. He covered ground quickly, and from the time he was a little boy surfing in his hometown of Oceanside, California, he was born to be a linebacker. His instincts were incredible. He could locate the football, anticipate the snap count, and appear to be playing at a different speed than any other player. Saying Seau was a smart player doesn't do him justice. He was beyond smart; he had a feel for the game and a natural way of being disruptive. By combining his natural smarts and skills with film study—understanding every single situation on the field—Seau became an elite player. Seau was also simply fun to watch. His passion and enthusiasm for the game jumped off the tape. He truly was one of those players who played the game because he loved it; he loved to compete and to win.

From watching him, I learned the difference between being a good fourth rusher and being a great fifth rusher. When Seau first entered the league, he was an outside linebacker, playing at the end of the line in a two-point stance and rushing in a three-point stance on a third down or two-minute defense. When I evaluated him against bigger offensive tackles, I realized he wasn't as impressive as the fourth rusher. He made plays and played hard, yet there wasn't magic or, say, talent like Lawrence Taylor had. But when he moved to inside backer and played off the ball in nickel defenses and two-minute drills, he came to life. He understood how to fit into the rush and how to wiggle and maneuver his way around the guards and centers, using his power and quickness. His relentless approach and his efforts to fit perfectly into the predesign rush made him effective on the two areas of the defense that matter the most—in the opposing backfield and behind the defensive line in coverage.

The best part of watching great players play is that they teach you something every single time. Seau was one of those great players.

82
JIM OTTO

1x AFL Champion

9x First Team All-AFL • 9x AFL All-Star •
1x First Team All-Pro • 1x Second Team All-Pro

AFL All-Time Team • All-Time Team: 100th NFL Anniversary Team

15-Year Career • 210 Games Played; 210 Started

Whenever the time was right (which was not often), I always loved getting Al Davis to share old AFL stories. Davis had an incredible memory of games, players, and plays, going as far back as the first AFL season. He would tell stories of the recruiting battles between the AFL and NFL over players, and the chaos between two leagues, one trying to protect their turf and the other trying to gain credibility and respect. One player Davis loved to talk about was his old center, Jim Otto, whom he respected as a player and a person. Otto was on the team before Davis arrived and was considered the original Raider, starting the first game in 1960. Davis admired Otto from his assistant's chair in San Diego, and when he took over the Raiders, he told Otto, "When I was with the Chargers, we felt if we could get you out of the game, the rest of the Raiders would quit because you are the leader of this team." Otto was an incredible leader and one of the toughest players ever to wear the silver and black.

With his signature neck roll, quarterback-style double face guard, and a metal nose piece hanging from the top of his helmet, Otto was a self-made player. He entered the league at 210 pounds and become one of the bigger players, tipping the scales at 255. Otto possessed what Davis would often refer to as the "will to win." He was never going to back down. Relying on his technique and fundamentals, along with the incredible power in his lower body, Otto constantly controlled the line of scrimmage. His legs looked like tree trunks. Even later in life, when he would be part of the traveling party to every Raiders away game, Otto was still an impressive-looking athlete in spite of the seventy-four surgeries he had endured. His hands, his legs, and the twinkle in his eye always relayed a love of the game that never went away, regardless of the battles he fought from his playing days. He was a man's man, and no wonder he became the symbol of what it took to be a great Raider.

81
CHARLES WOODSON

1x Super Bowl Champion • 1x NFL Defensive Player
of the Year • 2x NFL Interception Leader

4x First Team All-Pro • 4x Second Team All-Pro • 9x Pro Bowl

All-Decade Team: 2000s

18-Year Career • 254 Games Played; 251 Started

20 Sacks • 65 Interceptions; 11 Returned for Touchdowns

When Charles Woodson first arrived in Oakland, he was like many other Raiders corners—he was big, fast, and athletic; he could play bump-and-run man-to-man; and he was able to make plays on the football. Everyone in the Raiders organization thought he might be the next Willie Brown or Mike Haynes. He quickly became Defensive Rookie of the Year and a playmaker with the ball in his hands, even getting reps on offense. The future of the Raiders defense looked bright with Woodson.

Over the next six seasons, Woodson played well above the standard of excellence for most players, yet he fell below the expectations the Raiders had initially had for him based on his draft status and early display of talent. From 2001 until 2005, he failed to make a Pro Bowl or win any postseason honors. Woodson also didn't complete a full season, always breaking down because of injuries. In addition, he didn't score a touchdown or have double-digit pass breakups, and even though he recorded eleven interceptions, no teams were afraid to throw in his direction. He went from being a "stay away" corner to a "let's go after him, because something good could happen" corner. And it usually did; Woodson was flagged thirty-three times for penalties. He became a target because he was doing more grabbing and holding than covering when attempting to keep receivers from running away from him. He wasn't in great condition, and even though he was in the prime of his career in terms of age, his play wasn't anywhere near prime. Most of these problems related to off-the-field behavior and a lack of dedication to his craft. In 2006, he became an unrestricted free agent with only Tampa and Green Bay offering him a deal, both well below his franchise tag salary the prior year in Oakland.

But when Woodson arrived in Green Bay, his Hall of Fame career truly began. The game became important, and he worked at his craft, which then allowed his incredible talent to take over. Woodson was more than a coverage man, playing outside corner. He became a rare five-position player in the secondary, playing either right or left corner, either free or strong safety, and the slot coverage man in nickel, which highlighted his skills as a run supporter, a blitzer, and a coverage man. The star position created by Lions head coach Buddy Parker way back in the 1950s allowed Woodson to be near the ball with the potential to attack the passer. Had Parker seen Woodson play the star, he would be screaming, "This is what I was talking about!" Woodson was the perfect star. He was a strong run-force player, creating negative plays when the opponent attempted to run from their nickel formation. He was dynamic as a blitzer, with sensational timing, disguising his intentions and then being able to close down. Woodson had powerful arms, using them as billy clubs when he tackled to strip the ball and create turnovers.

During his seven seasons in Green Bay, Wooden became a dominating player, all because he had the courage to change his behavior. When he returned to the Raiders, he was the elder statesman, moving inside to the safety position. He shared his career experiences, helping young players understand the difference between being a professional athlete and becoming a pro player. From 2006 until he left the game, Woodson was a great pro.

LEVEL TWO: THE EXCELLENT

As we climb the ladder of our exclusive club, we enter the "Excellent" player category. Each player in this category had a superior skill that shined brightest on the gridiron in many ways. Their impact forced changes in the rules, their domination required other teams to develop new schemes, and most of all, their play delighted all who watched.

80
RANDY WHITE

1x Super Bowl Champion • 1x Co–Super Bowl MVP

7x First Team All-Pro • 9x Pro Bowl

All-Decade Team: 1980s • All-Time Team: 100th Anniversary

14-Year Career • 209 Games Played; 165 Started

111 Sacks (unofficial)

Being a Washington Redskins fan growing up meant I was also a Dallas Cowboys hater. Admit it: we all love one team and hate another. Do you know of any Kansas City Chiefs fans who will admit to loving the Raiders? When I got older, I discovered an Elie Wiesel quote that changed my thinking. He once said, "The opposite of love is not hate, it's indifference." And I was never indifferent to the Cowboys. Despite my loyalty to the Raiders, I admired the Cowboys' talent, respected their players, and became frustrated every time they added another top-five draft pick after winning ten games and making the playoffs. One of those top-five picks I respected was defensive tackle Randy White. Even as a Washington fan, I loved watching White, and when I played high school and college ball, I attempted (unsuccessfully) to duplicate his style of play.

When the Cowboys selected White, they wanted to convert him to their new middle linebacker, replacing Lee Roy Jordan. White had everything you would want in a middle linebacker—great speed, toughness, and a competitive spirit.

At 255 pounds, he was considered light for a tackle, but perfect for a hard-hitting, hard-charging, extremely fast middle linebacker. But White lacked natural instincts for the position. Middle linebackers are born, not made. It's a crib position. When your momma lifts you from the crib, you either are or you aren't. It cannot be taught. Junior Seau was born a middle backer at birth; White wasn't.

After two seasons, White moved back to his natural defensive tackle spot and all hell broke loose. Now when he was on the field, he looked as though he had been released from a cannon. Once he threw off the offensive lineman, his burst and acceleration toward the ball carrier was dynamic. And when grading any defensive lineman for the draft, or in free agency, this acceleration trait is most important. Not all defensive linemen naturally possesses the skill set. White did, and his speed from the blocker to the ball carrier was rare. He played with relentless passion, earning the nickname "Manster" (i.e., half man/half monster). White never slowed down, and the longer the game, the more effective he became in both run and pass.

If White played today, he might be slightly better, if that's even possible. He'd resemble the Rams' Aaron Donald in build, power, strength, conditioning, and ability to dominate the game. Had White been in a pass-rushing stance, moving him closer to the line of scrimmage and working up the field, his quickness, combined with his power, would have been a problem for most guards, much as Donald is today. Because of his upper-body strength, White could finish the tackle and take down any quarterback he got his hands on. As quarterbacks today move in both directions with a threat to run, White had the speed to chase and close. Thanks to Elie Wiesel, I knew I loved my rival team and players like White.

79
JUNIOUS "BUCK" BUCHANAN

1x Super Bowl Champion • 2x AFL Champion

6x AFL All-Star • 6xFirst Team All-AFL • 2x Pro Bowl

All-Time Team: 100th Anniversary

13-Year Career • 182 Games Played; 172 Started

70 Sacks (unofficial)

One of the main reasons valuing the horizonal board is critical is that it makes it possible to compare players at different positions. Junious Buchanan being slightly ahead of Gene Upshaw on my top 100 list isn't a criticism of Upshaw, but rather a tribute to the talented big man known as "Buck." Even Upshaw gave Buchanan praise, saying, "Out of every player I played against, Buchanan was the most feared, because he brought everything to the table. He was over six feet, eight inches, three hundred pounds. He was quick, he was strong, he was fast, he was dominating. If you were not prepared to deal with that it would be a long, long, long Sunday afternoon."

During the 1960s, the AFL held no bias toward the level of competition or players coming from predominately Black colleges. Under owner Lamar Hunt, the Chiefs wanted the best players, so when they took Buchanan in the first round with the first overall pick, they made a huge statement about their league. The NFL wasn't as liberal, and the Giants waited until the nineteenth round, the 265th pick overall, to select Buchanan. How does the first pick overall in one league go in the nineteenth round in another? The NFL's attitude and their belief that players would prefer to play in their league allowed the AFL to collect dominating players like Buchanan.

The pressure of being the first overall pick or carrying the weight of all the Black colleges on his shoulders never bothered Buchanan. He relished the opportunity to demonstrate skills few had, then or now. Buchanan's talent was uncommon for a normal-size defensive tackle, let alone someone his size.

Buchanan was a lean and trim tackle, even though he tilted the scales near three hundred pounds. He was way more than a run stuffer. His enormous wingspan made it hard for quarterbacks to throw the ball over his extended arms. His power and lateral quickness, combined with his speed, made him disruptive on every play. Upshaw would often tell his teammates to not piss Buchanan off with their trash-talking, as he had his hands full even when Buchanan wasn't angry.

Like White, Buchanan would have been even better today. His size, power, and ability to dominate the inside of the pocket, getting in front of the passer, would have made him an incredibly valuable player when defending the top quarterbacks. From a scouting standpoint, it's hard to find big, fast, athletic tackles with the wingspan of a giant. Clearly whoever was watching the tape for the Giants looked at the wrong games.

78
EARL CAMPBELL

1x NFL MVP • 3x NFL Offensive Player of the Year •
NFL Offensive Rookie of the Year • 3x Rushing Yards Leader •
2x Touchdown Leader

3x First Team All-Pro • 5x Pro Bowl

All-Decade Team: 1970s • All-Time Team: 100th Anniversary

8-Year Career • 115 Games Played; 102 Started

2,187 Rushing Attempts • 9,407 Rushing Yards Gained •
74 Rushing Touchdowns

121 Receptions • 806 Receiving Yards Gained •
6.7 Receiving Yards per Reception

In the early 1970s, college football didn't have recruiting services or nationally televised signing dates. The famous star system we know today hadn't been invented yet—no high school kids were ranked one through five stars. Football programs were not evaluated on how many stars they recruited, only on wins. Back then, recruiting was all word of mouth, gossip, perception, and tales of local legends. Running back Earl Campbell was one such local legend and became a national star. Campbell was the real deal, and then some. Had the star ratings been around, Campbell would have broken the record and been the first ten-star recruit; he was that good in high school. The pride of Tyler, Texas, nicknamed the Tyler Rose, dominated Texas high school football, leading Tyler High to their first state title in forty-three years. In the championship game, played at the Houston Astrodome (known as the "Eighth Wonder of the World"), Campbell carried the ball thirty-two times for 164 yards, scoring the winning touchdown to beat Austin Reagan High School in front of 16,375 fans. Four years later, Campbell would continue to dominate on the same turf, playing for the Oilers.

Campbell was the perfectly built running back—he was short, squatty with a low center of gravity, and no available surface on his body for tacklers to tackle. His thighs churned like two cannons, making it hard for anyone—including Bevo, the 1,800-pound steer who was the mascot of the University of Texas at Austin—to bring him down. During his senior season, in a game against Southwest Conference rivals the Houston Cougars, Campbell scored three touchdowns. In the corner of the end zone, Bevo had been taking in the game when all of a sudden a powerful force came storming in, and down Bevo went. That powerful force was Campbell. What onlookers—and Bevo—didn't know at the time was that Campbell had been bedridden the night before with a 104-degree temperature and it was questionable whether he would play. But he did, running for 173 yards and making Bevo wonder what hit him.

Campbell carried the ball 1,404 times in his first four years in the league, averaging 351 carries per season. That's in addition to the 765 carries he had during his Longhorn college playing days (with 267 of them occurring when he a senior). Without the benefits of modern medicine, nutrition, and training, the Oilers ran him into the ground. Why didn't anyone stand on a table and scream, "Less of Earl might be more?" Campbell wasn't the same back after those four seasons, as injuries affected his game. In 1983, he had a 322-carry season. Like heavyweight boxer Joe Frazier after two hard-fought battles with Muhammad Ali, the constant pounding took its toll. By the third fight, Frazier was a shell of his former self; by his last three-hundred-plus-carry season, so was Campbell. It's a shame the Oilers abused him. During Earl's time, grading backs was all about the runner:

- How does he run the ball?
- Can he break tackles?
- Will he be able to run the ball to protect the lead?

Today, backs are graded differently:

- Can he handle blitz protection?
- Can he catch the ball in space?
- Can he run the ball effectively from the shotgun formation?

Campbell would be just as great as dominating today. He would have altered his game and, with his soft hands, could have made a difference for any offense in the passing game. What smaller corner or safety would want to tackle Earl in the open field? And the more space was a factor, the less of a beating he would have endured. In any era, Campbell would be effective; his combination of power and speed was rare.

77
DAN MARINO

1x NFL MVP • 1x NFL Offensive Player of the Year •
5x Passing Yards Leader • 3x Passing Touchdown Leader

3x First Team All-Pro • 3x Second Team All-Pro • 9x Pro Bowl

All-Time Team: 100th Anniversary

17-Year Career • 242 Games Played; 240 Started

4,967 Passing Completions • 8,359 Passing Attempts •
61,361 Yards Gained • 420 Passing Touchdowns

Author Terry Pratchett once wrote, "A lie can run round the world before the truth has got its boots on." This quote sums up why Dan Marino had to watch his ranking in the 1983 NFL draft (often referred to as the "Quarterback Draft")

slip all the way to twenty-seven as he became the last of the six quarterbacks selected in the first round. Todd Blackledge of Penn State, Tony Eason of Illinois, Ken O'Brien of UC Davis, and Jim Kelly of Miami all went before Marino, which must have infuriated him. Hell, typing those names infuriates me. Only John Elway of Stanford, the first pick overall, could be considered more talented than Marino. According to Steelers head coach Chuck Noll, rumors of drug use, which originated from a suburban Pittsburgh newspaper, scared Marino's hometown team and kept them from drafting him. Though never confirmed, these alleged rumors were pervasive. Despite these rumors, Marino proceeded to have a remarkable career with the Dolphins.

Marino was one of the scariest players to face during my NFL career because of how he held the ball. With a bullet-like release, precision accuracy, and an uncanny ability to throw receivers open, Marino was impossible to slow down, especially when the game was on the line. Marino played the quarterback position with his arm and mind working in complete harmony. Never an elite athlete or fast runner, Marino relied on being quick minded to take down a defense. He understood the game and he saw things others didn't, much like John Nash, the code-breaking American mathematician and subject of the film *A Beautiful Mind*. With his arm wired to his beautiful mind, Marino broke every defense.

In his second season, he destroyed the NFL by throwing for over five thousand yards (unheard of during this era), averaging nine yards per attempt, and putting the ball in the end zone forty-eight times. That season, he led the 'Fins to their only Super Bowl season. But after scoring seventy-six points in the two playoff games before the Super Bowl, the team lost to the 49ers, who held Marino and the Dolphin offense to sixteen points, all scored in the first half.

The lack of more Super Bowl appearances is the only blemish in Marino's career. Why didn't this incredibly talented player, coached by the winningest coach in NFL history, Don Shula, never earn a Super Bowl ring? He went to the playoffs ten times over his seventeen-year career, yet he never broke through for that one shining moment. Quarterbacks alone cannot win the title; it takes the entire team, playing complementary football and working all three phases to perfection. When a team has someone as gifted as Marino, it becomes easy to put everything on his shoulders. As John Madden often said, "A great quarterback becomes a deodorant for all that ails a team." For example, instead of being tough minded and physical on third and short, you put the ball in old Danny Boy's hand and let him make the throw. That often works, but in playoff games and games against equal or better competition, the tougher team always prevails. A great player can make the team softer at times. Teams take the path of least resistance in every area, believing the great player can overcome any inadequacies. Miami's team building around Marino, not his play, cost him his Super Bowl.

There was no player I loved watching play more than Marino. He was the gift that kept on giving, and no matter who we played every single week, my eyes were on the Miami offense to study his beautiful mind and play.

76
SAMMY BAUGH

2x NFL Champion • 4x Passing Yards Leader •
2x Passing Yards Leader • 3x Passing Rating Leader •
8x Completion Percentage Leader • 5x Punting Average Leader •
1x Punting Yards Leader • 1x Interception Leader

4x First Team All-Pro • 4x Second Team All-Pro • 6x Pro Bowl

All-Decade Team: 1940s •
All-Time Team: 75th & 100th Anniversaries

16-Year Career • 167 Games Played; 84 Started

1,693 Passing Completions • 2,995 Passing Attempts •
21,886 Yards Gained • 187 touchdowns

31 Interceptions

When you study "Slingin'" Sammy Baugh, or Sam as he preferred, it's easy to understand how he received his nickname. The ball came off his hand like a slingshot. Baugh's three-quarter delivery launched the ball down the field with accuracy and touch. During his era, the ball—sometimes white in color— was harder to throw. Like a giant watermelon, it required big hands and a powerful arm to maneuver. The ball also became heavier as the seasons grew colder, yet that never deterred Baugh from making wonderful throws. No other sport has seen their ball change so significantly. The football has gotten smaller, more aerodynamic, and easier to throw, transitioning the NFL into a passing league.

In 1937, when the Washington Redskins drafted Baugh in the first round, as the sixth pick overall, they got a three-for-one deal—an elite quarterback, a safety, and a rare punter. Baugh's height and range made him a ball-hawking safety with great instincts. His leg, connecting with that watermelon-shaped ball, created booming kicks. Naturally, his talent at quarterback was sensational and he instantly impacted the league. In 1943, Baugh led the league with eleven interceptions, a 45.9-yard punting average, and 133 pass completions. This unorthodox triple crown will never be duplicated. By the time Baugh headed back to his ranch in Texas, he had set thirteen NFL records for the three positions.

Reminiscing about the first professional game he attended, Steve Sabol, son of NFL Films founder Ed Sabol, recalled, "I was nine years old and my father took me to Shibe Park in Philadelphia to see the Eagles play the Redskins. It was 1951. My dad said: 'See the man wearing number 33? That's Sammy Baugh.' That's all he said. It was like pointing out the Empire State Building, the Washington Monument, or Niagara Falls. 'That's Sammy Baugh.' That's all that needed to be said to anyone who followed pro football in the 1940s and early 1950s."

Baugh was an elite athlete, with the talent to play all three positions in today's game: incredible hand-eye coordination, which served him well catching poorly thrown balls; a powerful leg, and the ability to throw that oversized watermelon with pinpoint accuracy. According to *Washington Post* columnist Shirley Povich, when Baugh first joined the Redskins, Coach Ray Flaherty asked to see him throw, pointing to a player running down the field and saying, "Hit that receiver in the eye." Baugh responded, "Which eye?" Far from a fabrication, Baugh confirmed this exchange in the 1990s, acknowledging in his Texas drawl, "Yep, ah said it...First and last time in my life ah was cocky." From then on, Baugh let his triple-threat talents do the talking.

75
TONY GONZALEZ

8x First Team All-Pro ● 4x Second Team All-Pro ● 14x Pro Bowl

All-Decade Team: 2000 ● All-Time Team: 100th Anniversary

17-Year Career ● 270 Games Played; 254 Started

1,325 Receptions ● 15,127 Receiving Yards Gained ●
111 Receiving Touchdowns

A week before Christmas in 1984, I received my first scouting assignment while working for the 49ers, getting to work on my craft away from the offices. I had to travel to Montgomery, Alabama, to watch practices as college players participated in the annual Blue–Grey game held on Christmas Day. The game featured incredible draft eligible talent, including Jerry Rice and Bruce Smith (both future Hall of Famers), so naturally I was beyond excited.

As part of my assignment, I also had to travel to Auburn University to scout their prospects for the upcoming 1985 draft. On campus, everyone asked if I had ever seen Charles Barkley play. There was no Barkley on my scouting list, and I soon learned it was because he played on the Auburn basketball team. After I finished my film review, I went to the basketball court to find out why everyone had "Barkley Mania."

Inside that arena, I was reminded of the song "I Saw God Today," one of legendary country singer George Strait's many hits, which is about the miracle of birth and a father seeing his daughter for the first time. However, my "seeing God" moment, at least as it applies to athletes, was witnessing a football player's body running and jumping, soaring to levels above the rim. Barkley's movement was rare, his shape belied his skills, his big hands caught the ball with ease, and no one on that court could keep pace. This rare combination of skills belonged on the gridiron. It was the future of the tight end position. (Plus, Barkley quickly became my favorite basketball player of all time.)

Thirteen years later, Tony Gonzalez joined the Chiefs and my vision became a reality. As a college player at the University of California, Gonzalez had also been a star basketball player. Gonzalez wasn't as good at hoops as Barkley was, but some of the skills he displayed on the hardwood translated to the field and were magnified there. Gonzalez was fast, able to get in and out of his cuts, had soft hands and wonderful eye-hand control, and—like Barkley—could get the ball in the air, making the tough catch in traffic.

Gonzalez's athletic skill set made the tight end position a critical part of every down offensive football. Even though he wasn't a great blocker, he was willing and would attempt to box out the opposing defender. The Chiefs then added Jason Dunn as a dominating blocking tight end, allowing Gonzalez to play as a motion tight end. Aligning off the ball with motion enabled Gonzalez to get a free release into his patterns. Once this occurred, his athletic skill set took over.

Gonzalez took care of his body, working hard on his conditioning and nutrition, which allowed him to play seventeen years, only missing two games. He held onto the ball with great power, only fumbling twice during his entire career. His 1,325 receptions is an amazing statistic. What made Gonzalez special as a player are the same things that made my jaw drop watching Barkley. The only difference is you didn't have to convince Gonzalez to play football, or make him love the physical nature of the sport. He was a good basketball player who loved football. As the passing game turned football into basketball on grass, Gonzalez was the perfect player at the perfect time.

DEFINING THE F

A motion tight end later became designated as an F, essentially replacing the fullback position. The F tight end rarely had to position himself at the end of the line, and thus did not have to deal with bigger defensive ends coming off the ball.

74
WILLIE BROWN

3x Super Bowl Champion • 1x AFL Champion

2x First Team All-Pro • 2x Second Team All-Pro •

4x Pro Bowl • 3x First Team All-AFL • 3x Second Team All-AFL •
5x AFL All-Star

All-Decade Team: 1970s •
All-Time Team: 75th & 100th Anniversaries

16-Year Career • 204 Games Played; 186 Started

54 Interceptions; 2 Returned for Touchdowns •
7 Career Postseason Interceptions; 2 Returned for Touchdowns

The 1966 season produced the second straight ten-loss season for the Denver Broncos, a franchise that was just seven years old. All the losing caused owner Gerald Phipps to make changes to his front office and coaching staff, hiring Lou Saban as his football guru and giving him complete authority to run the Broncos, along with a ten-year contract. One month after becoming the head man in Denver, Saban traded his All-AFL corners, Willie Brown and Mickey Slaughter, to the Raiders for Rex Mirich and the Raiders' third-round pick.

A former linebacker at Grambling, Brown became a bump-and-run corner when he started his career with the Broncos. He was strong at the line of scrimmage, clearly a "breakfast corner," who must win early in the route, defeating the receiver as soon as the ball is snapped; the longer the extension of the play, the more challenging it becomes for a player with his skill set. His size, upper-body strength, and instincts were outstanding. In his era, the rules allowed for physical play, and Brown was always the most physical, starting a great tradition with the Raiders. When you spend time around the cornerbacks from Brown's time, the height and size of these men—including the Steelers' Mel Blount, the Chiefs' Emmitt Thomas, and the 49ers' Jimmy Johnson—are overwhelming.

Brown always played his best in big games. If Reggie Jackson earned the nickname Mr. October for his sensational postseason performances, Brown could have easily been called Mr. January, as he always saved his best for the biggest games. Brown played in a season's worth of playoff games and always responded to the big game moments with incredible production. In seventeen playoff games, which is now a full season in the NFL, he recorded seven interceptions and three touchdowns. Any defensive back would be satisfied with that unique production during the regular season. Brown played his best when the games mattered most. When Super Bowl XI highlights are replayed, Brown stepping in front of the Viking receiver and sprinting toward the end zone for a seventy-five-yard touchdown is the signature play of the game. The play is not only emblematic of the game, but also of Brown's big playmaking skills.

By the way, things never got much better for Saban after the trade. During his five seasons, Saban went 20–42–3 before returning to Buffalo in 1972. Meanwhile, Willie Brown became a lifelong member of the Raiders' family and coaching staff. He was also one of the nicest people you could ever meet.

TRADE FALLOUT

Brown's trade was confirmed by a Western Union telegraph, and the actual paperwork is archived at the Hall of Fame at Canton. The lopsided deal violated a stringent rule instituted years later by Al Davis, prohibiting the Raiders from trading with any other team in the AFC West or their upcoming opponents. Davis was self-assured when making any deal, yet he was always concerned about competing against former players who knew team secrets that could be used against the Raiders. Davis trusted no one, especially those he sent packing. Maybe this deal was the reason, as Davis figured he could not be as fortunate ever again.

73
JOE SCHMIDT

2x NFL Champion

8x First Team All-Pro • 2x Second Team All-Pro • 10x Pro Bowl

All-Decade Team: 1950s • All-Time Team: 100th Anniversary

13-Year Career • 155 Games Played; 151 Started

24 Interceptions

When something fundamentally powerful occurs that alters the world, the date must be time-stamped. Look at our cell phones. Let's admit it, the cell altered the world. First available affordably in 1997, the widespread availability of the cell phone is a moment in our cultural history that needs to be recorded—anything before 1997 would be tagged BCP (before cell phones) and anything after should be called ACP (after cell phones). One hundred years from now, anyone studying our time period would have a clear time stamp pinpointing this seismic shift and helping them to understand it.

Pro football has experienced many shifts in all three areas of the game—players, coaches, and schemes. Each shift requires time stamps to help football historians understand the game. When the forward pass rule changed in 1933, that gave us a time stamp for a change in the game's history. The same for when the T formation became commonplace in 1940. The creation of the middle linebacker position is also deserving of a time stamp.

The Bears' Bill George created the position of middle guard in a game against Philadelphia, but Detroit Lion Joe Schmidt became the first true middle linebacker. After losing to the Browns 56–10 in the 1954 Conference Championship game, Lions head coach Buddy Parker made a change to his defense. Parker loved watching Schmidt dominate the game from the middle of the defense each time he called for his short yardage unit to take the field. In Parker's short yardage defense, an extra linebacker entered the game, thus moving Schmidt from outside to inside linebacker. When the defensive linemen kept blockers from reaching Schmidt, he was instinctive and fast to make tackles. So Parker decided to move him permanently inside, and the middle linebacker position was created.

Before Schmidt lined off the ball, most defenses had six defensive linemen on the field, playing what was called a 6–2 defense: an eight-man front to stop the run. As the middle-of-the-field passing game became a problem for the defense, the middle guard was assigned to hug the center and drop into coverage, which Bill George was sensational at executing. On runs, George operated as a defensive lineman. On passes, he retreated with some depth to handle the inside passing routes. Schmidt, however, aligned deeper off the ball, playing on the second level of the defense. He was also assigned to the running back if he went out for a pass, guarding him man-to-man. Once this shift occurred, the defense became a three-level operation. The first level was the front where the defensive line operated. The second level was off the ball, with five-yard depth where the linebackers played in a two-point stance. The third level was where the safeties operated. In addition, Schmidt became the quarterback of the defense, making sure all three levels were functioning in unison. He set the front, understanding the formation and the tendency of the offense, and alerted his teammates. He called the defense from the huddle based on the game plan of the week.

By aligning off the ball, Schmidt was able to run from sideline to sideline, avoiding direct contact with the offensive linemen and relying on the "crib" instincts he possessed to find the football, run, or pass. He became an extra defender in the passing game, a role at which he proved to be extremely effective. Schmidt's style of play opened the door for future middle linebackers, like Dick Butkus, Willie Lanier, Ray Nitschke, and Ray Lewis. They have Schmidt to thank. The birth of the middle backer is now time-stamped.

72
DWIGHT STEPHENSON

4x First Team All-Pro • 1x Second Team All-Pro • 5x Pro Bowl

All-Decade Team: 1980s • All-Time Team: 100th Anniversary

8-Year Career • 114 Games Played; 87 Started

From his looming tower, University of Alabama head football coach Paul "Bear" Bryant believed Dwight Stephenson was the best center he'd ever seen play the game. With his amazing quickness, Stephenson was able to instantly gain the upper hand both in college and in the pros. When playing for the Dolphins, Stephenson demonstrated a burst off the ball normally reserved for the defensive linemen. (Controlling the line of scrimmage is determined by which lineman, offense or defense, closes down the distance the quickest. Whoever engages first, with hip roll and lower-body strength, then controls the action.) The "game within the game" in the trenches is usually determined by the first two steps after the ball is snapped. And there hasn't been a center since Stephenson to consistently win those first two steps. Alex Mack of the Browns and Falcons has excellent quickness, but can't match Stephenson's explosives two steps, nor can Jason Kelce of the Eagles, who plays with the same style as Stephenson—just not as well. If there were a quickness meter for offensive linemen, no one today, or in the past, would beat Stephenson.

On a Monday night game against the Jets in 1987, Stephenson badly injured his knee, forcing him to prematurely retire. The fact that he only played eight years in the league doesn't diminish his skills or minimize his place as the top center to play the game. The only blemish during his career in Miami was not winning a Super Bowl, losing to Washington after the 1982 season and the 49ers after 1984. He played in eleven playoff games during his career, winning six and losing five.

Stephenson was fortunate to play for two of the greatest coaches of the game—Bryant at Alabama and Don Shula in Miami—and gained their praise as the best center to play. When Shula presented him for the Hall of Fame, he said, "I've not seen a better football player on the field," which echoed Bryant's belief that Stephenson was one of the best linemen he ever coached.

THE LOYAL EDDIE CONYERS

Paul "Bear" Bryant wasn't going to rest on his laurels after winning the 1961 National Championship in his fourth season as the Crimson Tide's head coach. Bryant wanted the team to improve in every facet of the game, specifically cutting down on penalties. In the spring of 1962, Bryant told his staff to hire local officials to monitor each practice, an uncommon exercise for colleges at the time. Eddie Conyers, a local resident and employee of Allen & Jemison Hardware Company, received a phone call asking if he would be available to referee each afternoon during the fall. Conyers had only ever officiated two high school games, but wasn't about to turn down a request from the legendary coach. The next day, Conyers dressed in his official uniform and reported to the practice field. For the next sixty years, Conyers was present at every 'Bama practice on the field, having a front-row seat to some of the greatest players of all time, including Derrick Thomas, John Hannah, Ozzie Newsome, Kenny Stabler, and Joe Namath.

In late summer 2012, I attended an Alabama practice. Conyers was in his late eighties at the time, still fit, smiling, and letting everyone know he dominated on the golf course, shooting his normal even par. When we discussed the former players, he made it clear that Joe Namath, the kid from Beaver Falls, was by far the best player he had ever witnessed. Conyers had a gleam in his eye when discussing Namath and the impact he made the moment he stepped on the field in Tuscaloosa. I have a feeling Eddie is not going to be too happy with Broadway Joe's absence from my top 100 list.

71
KEN HOUSTON

2x First Team All-Pro • 10x Second Team All-Pro • 12x Pro Bowl

All-Decade Team: 1970s • All-Time Team: 100th Anniversary

14-Year Career • 196 Games Played; 183 Started

49 Interceptions; 9 Returned for Touchdowns

In 1973, when Washington Redskins head coach George Allen traded five players to the Houston Oilers for safety Ken Houston, everyone thought he had lost his mind. Not because of the five-for-one deal, but because Houston was only twenty-eight years old at the time of the trade and couldn't be considered an "over the hill" team member. The Washington players were not happy with their coach, as he traded away five of their friends and impacted the overall depth of the team. But Allen wasn't being stupid or hurting his team. He was keenly aware that Houston was the best safety in the AFL, even though the Raiders' George Atkinson and Jack Tatum always stole the spotlight. Houston was tall, lean, and athletic, and could deliver a hard hit. He had the skills to cover tight ends and backs, and was one of the best tacklers in the game.

Houston was a great player because he could do everything required of a safety. He had the skills and range to play on the third level of the defense. At times, when playing baseball in the deep part of the field, Houston looked like a Gold Glove center fielder, robbing hitters with his speed to get into the alley and make plays. Great safeties must be able to demonstrate range from the middle of the field to the sideline, protecting both sides. The great ones have an uncanny ability to start running before the ball is thrown, anticipating the throw—much like a center fielder who starts moving before the wood makes contact with the ball. This range allowed Houston to always be around the football and secure forty-nine interceptions over his fourteen-year career.

In addition to making plays in the passing game, Houston had the athletic skills to move from the third level of the defense (the deep part of the defense)

with great speed and body control and make an open-field tackle. This tackle is the most challenging for a safety to make in the open field, when there is a clear path to his right or left. Most of the time, the defense wants to use the sideline as an extra defender, forcing the back in that direction. When a running back has two options to exploit, the potential for a big run expands, unless the team has a safety like Houston. Open-field tackles and range define how well the safety impacts the defense, and Houston was great at both.

With quarterback Craig Morton having to fill in for the injured Roger Staubach, the Cowboys trailed the Redskins 14–7 late in the fourth quarter in 1973, only the fourth game of Houston's Washington career. With the ball on the Washington four-yard line, Morton sprinted right and hit running back Walt Garrison in the flat—the outside part of the field on both sides, from the line of scrimmage until five yards from a touchdown...until Houston grabbed Garrison around the waist and held the tough Cowboy from advancing the ball across the goal line. He preserved the win for the Redskins, and all the Washington players forgot about their five friends, who were now playing with the Oilers. Houston became a Redskin on that day.

70
MARION MOTLEY

1x NFL Champion • 4x AAFC Champion •
1x AAFC Rushing Leader • 1x AAFC Rushing Touchdown Leader •
1x NFL Rushing Leader

2x First Team All-Pro • 1x Pro Bowl

All-Decade Team: 1940s •
All-Time Team: 75th & 100th Anniversaries

9-Year Career • 105 Games Played; 78 Started

Playing fullback is not a glamorous position today. Rarely do you get the ball in the run game, or even play more than twenty plays a game. A fullback's role is usually restricted to special teams and grunt work. Many teams don't even carry the position; they borrow a linebacker or defensive lineman for a goal line or short yardage situation. San Francisco still uses two backs and relies on Pro Bowl fullback Kyle Juszczyk to have a role in the game. Juszczyk's role is still mild compared to the great fullbacks of the late 1940s, '50s, and '60s, when the position was another weapon in the backfield. There were as many running plays designed for the fullback as for the halfback. No one thinks of the great Jim Brown as a fullback, yet that was his designated position on the 1960s All-Decade Team, along with Jimmy Taylor of the Packers. The fullback position has always been a part of offensive football, dating back to the 6–4 Rutgers win against Princeton in 1869.

When you read fullback next to Marion Motley's name, don't equate his talent with Juszczyk's or that of the fullback position you view today—he was much different and more talented. He was a big, powerful runner, along the lines of Earl Campbell, who could plow over tacklers, run away from defenders, and dominate the game. Motley was labeled a fullback, but had he played now, the "full" part would be removed. Motley was forty pounds heavier than most players and used his great size to his advantage. He had soft hands, could catch a swing pass, and had the speed and open-field run skills to turn a short pass into a long gain. These multidimensional talents were on full display in a game in 1950. When facing the Steelers in Cleveland for the second time that season, Motley carried the ball eleven times for 188 yards, averaging seventeen yards a carry and catching a touchdown pass for thirty-three yards. On that day, the Browns dominated the Steelers, 45–7.

During Motley's era, many players played offense and defense. According to Bengals owner Mike Brown, the son of Paul Brown, "Motley was the best linebacker on the Browns." As a young twelve-year-old kid helping his father, Mike developed an affection for Marion and said that his father referred to Motley as "the greatest all-around player he ever coached."

Along with teammate Bill Willis, in 1946 Motley was one of the first Black players to break the color barrier. He dealt with racism on the field, but never let it deter his drive or passion, making those who uttered vulgar names pay a price each time he ran over them. His talents and skills as a runner and receiver would make any offense effective today. He would prove the point that a great talent from another era will be great in any era.

69
STEVE LARGENT

2x NFL Receiving Yards Leader

1x First Team All-Pro • 4x Second Team All-Pro • 7x Pro Bowl

All-Decade Team: 1980s • All-Time Team: 100th Anniversary

14-Year Career • 200 Games Played; 197 Started

819 Receptions • 13,089 Receiving Yards Gained •
100 Receiving Touchdowns

During season five of the hit television show *Seinfeld*, George Costanza accidently bumps into a modeling agent who finds his hands beautiful and wants to use him as a hand model. Afterward, he returns to Jerry Seinfeld's apartment and, pointing to his hand, declares, "This is a one-in-a-million hand." Like George, Steve Largent also has one-in-a-million hands...and more.

Largent's hands garnered all the attention because they allowed him to produce at every level of football, from high school to the pros. Yet his skill set extended beyond his great, soft hands. He had quickness, balance, and body control, all of which allowed him to make tough catches.

Great center fielders in baseball always catch with their feet, meaning they sprint as fast as possible to the location of the ball without extending their arms until the last minute, and then allow their glove to secure the ball. The same technique applies to catching footballs. It would be fair to say Largent caught as many balls with his feet as he did with his hands. While at the University of Tulsa in 1974 and 1975, Largent led the nation in receptions, scoring fourteen touchdowns each year. By the time he left Tulsa, he had accumulated 136 receptions, along with thirty-two touchdowns, for a 4.25 catch-to-touchdown ratio, which is beyond remarkable.

Largent's skill was the by-product of his hand-eye coordination. Much like Red Sox Hall of Fame hitter Ted Williams, Largent always had his eyes laser-focused on the ball. Largent caught the ball by trapping it in an unorthodox cradling, arms-under-the-ball style, which signaled the extreme level of concentration and focus he maintained. When the football was in the air coming toward Largent, it appeared to slow down to a snail's pace, allowing him to shift his body into the right position to make a catch. When the ball was just one yard away, he would be intensely focused, despite how fast everything was moving. He would zero in on the tip of the ball coming in his direction. He didn't need to wear gloves, as many players do today so they can grip the ball tighter and with stronger security.

Largent played outside receiver in a two-receiver era, and used his quickness and change of speeds to escape defenders. Had he played today, he would be much like Cooper Kupp of the Rams, playing inside and outside, and making clutch catches on third down. Had Largent been given the opportunity to play in the slot, with a receiver outside of him, his catch-to-touchdown ratio might have been even higher. Kupp averages a touchdown every 10.8 catches, which is not nearly as good as Largent, and Kupp is playing for passing game head coach Sean McVay. Largent had run game head coaches, especially Chuck Knox, who never saw a pass he liked, unless it was Largent in the end zone.

The NFL is filled with great receivers with the ability to make ridiculous one-handed catches. However, few have the focus and concentration to watch the ball in flight coming toward them, which is why some receivers with great hands will drop an easy catch. And even fewer can make the game slow down when the ball is three feet away. Largent had that rare skill, along with one-in-a-million hands.

68
MIKE DITKA

1x Super Bowl Champion (as player) • 1x NFL Champion

2x First Team All-Pro • 3x Second Team All-Pro • 5x Pro Bowl

All-Time Team: 75th & 100th Anniversaries

12-Year Career • 158 Games Played; 118 Started

427 Receptions • 43 Receiving Touchdowns

Former NFL commissioner Pete Rozelle's legacy is stained by his senseless decision to allow NFL teams to play in the days following the assassination of President John F. Kennedy on November 22, 1963. Rozelle later regretted his lack of judgment, humbly admitting he blundered. The nation was in shock, and watching football was the last thing most Americans had on their mind. But Iron Mike Ditka was ready for the game. He was playing for the Chicago Bears against his hometown Pittsburgh Steelers. Ditka grew up in nearby Aliquippa and played at the University of Pittsburgh, so this game had special meaning.

The significance of the day didn't distract Ditka or alter his style. On one play against the Steelers, Ditka demonstrated the signature toughness, passion, and playmaking skills that Bears fans had come to expect from him. Catching the ball in the "hook area" (the area between the numbers and the hash mark) from Bears quarterback Billy Wade, Ditka turned a ten-yard pass into a highlight reel as he destroyed would-be tacklers and maneuvered his way down the field. From that day forward, the sadness of remembering our former president will also be remembered by Bears fans as the day Ditka became Iron Mike.

He wore a face guard normally used by the placekicker, which barely covered anything. On the gridiron, Ditka behaved like a bull in a china shop, having little or no regard for his body as would-be tacklers bounced off him. He even played on the defensive side of the ball, making tackles and causing disruption with his willingness to exert physical toughness.

Ditka advanced the tight end position. Like Ron Kramer from the Packers, Ditka controlled the end of the line of scrimmage in the run game and then made explosive plays down the field in the passing game. His first year in the NFL, Ditka had a thousand yards receiving, and scored twelve touchdowns on fifty-six receptions. During his first four years, he averaged sixty-two receptions, gained 3,671 yards receiving, and scored thirty touchdowns. He set the league on fire with his ability to impact both the run and the pass.

Ditka's instant impact on the league helped other tight ends become a larger part of the offense. Instead of solely being run blockers, they were able to impact the passing game. In the 1950s, there were no tight ends on the All-Decade Team, and in the 1960s, only John Mackey of the Colts received a spot. Ditka wasn't as big as Mackey, or as fast, but he was an effective route runner, and once the ball got into his hands, he became a different player, looking to run over defenders instead of around them.

Ditka would have had a huge role in today's game. Because of his run-blocking toughness, he'd be able to get mismatches in the passing game, allowing him to be a third-down converter. He wasn't as big as Rob Gronkowski, or as fast as Travis Kelce, yet his overall toughness would have made up for any limitations in size or speed.

67
GALE SAYERS

2x NFL Rushing Leader

5x First Team All-Pro • 4x Pro Bowl

All-Decade Team: 1960s •
All-Time Team: 50th, 75th & 100th Anniversaries

7-Year Career • 68 Games Played; 65 Started

991 Rushing Attempts • 4,965 Rushing Yards Gained •
39 Rushing Touchdowns

112 Receptions • 1,307 Receiving Yards Gained •
9 Receiving Touchdowns

6 Kickoff Return Touchdowns • 2 Punt Return Touchdowns •
56 Total Touchdowns

Before Chicago's Wrigley Field became home to the Chicago Cubs, it belonged to the Chicago Bears for fifty years, until they moved into Soldier Field in 1971. Harry Caray's former hangout was not the ideal place to play a football game. The brick walls surrounding the playing surface became an obstacle for wide receivers and running backs, forcing them to stop quickly to avoid a collision. There were dangerous spots throughout, especially in the south end zone, which fell short of regulation size.

In December of 1965, the Bears hosted the San Francisco 49ers, trying to avenge their season-opening, ass-kicking loss, 52–24. A steady rain was falling, and once the tarp was removed, the field became what horse trainers refer to as a "mudder" track—so covered in mud that the players had difficulty changing direction and accelerating. The game slowed down for every player, except one. The muddy field should have limited rookie running back Gale Sayers's overall effectiveness. Instead, it made him better. He scored six touchdowns, including one on an eighty-five-yard punt return. Four were from running the football, and another was from catching a pass. All told, Sayers carried the ball nine times for 113 yards and caught two passes for eighty-nine yards. His six touchdowns led the Bears to victory.

But perception isn't reality. Many perceived Sayers to be a scatback, i.e., a smaller, change-of-direction, make-you-miss runner. The reality is that Sayers was a slasher, an edge runner with speed that could run through a man if he wasn't in the correct position. He was tall, with great lean and knee bend. Because of his length and running style, his quickness wasn't obvious to the viewer, only to the man attempting to tackle him. He had the uncanny ability to get on the edge of the tackler, slightly alter his balance, and then accelerate through his arm tackle. Sayers was like a great boxer who could bob and weave away from a punch. He was deceptive in his movement; he wasn't going to wiggle his hips, stop on a dime, and then burst. He was instantaneously fast, explosive, and would break the first tackler. His change of direction was subtle. Once he shifted, his instant acceleration took over. This style of running made him the perfect kickoff returner.

Sayers's talent shined independent of field conditions. He would be amazing on AstroTurf and on grass, wet or dry. He always had two feet solidly on the ground, which allowed him to stay in balance and work the edges of the tacklers. When he needed to shift, he was effortlessly in position.

After Sayers was hurt the first time in 1968, it became obvious that he lost speed and acceleration. Yet he still led the NFL in rushing when playing on a 1–13 team. Sayers's shortened career doesn't diminish his greatness. Unfortunately for him, the benefits of modern medicine didn't exist when he was injured, or he would have played longer without losing his speed and burst. When I watch Tony Pollard of the Cowboys, his running style and frame, along with his slashing style, remind of Sayers. Don't laugh: Pollard is a talented player who has all the characteristics of Sayers—he is a great kick returner, can catch the ball effectively, and demonstrates a burst and acceleration few possess. I love watching Pollard and I loved watching Sayers—nicknamed "The Kansas Comet"—on the run.

66
ERIC DICKERSON

1x NFL Offensive Player of the Year • 4x NFL Rushing Champion

5x First Team All-Pro • 6x Pro Bowl

All-Decade Team: 1980s • All-Time Team: 100th Anniversary

12-Year Career • 146 Games Played; 136 Started

2,996 Rushing Attempts • 13,259 Rushing Yards Gained •
90 Rushing Touchdowns

281 Receptions • 2,137 Receiving Yards Gained •
6 Receiving Touchdowns

Eric Dickerson was so formidable that the week before the 49ers faced him, head coach Bill Walsh grew nervous. Walsh used three simple words: "Eric is coming." Everyone on the team understood the challenge that awaited as Walsh prepared to play the Los Angeles Rams in week nine of the 1984 season. Stopping Eric Dickerson was the team's first, second, and third priority. Walsh stood in front of the room in his freshly pressed khaki pants and his white 49ers shirt with the logo on the right side. He never raised his voice and was complimentary to the entire Rams team, but he emphasized the point that Dickerson was not only a power back with rare speed, but that he also could shift his weight, get on the edges, and make people miss. Stopping Dickerson was going to be a team effort.

As I stood in the video room making sure the video recorder was working and listened to Walsh break down the talents of Dickerson, I was reassured we could win the game. Walsh was an outside-the-box thinker. He decided to move our starting free safety, Dwight Hicks, to corner and Ronnie Lott—one of the greatest players I've ever watched perform as starting corner—to safety. Walsh wanted a tackler in the middle of the field who could match Dickerson's physical size if he broke into the secondary. He wanted Dickerson to feel the tackler and receive punishment, and there was no better player than Lott to execute this plan. Walsh wasn't worried about Hicks playing corner. He reasoned that if the Rams wanted to take the ball out of Dickerson's hands and allow their quarterback, Jeff Kemp, to throw the ball, the 49ers' chances of winning increased. Not only did we win 33–0, we held Dickerson to thirteen carries for thirty-eight yards. It took the entire team.

Dickerson was a tall runner with a natural body lean. His bend with the ball in his hands allowed him to shift his weight, be in balance, and then reach high speeds instantly. His running style was all natural. Watching Dickerson run in his all-black Sealy High School Tiger uniform was no different from watching him run as a Ram or Colt. Many tall runners require a split second to reach full speed, and if they are deterred in the backfield, forcing them to shift in either direction, they become less effective. Not Dickerson. He had the shiftiness and foot quickness of a small back, his lateral movement was rare, and once he decided to head north and south, he would reach top speed.

Dickerson took the NFL by storm as his numbers for the first two seasons (1983 and 1984) with the Rams were amazing; they will never be duplicated. What makes his 1984 season so remarkable—gaining 2,105 yards in sixteen games—is that in the two 49ers games, Dickerson only gained 136 yards on thirty-nine carries. Imagine what Dickerson's numbers might have been had Lott not moved to safety.

In 2020, Derrick Henry of the Titans fell seventy-eight yards short of breaking Dickerson's single-season rushing record for sixteen games. Now, as the league plays seventeen games, the record might fall—with an asterisk. Henry runs differently than Dickerson; he doesn't have the same lean or instant speed, yet he is extremely effective. The big question is whether he will stay healthy and play in all seventeen. Only time will tell. As Walsh reminded the 49ers defense, Eric was coming all right, and it was fun to watch him.

65
JULIUS PEPPERS

3x First Team All-Pro • 3x Second Team All-Pro • 9x Pro Bowl

All-Decade Team: 2000s & 2010s

17-Year Career • 266 Games Played; 240 Started

159.5 Sacks • 174 Tackles for Loss • 186 Hits on Quarterback

In 1963, *Parade* magazine introduced their All-American High School Football team, honoring the best high school players throughout the United States. It was a great honor to be recognized as a *Parade* All-American and carried clout. Before every Raiders draft meeting commenced, I would watch as Al Davis, the owner, entered the draft room each morning and unpacked his bag, which included over twenty-five years of the *Parade* magazines neatly stacked together and held by a rubber band. He loved to refer to the *Parade* teams when scouting because he believed in pedigree. He reasoned that if a player was great in high school, chances were good that he would be great in the pros. This logic was true for Julius Peppers.

Peppers was another athlete who looked like a basketball player, with his great size, balance, body control, and quickness. He had natural bend, possessed a right-handed stance Davis would have loved, and could power an offensive tackle back. Because of his arm length and lower-body power, getting Peppers moved off the line was not easy. He had the talent to extend his arms, read and diagnose the play, and then shed the blocker to make the tackle. Defensive coordinators could count on him setting the edge of the defense, making it hard for the offense to run the ball outside of his alignment. Peppers was recruited as a football player in college, but he walked onto the University of North Carolina's basketball team, playing in a backup role. His athletic skills made him a versatile player, able to drop into coverage, which resulted in eleven career interceptions. It's a remarkable number for a defensive lineman, with Jason Taylor the next closest with eight.

When the twenty-two-year-old Peppers arrived in Carolina, he was instantly effective. As he grew in strength and experience, he became an even better player. When he left the Panthers at age thirty, he had another great career with the Bears, and then, at age thirty-four, was just as effective with the Packers. The longer he played, the better he became.

DEFENSIVE POWER

Powering a tackle back in pass rushing is the most important aspect of any defensive lineman's game. Many get caught up with spin moves, arm over, or a club move inside, which help. However, being able to walk a tackle back with power is the core of a great pass rusher.

64
ROSEY BROWN

1x NFL Champion

1x First Team All-Pro • 3x Second Team All-Pro • 9x Pro Bowl

All-Decade Team: 1950s •
All-Time Team: 75th & 100th Anniversaries

13-Year Career • 162 Games Played; 159 Started

When former New York Giants owner Wellington Mara was a young kid, he loved hanging around the team his father owned and was given the nickname "Duke" by the players. Mara was a scout by nature; he loved watching players play and often recommended talent to his father. One of his fondest memories was scouting Tuffy Leemans while he was still attending Fordham. He had watched Leemans, a running back at George Washington University in Washington, DC, dominate the University of Alabama and wanted to make sure his father signed this unknown star. In addition to discovering Tuffy Leemans, Mara will be remembered for finding a huge offensive tackle named Rosey Brown playing at Morgan State in Maryland.

Brown was selected by the Giants in the twenty-seventh round, the 322nd player overall, and became their starting left tackle. For the time, Brown was considered a huge man. Listed at six feet, three inches tall and 255 pounds, he appeared even larger in person. I can remember thinking the first time I met him, after his playing days were over and he worked as a scout for the Giants, "Wow, that's a huge man."

Brown was also athletic, he could run extremely well, and he didn't have an ounce of fat on him. If he played today, he would have carried 310 pounds easily. During his playing days, linemen could not use their hands, which meant they were on the ground more often, cut blocking in pass protection. With his huge hands, Brown would have been a deadly pass blocker, knocking the defensive lineman off his charge. Linemen with long arms, huge hands, and great lower-body power are effective today as they rhythmically time their foot movement with each punch. Had Brown played under the current rules, he would have dominated.

When Vince Lombardi served as the offensive coordinator for the Giants, one of his signature plays was the toss sweep, with the tackle having to pull and lead the halfback, Frank Gifford, around the corner, blocking the run-support players of the defense. Watching Brown pull and run with speed and body control as he cleared the path for Gifford was impressive. As Gifford fondly remembered, "Rosey is a Hall of Fame player, and I wouldn't be in the Hall of Fame if it weren't for him. Our two favorite plays were 48 pitchout and [Vince] Lombardi's 49 sweep, and Rosey was the key man in all of that."

63
LENNY MOORE

1x NFL MVP • NFL Rookie of the Year •
2x NFL Champion •
1x NFL Rushing Leader • 1x NFL Scoring Leader

5x First Team All-Pro • 2x Second Team All-Pro • 7x Pro Bowl

All-Decade Team: 1950s • All-Time Team: 100th Anniversary

12-Year Career • 143 Games Played; 118 Started

1,069 Rushing Attempts • 5,174 Rushing Yards Gained •
63 Rushing Touchdowns

363 Receptions • 6,039 Receiving Yards Gained •
48 Receiving Touchdowns

If video games had existed when Lenny Moore played, his rating on EA Sports' *Madden NFL* would have been off the charts. In an era of inflexible systems of offenses, Moore was *the* most versatile player. He played running back and wide receiver, and dominated at both positions. He paved the way for other multidimensional running backs, impacting the passing game. The biggest difference between Moore and other players was that Moore mastered both positions. He wasn't a halfback, extended from the formation, like Marshall Faulk, nor was he like the 49ers' Deebo Samuel, playing wide receiver and then occasionally running the ball from the backfield. On one play, Moore would look like Titans running back Chris Johnson, with power and breakaway speed. And on another play, he was like Colts wide receiver Marvin Harrison, running patterns. Whatever the position, when the ball arrived in Moore's hands, a big play was about to ensue. Moore led the NFL with twenty-six touchdowns of over fifty yards, the most by any running back in NFL history.

If Moore played today, the defenses wouldn't be able to match his skill set. If he were aligned in the backfield in a twenty-one-personnel grouping (i.e., two backs, one tight end, and two receivers), then the defense would have to decide to play their base or match his skill set in nickel, making them vulnerable to the run. If Moore's team were to send in twenty-two personnel (two backs, two tight ends, and one receiver), the defense could go with their short yardage and beef up the front or play their base and hope they had enough girth. Moore created a matchup problem either way back when he played, and he would create a bigger one today.

Moore was dynamic with the ball, displaying wonderful balance, and he had the ability to shift gears. He also was excellent in gaining yards after first contact, which is a huge indicator in evaluating running backs. Scouts must answer these questions: Does the back go down on the first contact? Moore rarely did. Does the runner run with a narrow base, getting tripped easily? Moore had a wide, powerful base. And finally, can the receiver make plays down the field on the ball? Moore was exceptional in this area. Moore was exceptional in all areas. That's why his *Madden* rating would have been off the charts.

62
DARRELL GREEN

2x Super Bowl Champion

4x First Team All-Pro • 7x Pro Bowl

All-Decade Team: 1990s • All-Time Team: 100th Anniversary

20-Year Career • 295 Games Played; 258 Started

54 Interceptions; 6 Returned for Touchdowns

Bobby Beathard, the general manager of the Washington Redskins, wasn't your typical scout or NFL executive. Health conscious, he was the type of person who would run the New York Marathon prior to attending a late afternoon game against the Redskins' fierce rival, the New York Giants. Beathard also loved finding talent late in the draft, from obscure schools, and he also was willing to trade away his first-round picks, a strategy similar to that of the Los Angeles

Rams today. During his eleven-year reign in Washington, Beathard (who was later selected for the Hall of Fame) only used first-round picks three times: first, in 1980, when he selected Syracuse wide receiver Art Monk; then, in 1981, when he picked the University of Pittsburgh offensive lineman Mark May; and finally, in 1983 Beathard combined his love of small schools with a first-round pick, when he selected a pint-size defensive back from a small school in south Texas: Darrell Green.

Green wasn't just football player at Texas A&I, he was also a world-class sprinter who ran the 50-meter dash in 5.76 seconds, the 100-meter in 10.08, and the 200-meter in 20.48. He dominated the Lone Star conference in track recording times, which are still the best in the conference. Green's incredible speed transferred to the football field when he played defensive back. Often in scouting, we look to track and field to find fast athletes who can become football players, and it typically doesn't work. The speed highlighted on the track never transfers to the field, as the track star plays slower than his times. Football requires thinking and reaction, and track requires hauling ass. And in that difference, speed is lost and all that remains is a player with great track numbers and poor football skills. Green could think, react, and maintain his lightning speed, appearing as if he were like Superman—faster than a speeding bullet.

Even though Green was diminutive in size, he played big. He had great leaping skills, which all sprinters possess and is why they also compete in the long-jump event. The power in their lower body creates explosive speed and vertical spring. You will never find a fast track athlete who cannot jump high. Green could soar high, and playing man-to-man he was smooth in his transition, always remaining in balance, which then allowed him to spring in the air. Green also had several gears of speed and could get into overdrive when needed. This extra gear was showcased to Washington fans in 1983, in the very first game Green played at RFK Stadium. Cowboys running back Tony Dorsett broke into the open along the opposite sideline from Green. Like a rocket, Green closed down on him, preventing the running back from scoring. Before this Monday night contest, Dorsett was always the fastest player on any field, but not anymore, not with Green in the NFL.

Green was the true definition of a coverage corner, blanketing his man from either the off or on position in coverage, and those extra gears of speed became important as he closed in on the ball at the top of the route. Green also had excellent instincts, which is a requirement for being a great corner—he could locate the ball in the air, had soft hands, and never appeared out of position. During his twenty-year career, he set the NFL record for most consecutive seasons with at least one interception: nineteen. His longevity was remarkable, and unlike many fast athletes, he didn't appear to ever lose a step.

For a man like Bobby Beathard—who loved to run himself—selecting the fastest and most durable runner in Green as his last first-round pick was his personal best.

61
ROB "GRONK" GRONKOWSKI

4x Super Bowl Champion • 1x NFL Receiving Leader

4x First Team All-Pro • 5x Pro Bowl

All-Decade Team: 2010s • All-Time Team: 100th Anniversary

11-Year Career • 143 Games Played; 128 Started

621 Receptions • 9,286 Receiving Yards Gained •
92 Receiving Touchdowns

When watching Rob Gronkowski play on the football field, I often wondered, "How could someone this big, this powerful, move with this much ease?" Each day, seeing Gronk with his long, powerful frame and huge hands (which when covered with white gloves looked like two giant toilet seats) was always entertaining. I can't imagine there will ever be another player like him.

With his size and speed, Gronk is a rare player who is never covered. Even when someone is near him, he will come down with the ball. His giant hands are soft, can extend from his body, and can catch the ball in awkward positions. He engulfs the ball and rarely has a drop. Never when watching him practice or play did I ever feel that he wouldn't make the play when the ball was thrown in his direction. His skills in the passing game made it impossible for anyone on defense to cover him man-to-man, and with his speed down the field, it was even harder to keep from making big plays. Gronk was a long-ball hitter, doing his best work down the field after five yards. Once he got that big body moving, he was—and still is—uncoverable, which is why he currently averages fifteen yards per catch. His touchdown-to-catch ratio is unrivaled, as is his ability to convert first downs. During his career, Gronk has accumulated 469 first downs from his 960 catches. And 48.85 percent of the time, when Gronk makes a catch, the chains are moving for another first down.

Because of his size, Gronk was a true tight end. He could block the end of the line, control the defensive linemen, and help the offense's running game succeed. Additionally, he created matchup problems for every defensive coordinator. Tight ends who dominate in the run and pass are like knights on the chessboard. When used correctly, they can checkmate quickly. Gronk is one of those knights, making many defensive coaches turn over their kings.

Gronk could rank higher on my board, but with his career still proceeding and his propensity for missing games, I've lowered his grade. He's at the ideal spot—for now. In ten years, I'm sure he'll grade higher. I feel blessed and honored to watch him work every day.

LEVEL THREE: THE EXCEPTIONAL

Twenty men—all from different eras and positions—deviated from the norm and demonstrated rare talent that impacted their respective teams and the game in ways that can never be replicated. Their relentless pursuit of exceptional play gave fans season upon season of incredible entertainment. Each man should have his name etched in the stadium in which he once played. His jersey number may be worn by others, yet all fans will know that number will forever be linked to him.

60
DERRICK BROOKS

1x Super Bowl Champion • 1x NFL Defensive Player of the Year

5x First Team All-Pro • 4x Second Team All-Pro • 11x Pro Bowl

All-Decade Team: 2000s • All-Time Team: 100th Anniversary

14-Year Career • 224 Games Played; 221 Started

25 Interceptions • 84 Passes Defended

A replica Viking ship sitting outside the Minnesota Vikings' former training facility in Eden Prairie welcomed players, coaches, and visitors as they entered. The wooden ship served as a reminder of the dangers Viking warriors encountered in the Middle Ages. In 1986, inside the building—built in 1980—the defensive staff were preparing for the upcoming season and trying to solve a conundrum. What they didn't realize was that the work being done that year would greatly impact a young Derrick Brooks, who at thirteen years old was playing peewee football in Pensacola, Florida. To understand the greatness of Brooks, you must understand how the defense that greatly highlighted his talents was formed.

All during the 1985 season, future Hall of Fame defensive end Chris Doleman and outstanding tackle Keith Millard were off the field when the opponents were in their nickel offense. Both players had pass-rush skills, but aligning in the 3–4 didn't showcase their talents. The staff, composed of defensive coordinator

Floyd Peters, linebacker coach Monte Kiffin, and secondary coach Pete Carroll, needed a revised defense that incorporated nickel as their base with an attacking emphasis in pass rush, yet could handle a two-back base offenses running game.

Essentially, Kiffin and Carroll professionalized the the college game with the Under 4-3 defense, which they both developed while at the University of Arkansas with head coach Lou Holtz. The Under 4-3 is a gap control defense that requires eight men near the line of scrimmage; each man has an assigned gap to control. The secondary relies on zone coverage, reading and reacting to the ball. The staff moved Doleman to right defensive end, aligning outside of the offensive left tackle. Millard moved to the three-technique, aligning on the outside shoulder of the guard. Talented safety Joey Browner moved near the line of scrimmage, and smallish linebacker Jesse Solomon became the Will Backer. They aligned their burly, big defensive tackle Joe Phillips in a tilt position on either side of the center, thus flipping Millard so he was always on the edge of the guard, running up the field, being disruptive. They relied on a cover three-zone system for their pass coverage that would transfer to man-to-man, depending on the route. They wanted fast players who could react to the ball, and most of all they wanted a pass rush that could disrupt the passer. Years later when remembering his time in Minnesota, Carroll said: "It was a one-gap principle defense way back then. Monte and I, when we were together in Minnesota with [former Vikings defensive coordinator] Floyd Peters, we were able to continue to build on and NFL-ize our scheme. And so, it's been a way to get guys to attack and play aggressive so that you can get good pass rush and still fit on the run. That's where the secondary fits and stuff like that really comes into play."

By 1987, this defense led the Vikings to the NFC Conference Championship game, falling one play short against Washington. What these three men did was not only create a system of defense, but create a prototype for the positions that were essential to making the defense successful. When Monte Kiffin became the defensive coordinator in Tampa in 1996, he found the perfect Will Backer entering his second year, Derrick Brooks.

The Bucs had several pieces on defense that fit the prototype of the Kiffin/Carroll scheme. Defensive tackle Warren Sapp was the ideal three-technique, and he became a Hall of Fame version of Millard. Brad Culpepper became the tilt nose, and John Lynch became the strong safety in the box, like Browner.

The defense was perfect for Brooks, and he became a human highlight machine, making every tackle and disrupting the pass game. Even though he was considered undersized for the position, as was Solomon, Brooks could use his instincts, intelligence, and tackling talent to become dominating. Having someone like Brooks playing the Will allowed the defense to take on a new evolution.

When head coach Tony Dungy, along with Kiffin, decided to slightly alter the coverage, making the middle linebacker responsible for the deep middle of the field in pass coverage and rolling the corners to each flat, they created what we all call Tampa 2 today, and Brooks became even more effective. His speed and knack for being around the ball had him covering areas of the field that weren't part of the original alteration. In Tampa 2, the safeties are split wider than their normal alignment in Cover 2. The middle linebacker has the middle of the field, which provides the defense with three players protecting deep. The Will (Brooks), the Strong Safety (Lynch), and the Sam, along with both corners, protect the second level of the defense, and the four down linemen are told to penetrate up the field and raise hell stopping the run along the way to the passer. Without a speed player like Brooks to cover the width of the field and react quickly to the quarterback's shoulder turn, the defense is vulnerable with large uncovered areas.

Dungy and Kiffin wanted their speed to dominate, not have players thinking of their assignments. Both believed the absence of thought creates instant reaction, and all great defensive players react quickly. Both men wanted every player in the secondary to focus on the quarterback's head and shoulders. As soon as the quarterback turned his shoulders to throw, before the ball was out of his hands, the defense was instructed to burst in that direction. They demanded movement before the ball was thrown. Brooks was remarkable in this area, covering ground vacated by the middle backer running deep. Tampa 2 only works effectively when the Will Backer can cover ground and be a surefire tackler. Great backers must be great tacklers, and Brooks was one of the best.

When the scheme enhances the player's talent and the player's talent enhances the scheme, then domination occurs. And the Bucs with Brooks dominated.

59
WALTER JONES

4x First Team All-Pro • 2x Second Team All-Pro • 9x Pro Bowl

All-Decade Team: 2000s • All-Time Team: 100th Anniversary

12-Year Career • 180 Games Played; 180 Started

The two most influential coaches in shaping my quest to enter the coaching ranks were Vince Lombardi and Bobby Bowden, the former head coach of Florida State. Lombardi died when I turned ten, so his influences in my life came from sharing the same last name (no relation) and reading about his work. But when I entered the coaching world, I was lucky enough to have Bowden became my pen pal. Having heard him speak at a coaching clinic while I was still in college, I started writing him letter after letter, hoping one day he would hire me as a graduate assistant coach. Bowden responded to every letter with a personalized note, making me admire him even more. Regretfully, I never got the chance to work for him during his remarkable career in Tallahassee. After my letter-writing campaign, I continued to pay attention to Bowden's program and loved spending time on campus watching him work, often apologizing for being an annoying pen pal. The Florida State roster in 1996 was loaded with future first-round picks, including Peter Warrick, Warrick Dunn, Andre Wadsworth, Peter Boulware, Corey Simon, Samari Rolle, and Tra Thomas. The Florida State practice field that year had more elite players than most pro teams. It's a good thing that colleges didn't have a salary cap, because no team in the NFL could afford all those great players.

Besides being a great coach, Bowden was a fabulous recruiter and judge of talent. Before a game against Clemson, Bowden told me, "Walter Jones is the finest offensive lineman I have ever coached. He will play a long, long time in your league." Bowden was right. Jones only needed one year at Florida State to make everyone in the NFL want his services. In the 1997 draft, Jones was the sixth pick overall, going to the Seattle Seahawks. Jones became a mainstay at left tackle, dominating the game, and according to the Seattle coaches, over his eleven-year career only allowed twenty-three sacks. Twenty-three sacks in 180 games meant that in 88 percent of the games Jones played, his man never sacked his quarterback. That statistic might be even more impressive than Joe DiMaggio's fifty-six-game hitting streak. Seattle head coach Mike Holmgren was once asked before a big game if he planned to help his left tackle in pass protection. Normally easygoing with the press, he grew incredulous with the question and called Jones "the best offensive player he ever coached." And for Holmgren, that's huge praise, since he coached Jerry Rice, Joe Montana, and Brett Favre during his career.

Jones had his fabulous career cut short because of a knee injury sustained in a game against the Cowboys in 2008. For a player who never played high school football and essentially began his football career at Holmes Junior College in Mississippi before enrolling at Florida State, he played the game without any difficulty. Regardless of whom he faced, Jones was able to protect his passer.

58
LEE ROY SELMON

1x NFL Defensive Player of the Year

3x First Team All-Pro • 2x Second Team All-Pro • 6x Pro Bowl

All-Decade Team: 1980s • All-Time Team: 100th Anniversary

9-Year Career • 121 Games Played; 117 Started

78.5 Sacks (unofficial)

Ron Wolf was highly prepared for the job. After spending twelve years working alongside Raiders owner Al Davis, Wolf was ready to build a team when the newly formed Tampa Bay Buccaneers hired him as their vice president of operations. Wolf was a well-seasoned scout, understood the NFL game, and knew the essence of team building. Preparing for the first draft, with the first pick overall,

Wolf had every intention of selecting a quarterback whom he could build his new franchise around.

The first problem—of many he faced in Tampa—was that the 1976 draft didn't have a quarterback worthy of the first pick overall or, in Wolf's evaluation, worthy of being a first-round player. If Wolf took a quarterback, he was ignoring the horizontal board and risking a mistake. By consensus, Richard Todd was the best quarterback in the class. He was a three-year starter at Alabama, running the wishbone, and only threw seventeen touchdown passes and seven interceptions during those three seasons. There was no game-playing evidence that he would adapt to the NFL, and if he did, his talent as a passer, along with his decision-making, would be questionable. Wolf knew Todd wasn't the man to represent his first pick. Todd's final grade could never justify being the first pick overall. For Wolf, there was only one man worthy of that distinction: Lee Roy Selmon.

Once Selmon became a Buc, his dominating skills and power took over. His feet were amazingly quick and could drive back any tackle into the quarterback's lap. His acceleration off the block was incredible, as his burst was explosive. Selmon's strength in his upper body and foot quickness made him unable to be blocked. In the early stages of the Bucs, their offense was so bad that it required their defense to be on the field constantly, almost as if they played a doubleheader each Sunday. They lost the first twenty-six games they played. But by Selmon's fourth year in the league, he was dominating and leading the Bucs to their first-ever playoff appearance. If Selmon were playing today, he would create havoc on every down. Selmon was similar in size to Khalil Mack, but more powerful and with a better burst and acceleration off the block point. Selmon had the kind of athletic skills that allowed him to easily move around, and unless the protection accounted for him with a chip block or the center sliding in his direction, he would win all the one-on-one matchups. As well as Mack plays now, Selmon would be in another class.

Years later, Wolf went on to restore the glory of the Packers and in recognition was later inducted into the Hall of Fame. He never had a fair chance in Tampa. Office politics, power-hungry head coach John McKay, and bad owner Hugh Culverhouse made his job impossible. But Wolf's short time in Tampa (he left in 1978) was still effective. He handpicked most of the players on the stout defensive team that made the playoffs. He remembered Selmon by saying, "Of all the great defensive linemen I have been around, from Howie Long, to Ted Hendricks and Reggie White, Selmon was the best." High praise from a man who knows.

PLAYING TRIPLE

Selmon played defensive end at Oklahoma when most teams in college football were running either the wishbone offense or Bill Yeoman's veer option. Both formations are triple-option plays—the veer begins from the split-back formation and the wishbone with three backs in the backfield aligned like the bone you break apart every Thanksgiving Day. To effectively play the triple option, most defenses used a 3-4 defense, with two defensive ends playing the run and the outside backers in a two-point stance forcing the option.

57
BRUCE MATTHEWS

7x First Team All-Pro • 2x Second Team All-Pro • 14x Pro Bowl

All-Decade Team: 1990s • All-Time Team: 100th Anniversary

19-Year Career • 296 Games Played; 293 Started

In American politics, the Kennedy family dominated the political landscape all through the twentieth century. The NFL football version of the Kennedys is the Matthews family. Patriarch of the family Clay Matthews Sr. played the defensive line for the San Francisco 49rs, his son Clay Jr. played nineteen years in the NFL for the Browns and Falcons, and his grandson Clay III played eleven years for the Packers and Rams. But Clay's (Sr.) younger son Bruce spent nineteen years in the NFL with the Oilers and then the Titans and was the best of the bunch. Had the family gone the political route, Bruce would have been the one elected as the U.S. president.

Bruce Matthews was one of the finest offensive linemen I ever watched play. He was a rare six-position player, which included every offensive line position as well as long snapper. Matthews not only had the skills to play multiple positions, but he could dominate each one. Even as the long snapper, he was one of the best in the NFL. He began his career at right guard, and then moved to center. In 1985, he moved to right tackle, in '86 to left tackle, and then for the remainder of his career moved back and forth among positions, from left guard to center, to right guard. When watching him play, I realized that the Oilers or Titans would benefit if they moved Matthews each week to the specific position required to block the opponent's best defensive lineman. Instead of sliding the protection to neutralize the best rusher, they should have Matthews align across from him and completely nullify the player's effectiveness in the game. It was an out-of-the-box thought, mostly because no lineman was capable of shifting positions...except for Matthews. He could move positions naturally and shift his fundamentals and techniques each week with ease. His rare balance kept him off the ground (he passes the clean pants test easily) and controlling the line of scrimmage.

Matthews had great size, with the ability to bend with great hip power. He made playing the position look effortless and easy. His fundamentals and technique were elite, which allowed him to execute his assignments perfectly. Today, Quenton Nelson would compare favorably to Matthews, even without being a six-position player.

Besides having talent, Matthews was competitive and tough. He played more seasons (nineteen) than any other offensive lineman and started more games (298). Matthews's skills over those eighteen years never diminished, and he destroyed Father Time just as he destroyed opposing defensive linemen. The Matthews family will probably add more players to their NFL lineage in the coming years, but it's highly doubtful anyone can be as dominating as Bruce.

56
WARREN SAPP

1x Super Bowl Champion • 1x NFL Defensive Player of the Year

4x First Team All-Pro • 2x Second Team All-Pro • 7x Pro Bowl

All-Decade Team: 1990s & 2000s

13-Year Career • 198 Games Played; 188 Started

96.5 Sacks • 4 Interceptions; 1 Returned for Touchdowns

When recalling drafts over a long career, one always remembers a player or players who caused regret, sorrow, unhappiness, and consternation. Being great at drafting talent means hitting on 75 percent of the picks (which, based on the Catholic-school grading system, is a C minus). This low success rate demonstrates how challenging selecting the right players can become. It's hard to evaluate talent, judge character, value competitiveness, and—most important—measure a player's heart. What continues to make me cringe whenever writing about Warren Sapp wasn't that we misevaluated his skills or that we were arrogant in relating his talents to our team. The Sapp draft in 1995 reminds me how bad information can haunt someone for a lifetime. And that makes me recoil.

Sapp was a sensational player at the University of Miami. He was uniquely talented with skills few possess in both defending the run and rushing the passer. Whenever a scout, personnel director, or general manager spends time at a school that regularly funnels high draft picks to the NFL, the obvious question is always, "How does this player compare to a player from a prior draft?" Most often, the coach being asked always answers that the current player is better, without fail. What matters more than the words echoing from his mouth are his mannerism, the inflection of his voice, and how his eyes shift when answering. During my visit to Miami, I asked a well-respected assistant coach on the Miami staff how Sapp would compare to former Hurricane Russell Maryland, the first-round pick and first overall pick in the 1991 NFL draft of the Cowboys. The coach's eyes shifted quickly, piercing me as he sent a stern, hard look in my direction. He then sneered, "Are you f***ing kidding me? There is no comparison." The body language and the answer were all I needed.

So why didn't this great defensive lineman become a Cleveland Brown? Rumors of drug use. Unlike Dan Marino, whose faulty information was linked to a local paper, Sapp was the victim of bad information emanating from the security office of the NFL. This history-changing, unscrupulously shared information forced us to trade down, a decision I've regretted for twenty-six years and will always regret.

When I was with the 49ers, Gary "Big Hands" Johnson was a defensive tackle toward the end of his career, after he had slightly lost a step. Big Hands was determined to get on the other side of the line of scrimmage before the ball hit the quarterback's hand from the under-center snap. He needed to be lightning quick, wired to the movement of the ball; if not, the lineman would block him. So Johnson hugged the ball as close as possible, essentially being a little off-sides. (Sidenote: Being offsides is like being pregnant—you either are or you're not. However, some line judges are a little lenient when calling the penalty, first offering a warning.) Johnson's quickness allowed him to gain the line of scrimmage thus being named All-Pro two times during his eleven-year career.

Every time I watched Sapp play, he reminded me of Johnson, only much quicker—if that's possible. Sapp appeared to be offsides, only because his re-action quickness was in perfect unity with the snap of the ball. Sapp didn't need that 1/8th of a second leeway, as he was explosive off the ball. Looking back and comparing the two, Johnson weighed around 265 pounds and was quick; Sapp was near 300 and quicker.

Sapp was the perfect addition to the Tampa defense, playing the under tackle, aligning on the guard's outside shoulder, and creating havoc using his incredible quickness off the ball. He was a cornerstone, a dominating player who made others around him better, except me. He gave me a lifelong regret. I still awake in the middle of the night with the Sapp nightmare in my head. Trust me, regrettable moments in drafts never fade.

55
BRETT FAVRE

1x Super Bowl Champion • 3x MVP • 1x NFL Offensive Player
of the Year • 4x Passing Touchdown Leader •
2x Passing Yards Leader • 1x Passing Completion Leader

3x First Team All-Pro • 3x Second Team All-Pro • 11x Pro Bowl

All-Decade Team: 1990s • All-Time Team: 100th Anniversary

20-Year Career • 302 Games Played; 298 Started

71,838 Passing Yards • 508 Passing Touchdowns •
336 Interceptions

In our first draft meeting with Bill Belichick in his role as head coach of the Cleveland Browns, we had the scouts read each player's report to start the process of setting our board. The scouts often concluded their evaluation by proclaiming that the player needed to be coached, as well as requiring more refinement and development. It became a fairly standard tagline, which annoyed Belichick a great deal, as he was the only coach in the room. Finally, without raising his voice, Belichick calmly asked, "What f***ing player doesn't need coaching or development? Are there any good players in this draft, independent of the coach?" Belichick understood all players need molding and that player development was essential for success. Scouts relied on this sort of assessment because it enabled them to position their grade perfectly. If the player performed well, the scout was correct. If he didn't, the scout was still correct, because the player must not have received good coaching.

I'm certain every scout in Atlanta proclaimed that Brett Favre was talented and that he received no coaching after he was drafted by the Falcons. Based on conversations and admissions of those in the building, Favre had no coaching in his rookie season. Falcons head coach Jerry Glanville was not enamored with Favre. He constantly ridiculed him, saying things like, "Hey, Mississippi [his nickname for Favre], you're not playing tonight. For you to play, we need two plane crashes and four quarterbacks to go down." Ken Herock, the Falcons' general manager, who drafted Favre, was at war with Glanville because the head coach was out to prove Favre sucked and was never going to allow him a chance to play.

Looking back on the trade he eventually made with Packers general manager Ron Wolf—his former working partner at the Bucs and Raiders—Herock said, "Maybe I lost sight of the thing, everyone was telling me how bad he was. That's all I kept hearing. And there was a possibility we could recover a first for a guy we drafted with a second. There was nothing there that said, 'Ken, you're right and they're wrong.' Everything was working against me."

In fairness to Glanville, Favre wasn't a model player when he walked into the Falcons' facility. By his own assessment, he was immature, trying to drink all the booze in the Atlanta area, and behaving like a kid the first time he leaves home for college. Only Favre was rich from his draft money. Once in Green Bay, playing for Mike Holmgren—a coach who specialized in developing quarterbacks—Favre found success and the right sort of coaching. During the 1992 season, when starter Don Majkowski injured his knee against the Tampa Bay Bucs in week three, Favre was called into duty. By the next week, he led the Packers to a come-from-behind victory in the last seconds of the game against the Bengals, 24–23. From that moment on, Favre became the player Herock had hoped—and Wolf knew—he could be.

Playing in the West Coast offense gave Favre the best of both worlds, throwing accurate short passes and allowing the receivers to gain yards after the catch. Favre played the game with a controlled recklessness. He took risks that few could take. He made throws that few would even attempt, and because of his skill and aggressive nature, he made more errors than most quarterbacks. Yes, Favre threw too many interceptions for an elite player—336 in his career compared to the 243 thrown by Drew Brees, who also played nineteen seasons. But he also made more plays than many. He would give some and take more. He played the game with great heart and competitive fiber. To rein him in would have curtailed his level of excellence. Atlanta's loss gave Green Bay their Titletown title back.

Like the scouts said, all Favre needed was good coaching development and someone who believed in his talents.

54
RON YARY

1x NFL Champion

6x First Team All-Pro • 2x Second Team All-Pro • 7x Pro Bowl

All-Decade Team: 1970s

15-Year Career • 207 Games Played; 180 Started

The greatest challenge any coach faces, and his greatest achievement if he succeeds in meeting it, is to instill his personality into the team. Whatever qualities the coach possesses, the team needs to adopt, becoming an extension of him. Bud Grant was a three-sport athlete, legendary before he entered into coaching, first as head coach of the CFL's Winnipeg Blue Bombers and then replacing Norm Van Brocklin as the head coach of the Vikings, in 1967. Once in Minnesota, Grant instilled a new team approach—forty players, playing together for sixty minutes—and insisted the team to handle the bitter cold without any heaters in the bench area. Grant wanted them to *become* Vikings.

No player represented Grant's idea of a Viking player better than tackle Ron Yary. He became the Vikings' first overall pick in the 1968 draft, a pick the organization acquired when they traded their starting quarterback, Fran Tarkenton, to the New York Giants for a first- and second-round pick in 1967 and a first-round pick in 1968. During this period, teams were willing to trade away high picks for a proven quarterback. Yary became the only offensive lineman ever selected first overall, an honor he held until Orlando Pace was selected in the 1997 draft.

Yary grew up in California, playing college ball at USC, where the temperature rarely dips below fifty degrees. He was extremely tough, only missing two games due to injury, and even played with a broken bone in his foot. He became adaptable to the cold when Grant insisted on practicing outdoors regardless of the weather. Yary was one of the bigger linemen for his time, weighing over 255 pounds. During his career, until the 1978 season, offensive linemen were still unable to extend their hands and punch, which limited their effectiveness when pass blocking. When the rule change went into effect, Yary became even a better player, using his long arms and foot quickness to pass protect.

Practice for Yary might have been harder than the games. Having to face Carl Eller, Jim Marshall, and the great Alan Page each day prepared Yary well for the games. His stance seemed awkward, never fully bending, and because of the era, he was always in a three-point stance. Had he played today, his hand would have never touched the ground, and he easily could have played left tackle.

When watching former Bengal and Super Bowl–winning Rams left tackle Andrew Whitworth play, I am reminded of the way Yary worked each Sunday. Both men could move and control the line of scrimmage and played the game with great toughness. And when the game was on the line, both men wanted to played their best. Yary personified the Viking and became an extension of Grant on the field—quiet, unassuming, talented, and tough.

53
MIKE HAYNES

1x Super Bowl Champion

2x First Team All-Pro • 6x Second Team All-Pro • 9x Pro Bowl

All-Decade Team: 1980s •
All-Time Team: 75th & 100th Anniversaries

14-Year Career • 177 Games Played; 158 Started

46 Interceptions

Since the rules of the game changed to forbid defensive corners from mugging receivers at the line of scrimmage, I have come to define their role in two ways. There's the "breakfast corner," who must win early in the route, defeating the receiver as soon as the ball is snapped; the longer the extension of the play, the more challenging it becomes for a player with his skill set. Then there's the "dinner corner," who isn't trying to jam or alter the route. He patiently waits for the receiver to get to the top of his route and then closes in. A dinner corner is a highly skilled athlete, with incredible quickness in and out of his cuts. When I watch Mike Haynes, I see the complete meal. He is both breakfast and dinner, and I get fatter watching him operate. He could win early or late, and even though he never wanted to beat up the receiver at the line, he was smooth, with no wasted motion, turning and running with ease.

Mike Haynes was like a big beach blanket covering tons of sand. He covered up every receiver he faced, preventing quarterbacks from throwing the ball. He was over six feet, two inches tall, and with his long, outstretched arms, it was impossible to get the ball over him.

Haynes was also extremely fast. With his combined height and speed, it was hard to throw the ball over his head. A six-foot-two corner who runs 4.40 in the forty is more like a corner who runs 4.20. Why? Because the difference between those two speeds seems large, but it isn't from the viewpoint of the quarterback. That .20 seconds is not greater than the length of a tall corner's wingspan. Arm length and speed work hand in hand.

Most important, Haynes played the game in complete balance; he never was on one foot or out of position. One of the greatest traits a man-to-man corner must possess is balance—he must remain in balance so he can extend his arms vertically and make a play on a ball thrown in his direction. Haynes had that. He could always spring vertically and grab the ball. He had the perfect blend of athletic skills and was one of the best corners ever to play the game.

52
EMLEN TUNNELL

2x NFL Champion

6x First Team All-Pro • 9x Pro Bowl

All-Decade Team: 1950s •
All-Time Team: 50th & 100th Anniversaries

14-Year Career • 167 Games Played; 137 Started

79 Interceptions • 10 Touchdowns

Serving in the Coast Guard in the South Pacific during World War II, Emlen Tunnell heroically saved a fellow crew member's life when their ship, the USS *Etamin*, was struck by a Japanese torpedo on April 27, 1944. The crew member, Fred Shavers, was engulfed in flames when Tunnell tackled him to the ground, stamped out the flames, and carried him to safety. For a man who made a living tackling, this one might have been his finest. Tunnell wasn't even supposed to be involved in the war effort. He was rejected by the Army and Navy because of a neck injury he suffered while playing college football at the University of Toledo, yet his efforts with the Coast Guard saved lives.

Tunnell was a great man and a great athlete who played two positions his rookie season: running back and defensive back. His main position was free safety, where his range and burst to the football was sensational. Like All-Pro safety Justin Simmons of the Broncos in stature and style of play, Tunnell possessed more skills and playmaking talent. A more favorable comparison would be fellow Hall of Fame corner Rod Woodson, when he moved inside to safety later in his career. Both were ball hawks and effective at making plays in the passing game. Like Woodson, Tunnell was a four-down safety, with punt and kickoff return ability, and he was capable of making instant offense, which resulted in ten touchdowns over his career.

Whenever Tunnell got the ball in his hands, which he did an amazing seventy-nine times, he was capable of scoring. (He averaged 5.64 interceptions per season, and in 47 percent of the games he played he had an interception.) He could close quickly on the receiver and, with his long arms and soft large hands, always seemed to make the play. Watching video of Tunnell with the ball in one hand and no face mask as he danced around the field heading to the end zone, it's easy to see his rare talent and skills.

Tunnell was also a great tackler, playing with physicality. Upon delivering a blow, he would often loosen the ball from the opposing runner. Tunnell forced at least twelve fumbles during his career, which could be more had they kept detailed stats during his playing days.

Tunnell was also the first Black player to enter the Hall, in addition to being the first defensive back. His seventy-nine interceptions stood as the most in the NFL until Vikings safety Paul Krause broke the record with eighty-one, playing in 226 games and over three full seasons more than Tunnell did.

When Vince Lombardi, the Packers' new coach, arrived in Green Bay, one of his first moves was to trade for Tunnell, even though he was nearing the end of his great career. Lombardi wanted Tunnell to be a part-time coach and player, and break the stigma of Green Bay being a horrible place for Black players to play. Lombardi paid Tunnell's rent at the Hotel Northland, making sure he was treated well in the town. Tunnell was able to educate the Green Bay players on Lombardi's demanding coaching style and eliminate the attitude of defeatism that permeated the team before Lombardi arrived.

Tunnell is rightly honored for all of his remarkable achievements on and off the field. There may never be another man with his infectious attitude, selflessness, and bravery. The Coast Guard and the NFL benefited greatly from his service.

51
RAYMOND BERRY JR.

2x NFL Champion • 3x NFL Receiving Yards Leader •
3x Reception Yards Leader • 2x Receiving Touchdown Leader

3x First Team All-Pro • 3x Second Team All-Pro • 6x Pro Bowl

All-Decade Team: 1950s •
All-Time Team: 75th & 100th Anniversaries

13-Year Career • 154 Games Played; 140 Started

631 Receptions • 9,275 Receiving Yards Gained •
68 Receiving Touchdowns

Imagine being slow, awkward in movement, with poor eyesight, and not being good enough to start for your high school team until your senior season even though your father was the head coach. With a description like that, a career in professional football might be the last occupation you would attempt. Raymond Berry Jr. didn't care what he lacked. He knew his heart was as big as his home state of Texas, and becoming great at something is as much about heart as it is about talent. Berry was living proof that absolutely anyone can become a self-made superstar.

After catching only thirty-three passes in college at SMU, Berry was selected in the twentieth round of the 1954 draft, pick number 203 overall, which would place him in the sixth round today and have him facing long odds to make the team. John Steadman, the legendary *Baltimore Sun* sports columnist, claims the Colts selected Berry with thoughts of moving him to defensive end, even though he only weighed 182 pounds. Berry had the height for end, but not the bulk, so he stayed as a receiver—his natural position—and became a fanatical worker.

Berry understood his limitations, making him the most trusted receiver for star quarterback John Unitas. He knew he wasn't the fastest, so he made damn sure he never played a game over his 182-pound playing weight, even taking his bathroom scale on all road trips to ensure he wasn't an ounce overweight. He knew he didn't have explosive quickness, so he choregraphed every single step of his pass routes, using head fakes and shoulder shrugs to deceive the defensive back, thus allowing separation. He knew he needed to make sure his hands could catch any type of pass thrown, never allowing one to slip away. Berry developed all sorts of practice methods, including letting one of his three children throw him the ball, knowing it would be a poorly thrown pass and force him to make a tough catch. There was no stone left unturned in his preparation and attention to his craft. In his playing contract, he made the Colts purchase him a Bell & Howell projector for his home, so he could prepare for the next opponent he faced.

In his greatest game—facing the Giants in 1958—Berry had twelve catches for 178 yards and one touchdown, leading the Colts to victory. After his playing days, Berry took his dedication and attention to detail to the coaching profession, leading the New England Patriots to the 1985 Super Bowl against the Chicago Bears. He coached six seasons for the Patriots, reaching the playoffs twice and having a 48–39 overall record.

When Berry retired in 1967, he was the NFL leader in career receptions, with 631. Had he played today, Berry might resemble DeAndre Hopkins of the Arizona Cardinals. Hopkins doesn't have great speed or elite quickness, but he has incredible body control and makes every catch, even though there are always defenders near him—which is how Berry played. What Berry lacked in God-given talent, he made up for with incredible heart and the desire to be the best receiver in the game.

50
JACK LAMBERT

4x Super Bowl Champion • 1x NFL Defensive Player of the Year

6x First Team All-Pro • 2x Second Team All-Pro • 9x Pro Bowl

All-Decade Team: 1970s & 1980s •
All-Time Team: 75th & 100th Anniversaries

11-Year Career • 146 Games Played; 138 Started

28 Interceptions

Steelers defensive line coach George Perles needed a way to prevent the team's best player, Joe Greene, from taking a constant pounding. He thought that if he shifted Greene's location—not to another gap, but if he positioned him sideways, along the line on either side of the center, tilted—then it would cause confusion for the offensive line. It would prevent the guard to that side from having free access to the rookie middle linebacker, Jack Lambert. Defensive tackle Ernie Holmes would then play a normal three-technique over the guard and flop from one guard to another, depending on the strength of the defensive call (the strength is always determined by what side the tight end aligns with). From the chalkboard to the grass practice field, Perles fully realized the "Stunt 4-3." Once this new front was introduced, Greene couldn't be blocked, weakside linebacker Jack Ham ran to the football, and rookie Lambert dominated. That week, their opponent, the Bills' running back O. J. Simpson, ran for a paltry forty-nine yards.

Lambert became middle linebacker for a new era. Instead of being a downhill thumper with size, like Ray Nitschke or Dick Butkus, Lambert became a backpedaling defender, helping out the pass and moving sideways to stop the run. He was still able to fill the gaps, but rarely were linemen free to block him because of the alignment of the defensive line. Lambert flowed to the ball and arrived at the carrier with power and punch, uncommon for someone who looked more like a safety. Undersized but tough, Lambert had incredible instincts for the position. He was smart, prepared, and could make the calls in the complex scheme Bud Carson was operating.

Lambert's game is perfectly suited for today's game, although his vicious hits of defenseless receivers coming over the middle would need to be curtailed. His skill set paved the way for Ray Lewis, Luke Kuechly, and Bobby Wagner to have great careers. After the Steelers found success with Lambert, teams changed their philosophy toward middle linebackers and lowered their size (i.e., weight) requirements, wanting pass-covering skills over run fits and fast flow over shed and attack. Today the down is not significant—every down is a passing down; therefore, if the middle linebacker cannot stay on the field regardless of the personnel the offense has elected to utilize, then his value dwindles. Lambert could play against any personnel grouping. His innate toughness would be welcome on any team and would set the attitude of the entire defense, who would follow his lead and play—hard down after hard down.

49
MEL BLOUNT

4x Super Bowl Champion • 1x NFL Defensive Player
of the Year • 1x NFL Interception Leader

2x First Team All-Pro • 4x Second Team All-Pro • 5x Pro Bowl

All-Decade Team: 1980s •
All-Time Team: 75th & 100th Anniversaries

14-Year Career • 200 Games Played; 189 Started

57 Interceptions • 2 Touchdowns

Standing six feet, three inches tall and weighing over 215 pounds, Mel Blount looked bigger than Steelers linebackers Jack Ham or Lambert on the field. He was physical with his jam at the line, never allowing the receiver to get into his pass routes. Blount could move his feet well, and turn and run. Because of his size, he covered up most receivers down the field, forcing the quarterback to look elsewhere. He supported the run with relentlessness and was not afraid to throw his body around to make the play. One of the many reasons the Steel Curtain became so effective was their ability to tackle the ball carrier, never allowing yards after contact or a catch.

The battles at the line against the receivers made Blount the greatest breakfast corner of all time, so much so that the NFL had to implement a rule to curtail the amount of breakfast he was serving. In 1978, the NFL passed their one-chuck rule inside of five yards, which was also known as the Mel Blount Rule since it grew from teams complaining that Blount was destroying their receivers. Blount still was effective after the rule change, in part because he was the perfect corner to play the ever-popular Cover 2 that was taking over the defensive secondary.

During the 1970s, the Steelers had curious coaches who developed different schemes to enhance their players' skills. With Bud Carson serving as the defensive coordinator, George Perles handing the defensive line, Woody Widenhofer overseeing the linebackers, and the great Chuck Noll as their head coach, the Steelers were as talented off the field as on. When the upstart Cincinnati Bengals began utilizing Bill Walsh's West Coast offense, the Steelers' defenses needed to adjust. For a coach like Carson, who loved to tinker with new ideas and schemes, Cover 2 became his newest invention. The technique came from Carson's intent to shifting run force (the player who forces the ball back into the heart of the defense). Cover 2 required corners to jam receivers at the line of scrimmage and support the run in the flat. And there was no one better at doing both jobs than Mel Blount, who tackled like a linebacker.

One of the reasons big corners like Blount don't normally exist in the NFL is that they lack the quickness, the fluidity of their hips, and the ability to break down and change direction. When measured for the 2016 draft, Jalen Ramsey of the Los Angeles Rams was six feet, one inches tall and weighed 209 pounds, with an arm length of 33 3/8 inches—huge for a corner and still much smaller than Blount. Ramsey is incredible, but he does not play the game with the same physical style as Blount. Ramsey does wins early in the route with elegance, foot movement, and ballerina-like flexibility. Blount was never elegant, and instead always forceful and obstinate in his play. Former Seahawks and Patriots corner Brandon Browner had the same size and style of Blount at the line, just without the speed and turn ability. Each day I watched Browner at New England practice, I was in awe of his size, which made me think of Blount and the uniqueness of his skill set.

COVER 2 UNCOVERED

Cover 2 is a seven-man front, with one of the defensive line assigned to two gaps. (Remember, in football at all levels, there are eight gaps that have to be defended at all times.) With seven in the front, the secondary now has four players to play pass defense. The corners have the outside flats, and the two safeties are responsible for half of the field, aligned fifteen yards away from the line of scrimmage, slightly outside the hashmarks. The three linebackers have the middle of the field, giving the defense five underneath players, thus taking away all the short passes. To run Cover 2 effectively, you'll need a corner, like Blount, who can tackle.

48
LADAINIAN TOMLINSON

1x NFL MVP 2008 • 1x NFL Offensive Player of the Year •
2x Rushing Leader • 3x Rushing Touchdown Leader •
1x NFL Scoring Leader

3x First Team All-Pro • 3x Second Team All-Pro • 5x Pro Bowl

All-Decade Team: 2000s

11-Year Career • 170 Games Played; 155 Started

3,174 Rushing Attempts • 13,684 Rushing Yards Gained •
145 Rushing Touchdowns

624 Receptions • 4,772 Receiving Yards Gained •
17 Receiving Touchdowns

John Butler walked into a mess. After leaving his general manager position with the Buffalo Bills, Butler headed west, looking for warm weather and constant sunshine—something that is not always available along the shores of Lake Erie.

The San Diego Chargers had gone 1–15 during the 2000 season, before he took over as their general manager. But there was a bright spot—he held the first overall pick in the 2001 NFL draft and he wanted to make the most of it. He traded down to Atlanta, able to stay in the top ten and secure both running back LaDainian Tomlinson as well as quarterback Drew Brees.

LaDainian became everything Butler could have envisioned, and more. Not solely a runner, Tomlinson was an offensive weapon, able to impact the game by both catching and running. When a team has a three-dimensional runner like Tomlinson—who can run, catch, and block—the offense becomes hard to shut down. Fans get enamored with the receivers in the spread formation, but the running back creates more headaches for the defensive coordinators. Tomlinson had the lateral quickness to make the tacklers miss and the power to run over them—which made him an amazing force coming out of the backfield. Who could cover him? Not a linebacker. And if the team placed a safety or corner in the box to cover Tomlinson, then the linemen would overpower them and make the running game hard to stop. The talent of the runner creates a quandary for the defense, in which they're damned if they do and damned if they don't.

Tomlinson was explosive with his shiftiness, sudden burst, and power. His low-center-of-gravity running style made him laterally quick, causing tacklers to grasp the air as he ran by them. He had great patience with the ball, allowing the hole to develop, then turning on the jets once he saw daylight. He was effective running from the deep I formation or the offset in the shotgun. Because of his power and shiftiness, running inside or outside didn't matter; he was great at both.

Tomlinson and former 49ers running back Frank Gore shared the same running style and dual-purpose talent. Tomlinson was a step quicker, slightly shiftier than Gore. Both were excellent, Tomlinson only better.

LEADING THE CHARGERS

While in Buffalo, Butler never had a first-round pick higher than fourteenth, so when he stepped into the spotlight with the Chargers, his main concern was making the most of the draft. When Virginia Tech star quarterback Michael Vick entered the draft, Butler had a tough decision. Vick was a multidimensional talent, and most assumed Butler would go for him. Not so fast. Butler preferred Purdue's Drew Brees, a more traditional player. Trading down his pick to Atlanta, Butler could get a solid starter and Brees. For Butler, the 2001 draft was like shooting pool—he knew he would make his first shot, gaining an elite player, but he also had to be in position to make his second one, acquiring Brees. Butler never was able to see his vision fulfilled, succumbing to cancer in 2003. His decision to trade down, selecting the great Tomlinson and being committed to his belief that Brees could be as good as if not better than Vick, allowed the Chargers to become one of the most talented teams ever to not win a Super Bowl.

47
LARRY "WILDCAT" WILSON

1x NFL Defensive Player of the Year • 1x NFL Interception Leader

6x First Team All-Pro • 1x Second Team All-Pro • 6x Pro Bowl

All-Decade Team: 1970s & 1980s •
All-Time Team: 75th & 100th Anniversaries

13-Year Career • 169 Games Played; 163 Started

52 Interceptions

When Vikings safety Harrison Smith times his blitz perfectly, accelerating off the snap of the ball toward the opposing passer, he should thank St. Louis Cardinals defensive coach Chuck Drulis. The same goes for the Steelers' Troy Polamalu, who entered the Hall of Fame. Why? Because without Drulis's creative thinking, the safety might never have vacated the deep part of the field to attack the passer.

Drulis thought the safety position was being underused. Drulis didn't think of football as a game of chess, in which only certain pieces move in certain directions. He felt every player had the capacity for "queen-like" movement, attacking from all directions. For several years, Drulis wanted to attack the quarterback, sending the safety into the heart of the offensive line, surprising the quarterback, because no one had ever done that before. He called the play "wildcat." But Drulis didn't have a player with the right amount of speed, toughness, and determination to attack and keep attacking even when blocked...until Larry Wilson arrived from the University of Utah in 1960.

Wilson played both ways for the University of Utah, running back and defensive corner. His willingness to tackle was impressive, and he became a seventh-round pick of the Chicago Cardinals (before they moved to St. Louis). A little under six feet tall and weighing around 190 pounds, Wilson wasn't considered big enough for safety and his foot speed wasn't ideal for corner. But from his first day, his toughness excited the coaches, and Drulis decided to move Wilson to safety. Wilson was a natural at the position. He demonstrated great range and playmaking ability. What he lacked in size, he made up for with his elite physical and mental toughness.

When Drulis started to send Wilson after the quarterback, it opened up a whole new world for the defense and created havoc for the offense. It also earned him a nickname that stuck for the rest of his life: "Wildcat" Wilson. Most of the protection schemes during this period were man schemes—the offensive lineman blocked the man over him and the running backs had the linebackers if they blitzed. Pass protections then were not as complex as they are today; no one ever considered sending a corner or safety toward the passer, as it seemed too risky, potentially making them vulnerable to allowing a big play. Once Drulis sent Wilson, all hell broke loose. Even though Wilson wasn't a big man, he put the fear of God into most quarterbacks. At the Pro Bowl, when Wilson went to shake hands with Y. A. Tittle, the Hall of Fame quarterback who suffered many hits from a blitzing Wilson, Tittle told him, "If I'd known you were this small, I'd never have been that scared of you." For a smaller man, getting as close to the line came with inherent risk, but using his former running back skills, Wilson avoided Powerful blows from the offensive lineman attempting to block. Wilson was willing to play through most any injury. In a game against the Pittsburgh Steelers in 1965, with two heavily bandaged, broken hands, Wilson still intercepted the ball, returning it for a touchdown and helping the Cardinals win, 21–17.

Today we see safeties hug near the line, forcing the offense to account for them in their protection schemes. Because of all the safety blitzes engineered by Wilson and copied throughout the NFL today, quarterbacks are prepared to handle a free blitzer from depth (ten yards off the ball, coming directly at the quarterback). Rarely do safeties now blitz from depth because the quarterbacks have seen it too many times and are prepared. Even if the safety is unaccounted for in the protection scheme, the quarterback will make a throw before the safety can reach him.

During his thirteen-year career, Wilson had a least two or more interceptions in a season and finished with fifty-three overall, which is amazing. The saddest part of Wilson's amazing career is that he never played in a postseason game. The Cardinals never finished higher than second place in their division, and they achieved that only twice—once in 1964 and again in 1968. Wilson also never won more than nine games in a season. That wasn't because Wilson didn't make plays, but rather that the Cardinals were a dysfunctional organization.

With help from Drulis, Wilson changed the safety position, benefiting future generations of players and coaches...and we all have benefited from watching.

46
AARON RODGERS

1x Super Bowl Champion • 1x Super Bowl MVP •
4x NFL MVP • 4x NFL Passing Rating Leader •
2x NFL Passing Touchdown Leader •
1x NFL Completion Percentage Leader

4x First Team All-Pro • 1x Second Team All-Pro • 10x Pro Bowl

All-Decade Team: 2010s

18-Year Career (and counting) • 230 Games Played; 223 Started

5,001 Passing Completions • 7,660 Passing Attempts •
59,055 Passing Yards • 475 Passing Touchdowns •
105 Interceptions

If you haven't heard of Phil "The Power" Taylor, he is the greatest dart thrower of all time. Taylor made darts a professional sport, advancing from local taverns to big arenas. The BBC rated Taylor as one of the ten greatest sportsmen over the last thirty-five years. And yet I am convinced Aaron Rodgers could beat him.

There are many factors that need to be evaluated when determining the talents of any quarterback. Accuracy is at the top of the list. Accuracy comes in a variety of forms, which is why throwing darts is applicable to throwing a football. On any dartboard, there are circles that surround the target, with the smallest one holding the most value. The same applies to throwing a football. According to former Packers quarterback Brett Favre, there are three levels of accuracy under pressure from the rush:

- Level one: Can the quarterback throw the ball through the door? Most can.

- Level two: Can the quarterback hit the doorknob? A smaller percentage of players are capable, as the list grows shorter.

- Level three: Can the quarterback throw the ball through the keyhole? Very, very, very few can.

The keyhole throwers are the elite passers, as their accuracy is pinpoint. It's why Rodgers is so effective. Rodgers throws the ball through the keyhole without touching the metal, much like basketball superstar Kevin Durant makes jump shots with the ball never disturbing the net. Rodgers controls the placement of the ball, effectively making it easier for his receivers to make the catch. He rarely misses the precise spot required to complete the throw, and harsh weather never affects his laser-like passes.

Rodgers also has the foot quickness to avoid the pass rush and the instincts to move laterally in the pocket to drive the ball down the field. His velocity on the ball and his ability to launch deep passes aren't affected when the pocket becomes tight. Rodgers can flick his wrist without his lower body becoming involved, driving the ball to any spot on the field. He doesn't require any space to make a throw.

The entire field was Rodgers's sweet spot; he could throw to anywhere in the stadium with accuracy. Defending a great passer is like defending a great shooter in basketball. Great shooters have sweet spots to stroke the ball, as do quarterbacks. Coaches in both basketball and football attempt to force the player away from his sweet spot and hope for the best. The problem coaches face with Rodgers is that the entire field is his sweet spot. He forces the defense to cover every single blade of grass on all downs, making it nearly impossible to slow him down.

Another incredible tool in Rodgers's arsenal is his ability to protect the football. Over his seventeen-year career, he has only thrown ninety-three interceptions, averaging 5.47 per season, which is beyond astonishing. Often quarterbacks who overly protect the football are reluctant to take chances, thus resulting in a lower yards-per-attempt number. They don't force the ball, settling for the checkdown, which keeps their yards-per-attempt number below a winning level. Not Rodgers. He does both: he protects the ball and has averaged 7.8 on every attempt over his career, which is sensational. Rodgers is rare in almost every aspect of his game.

I know Rodgers would love to be the host of *Jeopardy* one day, which is a wonderful goal, but I really want to see him challenge Phil Taylor to a round of darts. My money is on Rodgers.

45
GINO MARCHETTI

2x NFL Champion • 1x NFL Sack Leader

9x First Team All-Pro • 1x Second Team All-Pro • 11x Pro Bowl

All-Decade Team: 1950s •
All-Time Team: 50th, 75th, & 100th Anniversaries

13-Year Career • 161 Games Played; 151 Started

56 Sacks (unofficial)

During the winter months, if my father drove our family off the little island of Ocean City, it was to find restaurants open year-round. Ocean City was a seasonal town, busy in the summer, and deathly quiet in the winter. One Sunday afternoon, we crossed the bridge in my father's burgundy Mercury, beginning our travel along Highway 9, which singer-songwriter and fellow New Jerseyan Bruce Springsteen would make famous in his song "Born to Run." A brand-new burger place had opened and was the talk of the locals. "Welcome to Gino's," the bright sign flickered, as we made the right into the parking lot. Once inside, my father told me about the restaurant's origin. From research gathered talking with clients in his barber chair, my father learned that former Baltimore Colts players started this little hamburger chain in Dundalk, Maryland, and it grew in popularity across the mid-Atlantic states. Their television ads featured the catchy jingle "Everybody goes to Gino's, 'cause Gino's is the place to go." It only took hearing the jingle once, and it never left your mind for the day. Their burgers were sensational, their milkshakes even better, and they had the best fried chicken anywhere. The man behind all these tasty treats was the great Gino Marchetti. He wasn't the man making the burgers or frying the chicken, or even placing that extra scoop of vanilla ice cream in my shake. He was a dominating defensive lineman for the Colts.

Marchetti entered the 1952 draft and was selected by the Dallas Texans, which had relocated from New York and changed their name from the Yanks to the Texans. Seeing them struggling on and off the field, Commissioner Bert Bell convinced his former University of Pennsylvania player and Margate, New Jersey, summer neighbor Carroll Rosenbloom to purchase the team. Bell gave Rosenbloom the deal of a lifetime, and the Texans became the Colts, shifting from green and white to their now famous blue-and-white uniforms. Marchetti also was moving. When Weeb Ewbank became the coach in 1954, he shifted Marchetti from offensive tackle to defensive end, and from that moment on, Marchetti became the most dominating player on the defensive side in the league.

Marchetti was a workhorse, playing in 121 straight games, and he was selected to the Pro Bowl eleven times in a row. The only time he missed during his career was the last three minutes and the overtime portion of the 1958 NFL Championship game between the Colts and the Giants. In perhaps the most crucial play of this great game, the Giants were leading 17–14 and facing a third and three. Typically, in these game-deciding situations, the Giants loved to run to their left, behind their great tackle Rosey Brown. However, on the second-down play, they went against their tendency and ran their favorite play, 48 Power, toward Marchetti and gained five yards, giving them confidence. With the game on the line, the Giants were in the two-tight-end formation, with three backs aligned behind the quarterback, and once again ran 48 Power toward Marchetti. Running back Frank Gifford got stopped near the first-down marker. Marchetti screamed from the pile, with his leg trapped under Gifford and Eugene "Big Daddy" Lipscomb and two bones above his ankle broken. When the official came over to the pile, some believe he misplaced the ball nine inches short of the first down in his hurried attempt to help Marchetti. Marchetti believed he played the play wrongly, running toward Gifford, instead of anchoring the line, which would have prevented him from incurring the injury. Colts players believed Gifford didn't get the first down. And Giants players were certain he did. Without instant replay technology, the Giants were forced to punt.

Many who watched the game still wondered why the Giants would run the ball at one of the game's greatest run defenders and pass rushers. Marchetti may have only weighed slightly below 250 pounds, but he played with great strength and foot quickness, allowing him to shed and find the ball. His dominating play on the field made him a legend in the Baltimore area, which is why his first name was easily the choice when he started the hamburger joints with teammate Alan Ameche.

From his World War II service fighting in the Battle of the Bulge, to his incredible play in the NFL, and finally to his postfootball fast-food venture, Gino had a remarkable, long life.

Maybe the jingle should change a little: "Everyone wants to be like Gino, 'cause Gino is the man to be."

THE SAN FRANCISCO DON'S LAST STAND

Gino Marchetti began his professional career as an offensive lineman for the University of San Francisco, where he played for future Eagles head coach Joe Kuharich. The Dons were loaded with future Hall of Fame talent and were one of the few integrated teams of the era. Their ranks included running back Ollie Matson and offensive tackle Bob St. Clair. They defeated every team they played, outscoring their opponents 338 to 86. The closest margin of victory was six points, which occurred on October 21, 1951, when they were playing against the Fordham Rams at Randalls Island in New York. As a result of their perfect season, they were invited to participate in the Orange Bowl, one of only eight bowl games of the era, with one condition: no Black players were allowed to play. Matson and linebacker Burl Toler, who later became the first Black NFL official, had to stay home. The Dons' football program was in dire straits financially, and participating in this game would supply the funds the university needed to maintain their football team. The players voted unanimously against the game, which made their athletic news director (and future NFL commissioner), Pete Rozelle, extremely happy. Immediately after the vote, the school closed down its football program.

44
AARON DONALD

1x Super Bowl Champion • 3x NFL Defensive Player of the Year

7x First Team All-Pro • 8xPro Bowl

All-Decade Team: 2010s

8-Year Career • 127 Games Played; 123 Started

98 Sacks • 150 Tackles for Loss • 226 Hits on Quarterback

Witnessing greatness sometimes only costs the price of a ticket. When the Chicago Bulls opened their 1984 season, 17,374 fans packed Chicago Stadium to watch Michael Jordan, the highly publicized first-round pick from North Carolina. The "Madhouse on Madison" was rocking that night, as everyone was anxious to see this high-flying talent live and in person. Many Bulls fans had witnessed him dominate the 1984 Summer Olympics and now wanted to experience this human highlight machine with their own eyes. Tickets were in high demand for months, and the game instantly sold out. People knew they were going to see something extraordinary (and those who did can now sell the ticket stub for over $500,000).

If you're a Rams fan, watching Aaron Donald perform each week is like that. For the cost of a ticket, you are viewing a rare greatness that's simply priceless. Donald is playing in the perfect era for his game. He benefits tremendously from the advancements in weight training, nutrition, and medical science, which helped him develop his incredible power, conditioning, and explosiveness. His father, Archie, was an avid weightlifter and built a home gym in their basement. The pair started working out at a quarter to four each morning before school, and before long, Aaron became a fanatic about his body. The hard work paid off. Even though he was lightly recruited out of high school, with offers from Pittsburgh, Rutgers, and most of the MAC schools, Donald became a dominating force at Pitt by his sophomore season.

Though over the age of thirty, Donald is showing no signs of slowing down or becoming blockable by offensive linemen. If he stopped playing today, he would be a surefire first-ballot Hall of Famer. His dominance over an eight-year career is more than enough to welcome him into Canton. And now that we can quantify production accurately, we gain a numerical portrait of how Donald impacts the game. Donald benefits from us being able to keep score. His statistics are going to become the gold standard for generations of defensive tackles.

Donald combines great qualities of other Hall of Fame players—John Randle's quickness, Randy White's power and strength, Warren Sapp's foot quickness, Lee Roy Selmon's acceleration off the block, Joe Greene's explosive shedding ability, Bob Lilly's conditioning, Merlin Olsen's competitive drive, and Alan Page's intelligence—all wrapped into his body. Donald isn't lacking in any skill. His stamina, his ability to play relentless hard down after hard down—never slowing or needing to catch his breath—separates him from others. He is always charging and always getting stronger as the game nears the end. Many smart offensive coordinators have two game plans in one when facing an unblockable defensive lineman. If the lineman isn't in the game to start the series, they implement their no-huddle offense, preventing a personnel change by the defense. Then they throw the ball down the field, believing their protection will improve and they won't have to worry about handling the defensive star. With Donald, teams rarely get this chance. He plays down after down, each with the same intensity, making it hard for offensive coaches to scheme around him.

Greatness often occurs when great talent meets dedicated work habits. Donald exemplifies that quality.

43
JOHN ELWAY

2x Super Bowl Champion • 1x Super Bowl MVP •
1x NFL MVP • 1x Passing Yards Leader

3x Second Team All-Pro • 9x Pro Bowl

All-Decade Team: 1990s • All-Time Team: 100th Anniversary

16-Year Career • 234 Games Played; 231 Started

4,123 Passing Completions • 7,250 Passing Attempts •
51,475 Passing Yards • 300 Passing Touchdowns •
226 Interceptions

Other than Terry Bradshaw of the Steelers, no rookie quarterback entered the NFL with more fanfare than John Elway. New England Patriots personnel director Dick Steinberg said of Elway: "[He is] as good as I've seen since Joe Namath. He is a can't-miss in the pros." Tony Razzano of the San Francisco 49ers claimed he was "the best quarterback he ha[d] seen come out of college in twenty years of scouting." His college head coach, Paul Wiggin, declared Elway a "do-it-all quarterback," even though he never took the Stanford Cardinals to a postseason bowl game. Adding more fuel to the fanfare fire was Elway's blatant thumbing his nose at the Baltimore Colts, demanding a trade and wanting the right to select his new team. Everyone in Denver wanted Steinberg, Razzano, and Wiggin to be correct. Others—especially the Colts—hoped they were wrong.

Initially, the Broncos looked wrong. Elway struggled his first season, getting benched in the first game against the Steelers and allowing Steve DeBerg to lead the team to victory. In week two, against the Colts, Elway made a sensational throw to receiver Steve Watson for a big gain. For the next few games, Elway would start and then DeBerg eventually would take over, helping the Broncos win the game. Elway did not become a full-time starter until week eight, after DeBerg injured his shoulder. Despite the Broncos reaching the wildcard round of the playoffs in 1983, Elway's rookie season was a concern. But once Elway got comfortable and the game slowed down, he found his groove and proved his supporters correct.

Elway mastered the position and his natural skills took over the game. His powerful arm could throw to any point on the field. With his size and athletic skills, he was hard to tackle, and he wasn't going to always slide. Elway was willing to sacrifice his body, running over the tackler and dishing out the punishment. And no game was ever out of reach if Elway was playing; every teammate and coach believed Elway could win the game no matter the deficit. During his magnificent career, he led the Broncos to thirty-one comebacks and forty-one game-winning drives. As a former opponent of the Broncos, I always wanted the ball last, never wanting to risk having any time left on the clock for Elway to perform his magic tricks. Most times, Elway sent me home a loser.

Elway finished his career much like the character Billy Chapel (played by Kevin Costner) in the movie *For the Love of the Game*. After a wonderful career, the aging superstar pitcher is pitching in his last game at Yankee Stadium. He tosses a no-hitter and walks away from the game content. Prior to his last two seasons of his career, Elway was only 8–8 in playoff games, featuring three lopsided Super Bowl losses. But during those last two seasons, Elway won six straight playoff games, retiring with two big Super Bowl rings for his fingers. Elway was exactly who Steinberg, Razzano, and Wiggin thought he'd be. And all us football fans are forever thankful they were right.

42
PAUL WARFIELD

2x Super Bowl Champion • 1x NFL Champion •
2x NFL Receiving Leader

2x First Team All-Pro • 3x Second Team All-Pro • 8x Pro Bowl

All-Decade Team: 1970s • All-Time Team: 100th Anniversary

13-Year Career • 157 Games Played; 152 Started

427 Receptions • 8,565 Receiving Yards Gained •
85 Receiving Touchdowns

Art Modell, the former owner of the Cleveland Browns, was a seller of hope. After a bad season, his focus was on instilling hope in his fans for a better future, and often said to me, "Kid, we need to make a splash." Modell was like P. T. Barnum, trying to drum up excitement and anticipation, and wanting his team in the spotlight. Conversely, after a great season, Modell became the impatient farmer, constantly pulling up crops to make sure the roots were taking shape. After losing deep into the playoffs in 1967, 1968, and 1969, Modell was in full impatient-farmer mode, wanting to do something to give his team that one little push over the top.

The day before the 1972 draft, Modell and the Browns' front office, led by former *Cleveland Plain Dealer* sportswriter Harold Sauerbrei and head coach Blanton Collier, dug up some roots. In their minds, they agreed to trade their second-best receiver, twenty-seven-year-old Paul Warfield, to the Dolphins for the third pick and select Mike Phipps as their quarterback of the future. In 1969, Warfield had forty-two catches for 886 yards, averaging 21.1 yards per catch, and scored ten touchdowns. They believed their best receiver was twenty-eight-year-old Gary Collins, who led the team with fifty-four catches. Though he fell short of Warfield in yards (786) and average per catch (14.6), he scored eleven touchdowns.

What Modell and his staff didn't realize was that it was the combination of the two talented players that made them both exceptional. Years later, Al Davis always referred to this trade as a baseball trade, meaning when a baseball team has two great pitchers, and no hitting, they'd trade one pitcher for a hitter. But one hitter never improves a team, and by trading the great pitcher, a team's area of strength is weakened. That's exactly what happen to the Browns. Instead of having two great receivers, they only had one receiver and a rookie quarterback.

Warfield became the best receiver in Miami and, like John Mackey of the Colts, was underutilized for his talents. Miami's offense was run based, and during Warfield's seven seasons, he only caught more than thirty-five passes twice. Warfield was a smooth, effortless route runner who never looked like he was working hard or covering ground, yet he was running past everyone. He could change gears, extend his hands, and found the end zone in one of every five catches, regardless of touches. He was a tad slenderer than Davante Adams of the Raiders is now, but they both have the same power, exceptional hands, and big play ability. Warfield's best modern comparison would be Marvin Harrison of the Colts, who is also extremely athletic, with movement that is similar to a small forward on a basketball team. His touchdown-to-catch ratio is incredible, eighty-five touchdowns with only 427 catches, which translates to a touchdown every five catches. A touchdown every five catches is the strongest argument anyone can make for Warfield getting the ball more.

The Warfield trade is one Browns fans have always regretted and Dolphin fans loved.

41
JOHN MACKEY

1x Super Bowl Champion • 1x NFL Champion

3x First Team All-Pro • 5x Pro Bowl

All-Decade Team: 1960s •
All-Time Team: 50th & 100th Anniversaries

10-Year Career • 139 Games Played; 118 Started

331 Receptions • 5,236 Receiving Yards Gained •
38 Receiving Touchdowns

Former Colts general manager Ernie Accorsi was always a fan of the Colts before becoming the man in charge. Accorsi grew up in nearby Hershey, Pennsylvania, idolizing the Colts and knowing every detail about the team during the Unitas era. His instant recall of the Colts proved to be beneficial to Barry Levinson when the filmmaker was writing the screenplay for his 1982 movie *Diner* about his hometown Baltimore and the Colts. When I worked for Accorsi as the Browns' pro scouting director, he talked about the many talented players on the Colts, especially tight end John Mackey. Accorsi was always looking for the next Mackey because he understood Mackey's unique talents and how his skills impacted the game. When Mackey joined the Colts in 1963, their offense was loaded with future Hall of Fame players like quarterback Johnny Unitas, runner/receiver Lenny Moore, and wide receiver Raymond Berry. Once you add the dependable running backs Tom Matte, Tony Lorick, and Jerry Hill, the Colts were the best-scoring offense in 1964, finishing with a 12–2 record by Mackey's second season. With Don Shula as the head coach, the Colts could throw for over 250 yards per game, which was a significant amount in the mid-1960s, to running for over two hundred yards each game. With their talent level, they could dice up a defense any way they wanted. Mackey immediately became a big play factor in the Colts' explosive offense.

Mackey's skill of being able to gain yards after the catch and contact allowed Unitas to extend his career by throwing a quick five-yard slant to Mackey and then watching Mackey do the rest. Tacklers were always bouncing off Mackey like bowling pins, as his power in his legs and upper body made him a challenge to get on the ground. No play better personifies Mackey's running skills than the one he executed in November of 1966 against the Detroit Lions, when Mackey caught a short pass in the offensive flat, broke the initial tackle—and then broke four more—before reaching the end zone for a sixty-four-yard touchdown catch.

Watching Mackey play during his career, we can easily see that he was underutilized, not because of his skills, but rather because of the era and the run-first mentality prevailing in the NFL. Had he played today, he wouldn't have the height of Rob Gronkowski or Travis Kelce, but he would have their power, speed, and soft hands. If Mackey were playing now, he would be both a complete tight end with the power to block the edge in the run game and a mismatch receiver in the passing game. He would convert third downs at a high rate with his sure hands and excellent quickness. And even though the players are bigger and stronger, if Mackey were roaming the gridiron today, his power and ability to break tackles would still dominate.

LEVEL FOUR: THE EXTRAORDINARY

The smallest group of our exclusive club is filled with fifteen men who went beyond the usual and customary play on the field. Their impact extended years after they played because of their sustained domination. Their talents, will, toughness, and—most significantly—production were as consistent as the sun rising in the east.

40
TED HENDRICKS

4x Super Bowl Champion

4x First Team All-Pro • 2x Second Team All-Pro • 8x Pro Bowl

All-Decade Team: 1970s and 1980s •
All-Time Team: 75th & 100th Anniversaries

15-Year Career • 215 Games Played; 200 Started

61 Sacks (unofficial) • 26 Interceptions • 25 Blocked Kicks

Even though he was drafted by the Baltimore Colts in 1969 in the second round and helped them win a Super Bowl, Ted Hendricks was destined to become a Raider. Standing every bit of six feet, seven inches and weighing a lean 215 pounds, Hendricks played the game with great power in his hands. Once he engaged the offensive lineman with his powerful mitts, he was in complete control. Hendricks wasn't a 4-3 or 3-4 linebacker—he was an everything linebacker, capable of enhancing *any* scheme. He could play effectively going forward and moving backward. As tall and gangly Hendricks appeared, his movement was outstanding and his talent to make plays in space was sensational, earning him the nickname "The Mad Stork."

Normally tall players, particularly on defense, have a hard time playing with great pad level. They play erect, losing the battle of leverage, which is essential when attempting to shed the blocker. (Ideally, when their talent is evaluated, players with great height benefit because of their long arms and range, particularly if they are long trunked, meaning their legs are on the shorter side. Scouts love tall players with short legs and long trunks.) Hendricks defied all logic; he played tall with long legs. He wasn't always controlling the leverage with his knee bend, but he was always controlling the blocker. As light as he was in weight, he played strong, and his style of play was only suited for him.

After playing out his option with the Colts, Hendricks was briefly with the Jacksonville Sharks of the World League before being traded to the Packers along with a second-round pick for linebacker Tom MacLeod and an eighth-round pick. Hendricks didn't last long in Green Bay, even though he had an incredible season. Henricks intercepted five passes, blocked seven kicks, and made seventy-five tackles. When head coach and general manager Bart Starr didn't want to re-sign Hendricks, the player signed with the Raiders for two number-one picks. Al Davis would say of the trade, "I decided he was worth it, and I was influenced by several things. One was that he wanted to come here. Another was that the player limit was cut from forty-seven to forty-three, which was something I was against. I knew he could cover two positions." Davis would often tell me years later that Hendricks "tilted the field in the Raiders' favor."

If Hendricks played today, he would be the perfect 3–4 outside backer, with more height and versatility than T. J. Watt of the Steelers. He wasn't exclusively

THE ROZELLE RULE

In 1962, after R. C. Owens—San Francisco star receiver and the man who invented the alley-oop pass—signed with the Baltimore Colts, the NFL owners agreed to allow Commissioner Pete Rozelle to determine fair compensation if the two teams could not agree on it. The Rozelle Rule was born. Owens was coming off his best season as a pro, playing in fourteen games, catching fifty-five balls (the most in his career), and scoring five touchdowns. A free agent, he had just turned twenty-seven and was entering the prime of his career. With the Colts as one of the first teams to sign a free agent, they let Rozelle determine the compensation. After this historic signing—and until 1974—only thirty-four players signed with new teams, in part because of the high cost Rozelle imposed when he determined compensation. Rozelle sparked outrage when he awarded the 49ers two New Orleans Saints first-round picks for receiver Dave Parks, who had only caught twenty-six passes the previous year in San Francisco. It made players reluctant to enter the option market. Maybe that was Rozelle's intention all along.

a pass rusher; his twenty-six interceptions prove his talent as a zone- or man-coverage player. Watt is more of a pass rusher, whereas Hendricks could do both well. Plus, when it came time to kick a field goal, extra point, or a punt, Hendricks was able to get his big hands on the ball, batting down twenty-five kicks, an unofficial NFL record. (Sacks and blocked kick were not recorded during most of Hendricks's career.)

39
MERLIN OLSEN

5x First Team All-Pro • 5x Second Team All-Pro • 14x Pro Bowl

All-Decade Team: 1960s & 1970s •
All-Time Team: 75th & 100th Anniversaries

15-Year Career • 208 Games Played; 208 Started

91 Sacks (unofficial)

George Allen loved two things: coaching defense and having a dominating defensive line. The Rams became the perfect team for him to work his craft on when he became their head coach in 1966. And Merlin Olsen became an instant star for the Rams the moment he left Utah State and entered the league as the second of the Rams' two first-round picks in 1962. With Allen's defensive line, Deacon Jones and Lamar Lundy handled the end positions and newly acquired Rosey Grier and Olsen handled the inside. Olsen and Grier were both big men, standing over six feet, five inches tall and weighing nearly three hundred pounds. The combination of those four players gave Allen the basis of a great defense and doubled the Rams' win total from the prior year. The Rams were the second-best team in the NFL in points allowed and fourth in total defense under Allen in his first season as head coach. By his second season, they were first in points allowed, third in total defense, and no offensive line could handle the four defensive linemen.

Olsen was the glue that held it all together. He was fundamentally sound, played with relentless passion, and—for a man who went on to star as the titular

199

Father Murphy in the hit television show—displayed a nasty temperament. His disciplined play allowed Jones to take chances, moving out of his assigned area, and kept opposing teams from having any success running the ball. Olsen became the "Monarch of the Middle," impossible for any one man to block. He was a complete player on the field and a complete person off the field.

Olsen was remarkable in everything he attempted, from being a great color analyst after his playing days ended to becoming a wonderful actor, always playing roles befitting his quiet, outstanding character. Olsen would be a combination of two players today—Ndamukong Suh in terms of size and power and Fletcher Cox in terms of possessing the athletic skills and foot movement to attack the passer. Olsen never missed a game or snap, and he was beyond durable and dependable. Had Olsen not played under Allen, he still would be a Hall of Famer, but he might not have been able to win as many games or be part of a unit as dominating as the Rams' Fearsome Foursome.

GRIDIRON RULING

George Allen nearly didn't get to join the Rams as head coach. At the time he received the offer, he still had two years remaining on his contract with the Chicago Bears. Bears owner George Halas took him to court. On January 19, 1966, Judge Cornelius J. Harrington of the Circuit Court of Cook County ruled in favor of the Bears. Allen needed to complete his services with Chicago before accepting another position. But immediately after the ruling, Halas released Allen from the contract anyway. The suit was simply to prove a point about contracts. Halas said in court that day: "Validity of contracts was the issue here and your ruling will prevent the breakdown of organized sports and all sports. George Allen was a minor issue here." Like a great orator, Halas then took a long pause, and continued: "Now, I want to drop this suit and give Allen his full release. He can go to the Los Angeles Rams and he goes with my blessing." On that cold day in January, with the release of Allen, the Fearsome Foursome was born and Merlin Olsen's career was about to explode.

38
JIM PARKER

2x NFL Champion

9x First Team All-Pro • 1x Second Team All-Pro • 8x Pro Bowl

All-Decade Team: 1950s •
All-Time Team: 75th & 100th Anniversaries

11-Year Career • 135 Games Played; 133 Started

Former Ohio State football coach Woody Hayes loved reading military history and would often quote George Patton, his favorite general. Hayes loved a ground attack, punishing his opponents at the line of scrimmage by running the ball. He rarely liked passing, as he felt only three things could happen when the ball was in the air, and two of them were bad. Even as the college game began to incorporate more passing, Hayes remained steadfast in his resolve to keep pounding.

During his thirty-three-year coaching career (twenty-eight of them at Ohio), Hayes turned Ohio State into a national powerhouse. Jim Parker of Toledo, Ohio, had every school in the nation promising him the moon and the stars, but Hayes only promised him a great education and rewarding football career when they met. Parker said, "Woody didn't promise me the moon. He told me, 'You don't get anything on a silver platter here,' and I didn't. But I sent my brother Al to Ohio State after I left so he could be coached by Woody, and I want my son to learn football under him, too." Hayes loved Parker as a player and person, allowing him to stay at his home during his freshman year while acclimating himself to the college environment.

At Ohio State, Parker won the National Championship in 1954, the Outland Trophy, and even finished eighth in the Heisman, which was a rare feat for any offensive line. Parker then became the first-round pick of the Baltimore Colts in 1957 and a fixture in their offensive line at either left guard or left tackle, though Hayes told Colts head coach Weeb Ewbank that he felt defensive line was Parker's best position. Hayes wasn't wrong with his assessment. Parker was big, fast, strong, and had a defensive lineman's temperament. Opposing players bounced off him.

In his first game as a professional during the preseason, Parker pass protected more than during his four seasons in Columbus. His natural athletic talent allowed him to adapt to the pro game quickly, using his size and power to gain control of the lineman he faced. Playing on the left side of the line, in a right-handed stance, Parker was able to position himself and slide his feet in either direction quickly. In his game tape, he appeared larger than his listed six feet, three inches and 275 pounds. He moved with ease and was light on his feet. And even though he wasn't allowed to use his hands, he mastered the art of quickly controlling his man, and then readjusting his hands inside.

If Parker were in the game today, he would play guard, and his left hand would be on the ground. Larry Allen of the Cowboys is a good comparison. Even though Allen was heavier, they both were exceptional blocking for the run and manhandling their opponents.

Parker became the first offensive lineman selected for the Hall of Fame. He asked Hayes to present him. Hayes said, "Without question, [Parker] is the best offensive lineman in the ball game...Now, there have been a lot of great guards that have played football in those fifty years, but Jim Parker was picked as the best." Hayes was right.

37
WILLIE ROAF

6x First Team All-Pro • 3x Second Team All-Pro • 11x Pro Bowl

All-Decade Team: 1990s & 2000s

13-Year Career • 189 Games Played; 189 Started

Willie Roaf is alive because of football. Strange, but true. While at Michigan State, his father, Cliff Roaf, was friends and teammates with future Green Bay

Packers Hall of Fame defensive back Herb Adderley. Adderley's girlfriend at the time decided to set up Cliff on a blind date with Andree Layton, a deeply disciplined student who came from an intellectual family with high ambitions for her career. Cliff injured his knee in a game on the day of their date. But he ignored the pain and soldiered on to spend time with Andree. The knee injury eventually curtailed his playing career, but the date lasted a lifetime. Both found success in their professional lives—Cliff as a dentist and Andree as the first Black woman judge to sit on the Arkansas Supreme Court. Of their four children, their son Willie followed in his father's footsteps by playing football, despite his mother's plea to the contrary. Willie would hear his mother tell him, "Son, you better be glad I'm not God, because I would wave a wand over you, and football would be history." Fortunately for football fans from New Orleans and Kansas City, Judge Roaf didn't have that power.

In 1991, the Saints were experiencing changes all throughout their organization. Their team was getting older, their best players were no longer playing their best, and their general manager, Jim Finks, was battling lung cancer. Prior to the draft, they traded one of their superstars, outside linebacker twenty-nine-year-old Pat Swilling, to the Lions for the eighth pick overall in the draft. Finks believed the game was won in the trenches and with this top ten pick was going to select the best offensive lineman in the draft. Even though Lincoln Kennedy was playing at a higher level of competition at the University of Washington, Willie Roaf was the best player in all aspects on tape. Roaf was tough, smart, strong, and had the foot quickness to slide and secure the edge against any pass rusher in the league. It was hard to get through him or around him, as he could block out the sun.

Suffering an injury in 2001, Roaf considered retiring before being traded to the Chiefs for a conditional fourth-round pick that could become a third, if Roaf met certain playing time requirements. In addition, Roaf received a new contract, which made him one of the highest-paid linemen in the game. As Roaf played next to Pro Bowl guard Brian Waters in Kansas City, the Chiefs had one of the best run blocking and pass protection lines in football. During his four seasons in Kansas City, Roaf made the Pro Bowl each year. Unfortunately, his stellar performance didn't allow the Chiefs to win many playoff games, and they lost in Roaf's only appearance, in 2003. Roaf only played in three total playoff games, winning one and losing two. With Roaf and the surrounding talent on the Chiefs, along with a Hall of Fame coach in Dick Vermeil, one playoff win seems light.

At his Hall of Fame induction speech, Willie paid tribute to his deceased mother in closing his remarks by saying, "Finally, to my mother, the Honorable

Judge Roaf, looking down on this ceremony. No, Mom, I did not become a doctor, a lawyer, or a brain surgeon, but I did become a Pro Football Hall of Famer, and I know you're proud of me, and that's what matters to me the most." His mother would have been more than proud of her son, as Willie showed great dedication and attention to detail. He gained a doctorate in protecting the passer, and that diploma now resides in Canton.

36
BOBBY BELL

1x Super Bowl Champion • 2x AFL Champion •
1x NFL Defensive Player of the Year

1x First Team All-Pro • 1x Second Team All-Pro •
3x Pro Bowl • 6x AFL All-Star • 5x First Team All-AFL •
1x Second Team All-AFL • AFL All-Time Team

12-Year Career • 168 Games Played; 159 Started

26 Interceptions

Lamar Hunt came from a family of oil tycoons, but his interests were elsewhere. Seeing the promise of football—especially televised football—Hunt tried to leverage his family's wealth into the opportunity to join the old boys club of NFL ownership. Each time, he was rebuked, so he decided to invest in his own league. Along with seven other founders, known collectively as the "Foolish Club," Hunt formed the American Football League. Competing with the NFL for players was never part of Hunt's vision. As he recalled, "I told myself I didn't want to go into this if it meant some kind of battle." But that's just what happened. Once the league was formed, the fight for talent began.

In 1963, a battle raged between the NFL's Vikings and Hunt's Kansas City Chiefs over a University of Minnesota standout linebacker, Bobby Bell. Bell was a second-round pick of the Vikings in 1963, the sixteenth player selected overall. The AFL held their draft two days before the NFL and selected Bell in the seventh round, fifty-sixth overall. Minnesota fully expected to win this clash, offering Bell a three-year $62,000 contract, not fully guaranteed. But Hunt and the Chiefs countered with a five-year contract, $150,000 fully guaranteed, and Bell became a Chief. This investment might be the best one that Lamar Hunt ever made.

Standing six feet, four inches tall and weighing 220 pounds, Bell was the best athlete on the field, regardless of position. In college, his athletic skills were so recognizable that the Minnesota hockey and golf coaches asked him to join their teams—even though Bell had no experience in either sport. Bell aligned at outside linebacker, would drop into coverage, and was one of the best open-field tacklers in the game. Bell also played over the tight end, using his long arms to quickly shed the defender, and then burst to make the tackle.

During the 2022 season, Cowboys rookie Micah Parsons was playing lights out and dominating the game, causing writers to compare him to former Giants great Lawrence Taylor. When an NFL reporter asked his opinion of the comparison, Patriots head coach Bill Belichick was indifferent, saying, "There's nobody that really I could put in his category that I've coached." And he is right: Parsons doesn't play like Taylor; his game is like Bobby Bell's. The problem is that most writers don't remember Bell, or how amazingly Bell played. Had Bell played for the Chiefs today, he would do everything Parsons does, from rushing in a three-point stance to being the fifth rusher, off a two-point stance from his backer position, to dropping into coverage, defending the pass, and playing man-to-man on any potential back in the passing route. Bell would have benefited greatly from today's schemes and the need for athletes to be multidimensional in their skills.

"I can honestly say that Bobby Bell had as much talent as anyone I ever coached," Hank Stram, the Chiefs' longtime coach, once said. And Stram was correct. Bell helped the Chiefs win a Super Bowl in 1970, and more important, he helped the AFL become a legitimate league with his amazing play.

NUMBERS MATTER

Had I been at Minnesota or Kansas City, Bobby Bell would have worn a number more fitting for his rare skills. A player's number defines their skills and—trust me—there has never been a number 78 in all of football that had the skills, speed, and talent of Bell. There also will never be one in the future. When Bell played, offensive linemen had to wear a number from 50 to 79. Bell would have been the perfect 55, or even 51.

35
ALAN PAGE

1x NFL Champion • 1x NFL MVP, 1971 •
2x Defensive Player of the Year

6x First Team All-Pro • 3x Second Team All-Pro • 9x Pro Bowl

All-Time Team: 75th & 100th Anniversaries

16-Year Career • 218 Games Played; 215 Started

148.5 Sacks (unofficial) • 28 Blocked Kicks (unofficial)

In 1967, Notre Dame defensive tackle Alan Page joined defensive ends Carl Eller and Jim Marshall and fellow tackle Gary Larsen on the Minnesota Vikings defense, creating what would become the famous Purple People Eaters. Page was the missing link needed to take this talented group to the highest levels. He also became the only defensive lineman to be named MVP in 1971 and was a member of four Vikings Super Bowl teams. Page was highly intelligent and instinctive, and he would burst off the ball with insane quickness. Studying Page was a sheer joy, as his quickness was unlike that of anyone I've evaluated before, or since. I thought John Randle, Michael Dean Perry, and Warren Sapp had elite quickness, and they did, but Page was slightly quicker. In fact, there should be a term in scouting dedicated to his quickness, called "Page-turner quickness," and if any player comes close or matches his talent, then he gets the highest grade. We might be waiting a long time to see another six-foot-five man get off the ball like Mr. Page.

Playing in a nontraditional, left-handed stance for a defensive tackle, Page was an incredibly well-conditioned athlete. He could shed blocks and had an uncanny knack for batting passes down and blocking kicks. Unofficially, Page is credited with blocking twenty-eight kicks and numerous passes. Even though sacks were not officially recorded until after he retired, Page amassed 148.5 sacks over this sixteen-year career. That startling number doesn't include the quarterback hurries, which are far more important than sacks; sacks are often a result of the coverage or the quarterback holding the ball too long, but hurries create turnovers. When the quarterback feels the pressure, he throws the ball too early, thus allowing the defensive player to make a play on the ball as the receiver is not expecting the throw. Page was one of the best at hurrying a quarterback to throw the ball over his long arms, which was almost impossible.

During his career, Page became fanatical about his conditioning. When his wife, Diane, wanted to stop smoking, Page helped her quit her addiction by running with her each day in the off-season. Their joint runs became longer and longer, and eventually Page was running marathons. The constant running reduced his weight, causing a concern for the Vikings, to the point where they released him after six games in the 1978 season because they felt he could no longer play due to his lack of bulk. Immediately, Page was claimed by the rival Bears and went on to play three and a half seasons, starting every game and continuing to pressure and sack quarterbacks. It's hard to compare anyone today with Page because of his quickness and length. He would have been an amazing nickel rusher, creating havoc inside, and his skill set was ideally suited for playing in a spread offense game. Richard Seymour of the Patriots and member of the 2022 Hall of Fame might be a fair comparison in height and style, but not in domination.

Page became a lawyer, going to law school in the off-season, and he eventually became the first African American to ever sit on the Minnesota Supreme Court. He was awarded the Medal of Freedom in 2018 and continues his community work through the Page Education Foundation, whose mission is to encourage students of color develop their critical thinking skills. Page was a remarkable player and is a remarkable man.

BEDSIDE DRAFT

With a little more than a month left before the 1967 draft, the Vikings and general manager Jim Finks were in rough shape. Their Hall of Fame quarterback Fran Tarkenton was unhappy with the team and wanted to be traded. During his six years in Minnesota, Tarkenton only had one winning season. For much of his time, he was at war with Coach Norm Van Brocklin and the organization, but even after Van Brocklin surprisingly quit on February 12, 1967, Tarkenton remained steadfast in his desire to no longer be a Viking. He stated, "It comes as a great surprise to me that Norm has decided to resign, but in no way does it affect my decision." It's a good thing talk radio didn't exist then, or Jim Finks would have been feeling hotter than the inflamed gallbladder from which he was suffering at the time.

On March 8, six days before the draft began, Finks traded Tarkenton to the New York Giants for a first- and second-round draft choice in '67, a first-round choice in '68, and a second-round selection in '69. Two days later, he hired Winnipeg Blue Bomber head coach Bud Grant as his head man. While recovering from gallbladder surgery—while also in the throes of a painful tooth infection that would soon require multiple root canals—Finks turned his hospital room into a makeshift draft room. As he swabbed pain reliever on his sore teeth, he made his moves. With two picks in the first round, the Vikings look primed for a turnaround. After selecting running back Clint Jones from Michigan State with the pick acquired for Tarkenton, Finks then selected wide receiver Gene Washington with his original pick. Now, with the Rams holding the fifteen pick overall, Finks negotiated a trade, sending three-time Pro Bowl running back Tommy Mason and tight end Hal Bedsole, along with a second-round pick in 1967, to the Rams, and—with less than a minute remaining on the clock—selected Alan Page. That selection would eventually cure everything that ailed Finks.

With sore teeth and a healing wound, Finks created a roster that was able to compete at the highest level for the next decade. What looked like a doomed off-season in 1967 became the foundation for a team able to reach the Super Bowl four times, cementing Finks's legacy.

34
JACK HAM

4x Super Bowl Champion

6x First Team All-Pro • 2x Second Team All-Pro • 8x Pro Bowl

All-Decade Team: 1970s •
All-Time Team: 75th & 100th Anniversaries

12-Year Career • 162 Games Played; 160 Started

32 Interceptions

Steelers linebacker and second-year starter Jack Ham was the perfect Will line-backer, playing off the ball, away from the tight end, using his quickness after reading and diagnosing the play. Ham was a great tackler, though not the biggest backer. His foot quickness and burst allowed him to be in perfect position to bring the ball carrier to the ground. His style of play was clinical. When coaches wanted to show young players the art of playing linebacker, Ham's Steelers tape was the best example.

During the 1970s, Penn State earned the nickname "Linebacker U" because of Ham's sensational play. The Nittany Lions won twenty-two straight games in Ham's sophomore and junior seasons. In 1968, Penn State limited opposing teams to 10.9 points per game, and in 1969 that number shrunk down to 8.2 points per game, which is remarkable. With the stellar play of their linebackers and their dominating defense, Penn State became a destination spot of any young high schooler wanting to carry on their linebacker tradition. Charlie Zapiec, John Skorupan, Ed O'Neil, Greg Buttle, Kurt Allerman, Shane Conlan, Andre Collins, and LaVar Arrington all followed Ham at Penn State.

Because Ham was the gold standard, scouts and coaches often asked the Penn State staff if anyone was better than Ham, and the answer was always a surprising yes. As a young scout in 1986, not really understanding Ham's greatness was, I asked to see tape of Ham after the coaches openly claimed Shane

Conlan was a better player. I felt Conlan didn't have that Hall of Fame shine and needed to compare both players myself. After watching the Penn State Kansas Orange Bowl from 1969, I knew Ham clearly was the better player; it wasn't even close. That day, I learned Penn State coaches used Ham as their comparison to enhance their new players' value. It was a lie, as anyone who watched Ham's tape would know.

Ham's game was era proof. Reading, running, and making tackles on all levels of the defense is an ageless skill set for the NFL. Ham would be a three-down starting backer today, exceling in his coverage skills, and the offense could never remove him from the field regardless of the personnel group they enlisted. Devin White of the Bucs has a skill set that compares to Ham's, though he is not as consistently productive in impacting the passing game. In three seasons with the Bucs, White had one interception; Ham had eleven. In the NFL, we can compare many to Ham, and even tell the same lie the Penn State coaches told, yet in the end, few exceed Ham's talent.

THE IMMACULATE RECEPTION

Jack Ham participated in one of the most infamous games in football history. On December 23, 1972, Steelers running back Franco Harris caught a deflected pass for a sixty-yard touchdown reception against the Raiders. John Madden, coach of the Raiders, never saw an official signal touchdown, which always takes place whenever a player crosses the goal line. Fred Swearingen, the official for the game, and the other five referees huddled near the three-yard line where Harris had crossed to get their story straight. When the huddle broke, Swearingen went to the dugout to take a phone call. Whomever Swearingen talked to has been a highly classified secret since then, causing more conspiracy theories to emerge than the two phone calls that the accused presidential assassin Lee Harvey Oswald attempted to make from the Dallas police station. Who was on the other end of that call? It was shrouded in secrecy, and many (Al Davis and John Madden for sure) believe the call determined the outcome of the game—with the Steelers getting the win. That play is forever known as the "Immaculate Reception."

33
EMMITT SMITH

3x Super Bowl Champion • 1x Super Bowl MVP •
1x NFL MVP • 4x Rushing Leader •
3x Rushing Touchdown Leader • 1x NFL Scoring Leader

4x First Team All-Pro • 2x Second Team All-Pro • 8x Pro Bowl

All-Decade Team: 1990s • All-Time Team: 100th Anniversary

15-Year Career • 226 Games Played; 219 Started

4,409 Rushing Attempts • 18,355 Rushing Yards Gained •
164 Rushing Touchdowns

515 Receptions • 3,224 Receiving Yards Gained •
11 Receiving Touchdowns

University of Florida running back Emmitt Smith was the best player in the 1990 draft, if you had asked my dear friend and mentor Jerry Angelo, who was assisting Bucs head coach Ray Perkins at the time. Smith had impressive rushing numbers on the field, although many questioned his speed. When he didn't run at the NFL Combine, those questions were further ignited, until Smith worked out on the campus of Florida and displayed his talents. After the workout, the media cornered Bobby Beathard, general manager of the San Diego Chargers, for his opinion. He stated, "The one thing we wanted to see was if Emmitt can run, and he can run. What he did today confirms our suspicions that he can run fast. He did very well. He has good speed."

As Bill Walsh always said whenever discussing a college player's chances of success in the NFL, "Past performance predicts future achievement." Walsh was obsessed about learning every single detail about what a player accomplished during his high school career; the past mattered to him. For the rest of my scouting career, reviewing a player's past was the beginning of every player evaluation. Reading the media guides to understand the playing journey of a player became as important as the game film.

When you read about Smith's accomplishments in high school, it soothed any concerns. He won two state championships, gained 8,804 rushing yards, and scored 106 touchdowns. What more could one player accomplish? But Angelo couldn't sell Perkins on drafting Smith, who slid all the way down to the seventeenth spot, where the Cowboys' Jimmy Johnson made him their pick. Johnson had tried in vain to recruit Smith out of high school for his Miami Hurricanes and wasn't concerned at all about Smith's speed or lack of size. Once Smith arrived in Dallas, he did what he did in high school and college: he dominated.

Running back is an instinctive position, and Smith might not have timed the fastest, but he played the fastest. Playing speed over timed speed matters because players with great instincts always look faster on tape. Smith's natural running style, shiftiness, and ability to break tackles wasn't just good; it was rare. He had a burst in and out of the hole, with a sudden change of speed, and the balance to remain on his feet was incredible.

Smith was a workhorse who became an even better player in the fourth quarter. Even at the age of thirty, which is old for a running back, Smith still carried the ball 329 times and gained 1,397 yards in fifteen games. The longer the game, the stronger Smith became. Angelo's instincts on Smith were correct. Smith proved the Buccaneers' loss was the Cowboys' gain.

32
RAY LEWIS

2x Super Bowl Champion • 1x Super Bowl MVP 35 •
2x Defensive Player of the Year • 3x NFL Tackle Leader

7x First Team All-Pro • 3x Second Team All-Pro • 13x Pro Bowl

All-Decade Team: 2000s • All-Time Team: 100th Anniversary

17-Year Career • 228 Games Played; 227 Started

"Michael, you have a second?" asked Jim Schwartz, the scouting assistant who shared the office next to mine back in 1995. Schwartz oversaw reading every Cleveland Browns scouting report written to ensure they were free of error and utilized the grading system correctly. After reading, Jim would develop a profile reel showcasing the player's talents. The words on the paper needed to match the screen, and Schwartz was excellent at monitoring the quality control of the scout's work. I strolled into his office, where a TV glowed with a game involving Virginia Tech and the University of Miami. Schwartz hit play on the remote, with his index finger pointed to the player on which he wanted me to hone in. The Virginia Tech ball carrier started to the left, then pivoted right and escaped down the sideline, appearing to have a clear path toward the end zone. But then Miami's number 52 jumped off the screen with his burst and acceleration, running down the ball carrier at the ten-yard line from across the field. It was an amazing display of speed and relentless determination from the one and only Ray Lewis, whom Schwartz had loved since the prior spring, when he had observed all the college players at the Playboy All-American. Lewis displayed a magnetic personality and leadership ability. After rewatching the play multiple times, we looked at one another and said, "Let's hope he makes it to our pick."

Schwartz later moved over to the Baltimore Raiders, where he was able to realize his vision and bring Lewis on. There were some concerns about Lewis's size, that he might be too small or light—like the concerns people once had about Jack Lambert—but that went away as soon as Lewis arrived. Lewis had great instincts for the position, combined with his power and great balance—he also won the Florida 4A wrestling championship in high school. Understanding his size limitations, Lewis carried his wrestling skills over to football. He would say, "Wrestling is still one of the reasons why I swivel my hips; it's been everything for me. The principles that you learn in wrestling, none of that changes. It carries over, and if you stick to those things, the low man always wins." And Lewis was always the low man.

Lewis's intense, competitive personality became the personality of the Ravens. They became his team, and even though they struggled to consistently move the ball on offense, their defense was able to gain control of games. Lewis made those around him better, which is hard for any position on the field other than quarterback. Though Lambert paved the way for slender middle linebackers to have a place in the game, Lewis took it to another level. There might be another middle linebacker with his instincts, competitive drive, and speed, but it is doubtful there will be another one who can transform an organization.

EVALUATE IN PERSON

One of the hardest and most critical evaluations occurs when attempting to judge the overall speed of a specific unit. For example, when the Raiders were getting ready to host the Ravens in the 2000 AFC Championship game, everyone knew the Ravens were great on defense with explosive players on all three levels. The coaches and scouts watched them dominate the Broncos, then go on the road and soundly beat a good Tennessee Titans team before our matchup. We knew the game was going to be a challenge from start to finish. What I personally didn't realize from studying the tape was how much faster they were in person. The tape didn't do them justice: they were far more explosive than I had imagined, and at times there appeared to be two number 52s on the field, as Lewis was all over. Without seeing the Ravens live and in person beforehand, judging their speed off the tape proved diagnostically wrong. They held us to three points, knocked our starting quarterback, Rich Gannon, out of the game in the first quarter, and soundly beat us in all facets of the game. During that playoff run, the Ravens allowed twenty-three points in four games, 5.7 per game, which is insane. From that moment, I made it a rule to always evaluate in person—which two years later I violated because of a scheduling quirk. And it proved costly.

31
FORREST GREGG

3x Super Bowl Champion • 5x NFL Champion

7x First All-Pro • 2x Second Team All-Pro • 9x Pro Bowl

All-Decade Team: 1960s •

All-Time Team: 75th & 100th Anniversaries

15-Year Career • 193 Games Played; 156 Started

In the 1966 Green Bay Packers offensive playbook, head coach Vince Lombardi detailed his requirements for each position. Below is the offensive tackle position, quoted directly from the book:

Offensive Tackle

Largest - Bob Brown, Philadelphia	*6'5" 280*
Average	*6'4" 249*
Smallest - Frank Varrichione, Los Angeles	*6'1" 235*

Basic Requirements and Information:

Pass protection is the most important quality. He needs the agility and balance to handle good defensive ends. Pass blocking will occupy 50% of his time. Quickness and strength at the point, plus speed to pull on pitchouts are necessary.

Speed: 5.4 seconds for 40 yards in shorts and football shoes.

Forrest Gregg met all these requirements, and then some. He was the gold standard for offensive linemen from his era because he could do everything on the Lombardi criteria list at guard or tackle. His ability to run and block in space allowed the Packers sweep to become their defining play, which was a priority for Lombardi when he arrived in Green Bay. He loved the sweep because it was a hard-nose play. Lombardi said, "Gentleman, this is the most important play we have. It is the play we must make go. It's the play we will make go. It's the play we will run again and again and again."

Gregg was a key component of making the sweep effective, and often played guard when the situation warranted. Offensive linemen from the "no extension of hands" era often appeared off-balance and always in danger of losing the block, which is natural, considering they had to keep their hands inside with their forearms doing most of the work. They had to lead with their heads and shiver their forearms to gain control of the man they blocked. Gregg was excellent at doing both. With his toughness and balance, he could even handle the Rams' Deacon Jones's famous head slap, which tormented offensive linemen throughout the league.

When I was fourteen years old, I found just one present waiting for me under the Christmas tree. This was highly unusual for my mother. Though we weren't poor (nor were we rich) Christmas was a special time for our family, and my mother normally overspent. This one gift was so expensive and valuable that it was all I needed or wanted—the two-volume *Lombardi on Football*, housed in a green slipcase. Those volumes allowed me to enter a world I had only dreamed about, making it all seem achievable. The color pictures were amazing. I stared at those beautiful green jerseys on the field for hours. On page 105, there was a black-and-white closeup picture of Gregg's face, with mud everywhere from his neck to above his eyes. Blades of grass were still attached to his helmet, his chin strap was unbuttoned, and his eyes peered back, oblivious of the camera. The accompanying page featured the following quote from Lombardi: "Forrest Gregg is, quite simply, the finest football player I ever coached." Today, the book still sits on my bookshelf.

THE PACKERS SWEEP

Even though Lombardi highlighted the hole for the back to run, the essence of the play was to run to daylight. Once the back determined the point on the field where the defense was cut in half by Lombardi's famous seal, then he would plant and run. The Packers sweep is a version of the outside zone today, with slightly different blocking from the line in terms of techniques and pulling, but the planting to run off the cut of the defense is vintage Lombardi. Every team knew the sweep was coming, and yet they were defenseless in stopping the play, solidifying the point that to be a great team you must have tendencies. Great teams don't trick their opponents; they outexecute them with their talent, performing at the highest level.

30
JOHN HANNAH

7x First Team All-Pro • 3x Second Team All-Pro • 9x Pro Bowl

All-Decade Team: 1970s & 1980s •

All-Time Team: 75th & 100th Anniversaries

13-Year Career • 183 Games Played; 183 Started

If Michelangelo sculpted the prototypical guard, John Hannah, with tree-trunk legs and thighs thirteen inches in diameter, would've been his model. He might not have met the height standard for the guard position, but he exceeded in every skill set needed for the position. Hannah was perhaps the finest offensive linesman in the game.

Besides being strong, powerful, and able to leap tall buildings in a single bound, Hannah was fast. I mean, really fast. He ran effortlessly. He could generate raw power from his lower body because of his ability to bend. Hannah had the flexibility of a four-year-old, and was able to sink his hips all the way to the ground. Had he been a catcher in baseball, his ass would touch the dirt. The older a player gets, the harder it is to remain flexible, but not for Hannah. When they ran his favorite play, Flow 36—which required him to pull and run to his right and lead the back off tackle—Hannah was a dancing bear, with great speed, body control, and power. New England Patriots personnel director Francis Joseph "Bucko" Kilroy once said, "For all his size and explosiveness and straight-ahead speed, John had something none others ever had, and that's phenomenal, repeat phenomenal, lateral agility and balance, the same as a defensive back."

Hannah was gifted in everything he did athletically. He won the SEC discus and shot put championship as a senior and won the National Prep Championship as a wrestler. The shot, discus, and wrestling can all translate to playing offensive line. It takes foot quickness and lower-body power to throw both the

BUCKO'S LEGACY

From his hometown of Philadelphia, Francis Joseph "Bucko" Kilroy lived a life of football—he was a top-level guard at Northeast High School and one of the best players in Temple football history. During the war, he played for the "Steagles," a combination of Eagles and Steelers players, and then made the All-Decade team with the Eagles from 1944 to 1955. In his fourth game as a pro, Kilroy faced off against the Bears, who had just brought Bronko Nagurski back after a five-year layoff. Kilroy lined up against Nagurski—matching his power and toughness—and at that moment, he knew he belonged in the NFL. He was tougher than nails; some might say dirty. He played in 147 consecutive games, only missing one game over his 203-game NFL career. He started both ways for the 1948 and '49 Eagles, leading their running game. And over his career, he had five interceptions. Leaving the City of Brotherly Love, Kilroy helped the Cowboys develop their famous grading system, and then became the director of player personnel for the New England Patriots, where he drafted two Hall of Fame players for the Patriots—John Hannah and later cornerback Mike Haynes in 1976.

Everyone had a funny story about Bucko, from his playing days to his career as an executive. When you attended college all-star games before the age of computers and digital video, you'd experience a great deal of dead time between practices and interviews with the players. Scouts from other teams would hang with one another, often sharing a meal. The bond those men shared was undeniable, and they maintained their friendships, even as competitors. In a restaurant booth in downtown Mobile, Alabama, current and former Cowboys employees were preparing for their annual get-together. (The Cowboys had an incredible farm system of scouts and developed a complex grading system so sophisticated that rival teams would hire one of their scouts, and then promote them to a director position.) The group included Cowboys vice president Gil Brandt, Seattle personnel man Dick Mansperger, Cowboys scout Red Hickey, and our man Bucko Kilroy. When Kilroy went off to the bathroom, the other three men decided to play a little joke on him, inventing a player from a small school in North Dakota. Kilroy, who prided himself on knowing every single detail about every player, would be caught off guard, or so they thought. When Kilroy returned to his seat, they continued to talk positively about this fabricated player, discussing in detail the positive traits he possessed. When Brandt finally asked Bucko what he had on the player, Bucko said, "low test score," without blinking.

The stories about Kilroy sometimes take away from the impact he made on the Patriots, particularly the 1985 team, which played the Bears (and lost) in Super Bowl XX. I loved shaking his hand, a hand that still had the wear and tear of an offensive lineman or a seasoned construction worker—large, hardened, and with fingers that had been broken several times and pointed in various directions. We shared a common bond of our love for Philadelphia, and I loved hearing him tell stories of the past and how scouting developed. The man did it all, and then some.

discus and the shot. It takes balance, power, and quickness to wrestle. No wonder Hannah dominated on the football field. With his rare traits, Hannah could have played any position. There are times when I watched him run, leading the sweep, that I thought that had he been a running back, he might have been the best ever. I am not kidding.

29
ED REED

1x Super Bowl Champion • 1x NFL Defensive Player
of the Year • 3x NFL Interception Leader

5x First Team All-Pro • 3x Second Team All-Pro • 9x Pro Bowl

All-Decade Team: 2000s • All-Time Team: 100th Anniversary

12-Year Career • 174 Games Played; 169 Started

64 Interceptions; 7 Returned for Touchdowns

64 Interceptions • 7 Touchdowns • 9 Career Postseason
Interceptions (tied for NFL record); 1 Returned for Touchdown

There are three types of drafters. The first is "The Static Drafter." This person rarely trades during the draft, up or down. They remain inactive during the day, and other teams know they can maneuver around them, as they are unwilling to trade. The Cincinnati Bengals under owner Mike Brown fell into this category, as did the New York Giants when former general manager George Young was in complete charge.

The second is "The Lover." This person falls in love with one player and will move mountain and earth to acquire him regardless of the cost. Al Davis was a lover, and so was Bobby Beathard of the Washington Redskins and San Diego Chargers. When Sean Payton was head coach of New Orleans, he would often fall in love and make a deal to acquire the team's perfect love partner.

The third is "The Flockier." This team values the horizontal board, never loves one player, and is willing to move down if there is a flock of players available, not caring about one position. Being a Flockier helps remove internal bias, which often ruins a draft. Currently, the Eagles, at times the Patriots, and the Ravens fit this category.

So how do the three drafting profiles apply to Ed Reed? Let me explain. During the 2002 NFL draft, Ozzie Newsome, the man in charge (written in his contract) for the Ravens, held the twenty-fourth pick in the first round. Newsome never fell in love with one player and always ran his draft with a flocking mentality. In 2002, he had twenty-three players with first-round grades on his board, preferring Arizona State offensive tackle Levi Jones, Boston College running back William Green, or Northwestern linebacker Napoleon Harris. When the Raiders took Harris (that's another story), Newsome was left with no one worthy to select based on his board, which for Newsome meant he had to trade down. Newsome needed to get to an area that justified his grades, or else he would be reaching. Newsome is a Flockier as is evidenced by his not overreacting and becoming impatient when all three players were quickly picked by other teams. If a team with a Lover philosophy had seen Jones go at ten and Green at sixteen, they would have panicked and made a deal to move up to acquire Harris. Not Newsome. He would either pick Harris or trade down to another flock, never believing he might be static.

Trading down is a wonderful idea until you can't find a team to trade with. As Bill Walsh would often say, "We can't pass." After exhausting all options to move down, if none are available, a player needs to be selected. "We got wiped out," Ozzie Newsome said on April 20, 2002. With no trade partner, the Ravens selected safety Ed Reed from the University of Miami, a player who wasn't the biggest, or fastest, but who ended becoming the only Hall of Fame player from the draft (so far, as Julius Peppers will join him shortly, when eligible). All three players Newsome originally wanted ended up not being worthy of the pick. Some might say Newsome got lucky, which to a degree is true, yet he still thought highly enough of Reed to have him in his flock.

Ed Reed's draft story is a glaring indication of how broken the draft process has become over the last twenty years. Perception rules, and if a team doesn't follow the expected route, their draft grade becomes bad, and their fan base becomes outraged. After Reed was drafted by the Ravens (the twenty-fourth pick in the first round), the headline in the *Baltimore Sun* read: "Reed: Solid, not sizzling." Two years later, he wasn't just sizzling—he became the NFL's defensive player of the year.

Reed played the game as if he had a listening device in the opponent's huddle. He never wasted a step, was always in the right place at the right time, and controlled the middle of the field, making quarterbacks aware of his location. He covered ground from one sideline to another, played faster than his timed speed, and hit harder than his weight. He was someone the quarterback had to account for on every single play, run, or pass.

The number one job of any quarterback—pre- or postsnap—is to determine if the middle of the field is open or closed. Open means there isn't a center fielder; closed means there is. Not too complicated, correct? Reed often fooled the quarterback by being near the line of scrimmage, and instead of running toward the deep part of the field, he would ignore his assignment and play the play. To imply Reed was guessing would be a mischaracterization. He never guessed; he knew. Reed played football the way Arnold Rothstein, the man who fixed the 1919 World Series, gambled. Rothstein once said, "I create my luck. I'm a successful gambler because I never bet on an event I'm not sure of in advance." Reed was always sure, which is why he is tied for the most interceptions in the postseason and leads the NFL in return yards off interceptions. You don't make as many plays as Reed made by guessing.

Reed played the game with incredible passion and enthusiasm. He made every quarterback nervous. Tom Brady, sitting in Bill Belichick's office while breaking down the Ravens' defense, said, "Every time you break the huddle, Reed is who I am looking for." Reed defied logic within the structure of the defense. He made life impossible for people like Belichick and Brady, who want to attack the logic of the defense. Reed never allowed them to hack his code. He was the antispyware safety, predictably unpredictable, and he infuriated perfectionists like Belichick and Brady.

What Reed lacked in measurables, he made up for in his uncanny understanding of how to play the game in all phases. His hands were incredible, and once he had the ball, he was hard to tackle. No one today can duplicate how Reed played. His uniqueness of play, attention to detail, and understanding of the game are rare, and we might never see anyone like him again.

28
LARRY ALLEN

1x Super Bowl Champion

7x First Team All-Pro • 11x Pro Bowl

All-Decade Team: 1992s & 2000s •
All-Time Team: 100th Anniversary

14-Year Career • 203 Games Played; 197 Started

Throughout my years of scouting, I have learned that no skill result or test score can tell the entire story of a player. Any result becomes a starting point, especially when dealing with the Wonderlic test score and Cowboy great Larry Allen.

Eldon E. F. Wonderlic, working at the Household Finance Corporation in 1936, was tasked with finding a more efficient way of predicting the success rate of potential hires. Wonderlic understood past performance predicts future achievement, but how can you predict someone's ability fresh out of college or entering the workforce for the first time? Wonderlic dove deep into understanding cognitive behavior, discovering that different jobs had different cognitive demands, ranging from very low to very high, and that there were distinct IQs associated with each job. With this knowledge, Wonderlic developed a twelve-minute test that was easy to administer and grade and became a popular measuring tool of intelligence for corporations across the country.

In 1961, the Wonderlic test gained interest from the Dallas Cowboys personnel director Gil Brandt. Brandt and the Cowboys were ahead of their time, developing a grading system for players by using military concepts and giving the Wonderlic to potential prospects. Other NFL teams followed suit and the Wonderlic became a standard testing instrument for deciding a player's level of intelligence based on certain positions.

The test results offered a starting point, but not the full picture, and each team viewed them differently. Some treated the results as the gospel and would remove players from their draftable board if their score didn't meet the acceptable level for the position. Others, like the Raiders' Al Davis, ignored the test completely, believing coaches needed to find ways to teach the players the system, regardless of their innate intelligence. In Cleveland, Bill Belichick had each position group assigned a threshold of acceptance, and if a player scored below, he was given a letter grade of M (signifying a mental concern). The M didn't remove the player from our draft board, but it required we do more work. Offensive linemen normally scored high on the test, which is why, in Cleveland, we wanted at least a grade of correct answers to prevent the M from being assigned. Besides the mental aspect of the grade, the score also indicated an ability to focus and concentrate, which is a critical for all linemen. All linemen suffer aches and pains because of the violent nature of the position. If the pain detracts from their ability to focus, resulting in misassignments or false starts, that needs to be fully analyzed. For example, if a player has a low test score and a high number of penalties, mostly false starts, then the two combined indicate a problem, requiring more investigation.

Hoping to enhance our player development, we blended coaching and scouting together in Cleveland. Scout Pat Hill also worked in coaching to help Kirk Ferentz with the offensive line. Hill would work out players during the spring as we prepared for the college draft. Larry Allen from tiny little Sonoma State was on Hill's list, but with a caveat. Though our grade on Allen was high and perfectly represented his talent in the field, Allen scored low on his Wonderlic text, resulting in an M being placed next to his name. When researching Allen's background, Hill learned that academic trouble followed the player from school to school, preventing him from attending a Division I program worthy of his enormous talents.

We wanted to avoid what we called a "national anthem player," which was a player who learned something one day and forget everything by the next—each day was like the start of a new game, beginning with the national anthem being performed. Hill visited Allen and administered a recall test about our run game and pass protections. If Allen could handle this assignment, then we would remove the M from his grade. Sure enough, he did. Allen wasn't a national anthem player. Though he wasn't a great test student in the classroom, he was a great football player who could learn and retain.

Allen was selected in the second round of the 1994 draft, and dominated from his first day. With his powerful upper body, Allen controlled defensive linemen much in the way that Hakuhō Shō, the greatest sumo wrestler of all time, controlled his opponent. Allen, who once bench-pressed 225 pounds forty-three times, was able to translate that power to the field. Even though the bench press is used as an indicator of strength by NFL teams, some players are unable to convey the power to the field. Allen could roll his hips and uncoil, which then allowed him to use the bench-press power on the field, making him an explosive blocker. Combining his power with toughness and competitive drive, Allen, like Shō, would pin his man to the turf and never stop until the whistle ended the play. The success of the Cowboys' running game had as much to do with Allen's domination as anything. Even though Allen was shorter than most teams would want for left tackle, he could handle the assignment with his quick feet and lateral movement. He wasn't the ideal height; he was the ideal athlete.

The results of the Wonderlic were never foolproof. The grade only offers a starting point, proven by Allen being able to function at an incredible level with a lower score. What the Wonderlic has taught me over the years is the same thing that college test scores reveal—some people can take tests; some can't. Don't just accept the grade.

27
BOB LILLY

1x Super Bowl Champion

7x First Team All-Pro • 2x Second Team All-Pro • 11x Pro Bowl

All-Decade Team: 1960s & 1970s •
All-Time Team: 75th & 100th Anniversaries

14-Year Career • 196 Games Played; 196 Started

95.5 Sacks (unofficial)

In 1967, on a Wisconsin day so bitter cold that Cowboys personnel director Gil Brandt bought the fur boots off his driver on the way to the game, the 'Boys faced off against the Packers. It was New Year's Eve, and with temperatures reaching eighteen degrees below zero, the game went down in history as "The Ice Bowl." Every inch of Cowboys defensive tackle Bob Lilly was cold. But Lilly was the ultimate warrior, never missing a game during his amazing fourteen-year career, and the bitter cold on this day, before America welcomed in 1968, wasn't going to prevent him from playing his best.

Seven years earlier, on December 27, 1960, the Cowboys made their first-ever draft selection, picking thirteenth in the first round and securing defensive linesman Bob Lilly. He was the perfect player for the Tom Landry Flex defense and the foundation for the Cowboys' "Doomsday Defense." Standing six feet, five inches tall and weighing a lean 270 pounds, Lilly was tremendous in every facet of the game. He was strong and sturdy at the point. He had excellent quickness to penetrate. His speed was outstanding for running plays down from sideline to sideline, and he had amazing burst off the blocker to the ball carrier. Lilly was also an excellent tackler, which is often an overlooked quality in defensive linemen. Due to the close nature of the area defensive tackles operate, tackling isn't emphasized as a necessary skill. The back comes rambling into the hole, which is filled with bodies, allowing the defensive tackle to use his full body to bring down the ball carrier. Lilly exceled by extending his long arms and using the power in his hands and upper body to bring down the quarterback. Too often today, defensive linemen "just miss" the quarterback; they get their hands on him without being able to bring him down. Great defensive linemen are great tacklers because of the power in their hands, and Lilly was the shining example of this rare quality.

Lilly was consistent in his play on the field as well as in his behavior off the field, and he continued to improve his conditioning, quickness, and strength. By his sixth season, he began to incorporate weight training into his off-season program, allowing him to augment his natural strength. His quiet determination and toughness never stopped from the moment the whistle started the game until the end. The bigger the game, the better Lilly played. He became known as "Mr. Cowboy" for his perfect representation of the Cowboys on and off the field—the model of consistency.

On that frozen field on New Year's Eve, Lilly behaved like a hitter stepping into the batter's box, using his spikes to soften the field, giving him more traction. Thirteen seconds were left on the clock and the ball was on the Cowboys' one-yard line. Lilly kicked back his legs, got as low as he could, aligning in the A gap to the defensive right (Packers quarterback Bart Starr's left). Starr barked out the cadence, and once the ball entered his hands, he moved in the other direction, away from Lilly. Starr's Hall of Fame guard Jerry Kramer and center Ken Bowman blocked left defensive tackle Jethro Pugh, allowing Starr to make a historic dive for the score, winning the game. Had Starr run the ball in Lilly's direction, the course of NFL history would've been altered, because Lilly, with his amazing quickness and strong hands, never would've let Starr get by.

26
ROD WOODSON

1x Super Bowl Champion • 1x NFL Defensive Player
of the Year • 2x NFL Interception Leader

6x First Team All-Pro • 3x Second Team All-Pro • 11x Pro Bowl

All-Decade Team: 1990s •
All-Time Team: 75th & 100th Anniversaries

17-Year Career • 238 Games Played; 229 Started

71 Interceptions; 12 Returned for Touchdowns

From the first day Rod Woodson made the trip south from his home in Ft. Wayne, Indiana, to the football office of Purdue, he requested, then begged, and finally pleaded for head football coach Leon Burtnett to allow him to play offense. During his senior season, Woodson played off and on at receiver, catching twenty-two passes, but in the last game, he became a two-way player. "The plan was to play him as many plays as he wanted," Burtnett said.

Woodson's stat line for the game featured the following:

- Ten tackles, including seven unassisted
- One pass breakup
- One forced fumble
- Fifteen rushing attempts for ninety-three yards
- Three receptions for sixty-seven yards
- Two kickoff returns totaling forty-six yards
- Three punt returns for thirty yards

To label Woodson strictly a defensive back would be unfair. Yes, it was the position he played during his seventeen-year NFL career, but his talent extended way beyond a single position. Woodson was a Hall of Fame player who happened to play defensive back. He would have been a Hall of Fame player in any position he played because of his dynamic athleticism.

Woodson's elite talent made him the definition of a four-down player. With his ability to return punts and kicks, he was dangerous any time the ball reached his hands. His running instincts were exceptional, combining with his great balance and speed, which made him hard to tackle. (He was also the Big 10 five-time champion in 60- and 110-meter hurdles, and in 1984, he went on to qualify in the Olympic trials.)

When Woodson played defensive corner, he was always willing to take chances, and often an offensive team would attempt a double-move pass route (this occurs when a receiver runs a short or intermediate route and suddenly converts to a deep pass), causing Woodson to guess wrong. It might've happened once, but never twice. Woodson was too smart for that. When Woodson moved from corner to safety, he did so effortlessly because his instincts were sensational no matter the position.

In 2002, the Raiders started the season 4–0, and then suddenly lost four in a row. On Monday night in Denver, as they played their rival, the Broncos, head coach Mike Shanahan was convinced a loss would send the team home for the season without a playoff appearance. On the opening drive of the game, the Raiders took a 3–0 lead. The Broncos then drove the ball down the field, ready to take the lead. From the Raiders' four-yard line, Bronco quarterback Brian Griese attempted to throw a pass over the middle to running back Clinton Portis, and out of nowhere comes Woodson, intercepting the pass and taking it to the house for a Raiders touchdown and a 10–0 lead. The play saved the Raiders' 2002 season and propelled them to making a Super Bowl appearance against the Tampa Bay Bucs. It was emblematic of so many of Woodson's plays during his career.

Woodson was amazing to watch from a competitor's chair while I was in Cleveland and more fun to observe when we were on the same team in Oakland. Anywhere Woodson played, Canton was always going to call.

SEEING THE GAME THROUGH BOTH EYES

Woodson was successful because he was able to see the entire game visually through both eyes. For example, when a right corner (right and left are determined from the back of the defense looking toward the offense) aligns, the bulk of the action takes place to his inside; therefore, he sees the game through his left eye. Every play comes from his left, and his peripheral vision streams through his left eye. When a team attempts to move a corner with only one eye of vision inside, he lacks the awareness to compensate. He has become accustomed to seeing the game one way, and when moving to safety, the game is now harder to understand. This is because moving from corner to safety the width and the length of the field are entirely different and the corner's view of the ball becomes impaired. Woodson saw the game, regardless of his position, through both eyes.

LEVEL FIVE: THE ELITE

What is the common thread that makes the simple distinction from great to being one of the game's best ever? Many players have graced the gridiron with Hall of Fame talent, but they don't have a bust in Canton because they didn't have a Hall of Fame career. The players in the elite section of this book have one commonality: longevity. Athletes who become elite in their chosen sport constantly perform at a high level, impacting their game, the team, and most of all, the scoreboard.

Elite players don't need an explanation for their athletic skills. Their drive, their motivation, and their pursuit of greatness are what make them unique. Seriously, how many times can a person describe Barry Sanders's lateral quickness or Deacon Jones's favorite head slap? Their exclusive stories speak for themselves in terms of how they impacted the sport when they played and after. As we discuss the top twenty-five players, their stories will vary—from history lessons to journeys players endured to become the best of the best—to illustrate why these titans of the sport are truly elite.

25
WALTER PAYTON

1x Super Bowl Champion • 1x NFL MVP •
1x Rushing Leader • 1x Rushing Touchdown Leader

5x First Team All-Pro • 3x Second Team All-Pro • 9x Pro Bowl

All-Decade Team: 1970s & 1980s •
All-Time Team: 75th & 100th Anniversaries

13-Year Career • 192 Games Played; 184 Started

110 Rushing Touchdowns • 15 Receiving Touchdowns

Sometimes the result of heads or tails can make all the difference in the world. For example, determining the selection order of the 1975 draft between the Browns and the Bears required a flip of the coin. Whoever won the toss would pick fourth overall and the loser would select fifth. Bears owner George Halas knew not only that one player with unique talents could make all the difference in his team, but that one spot could make all the difference in the draft. Halas also knew from talking to Cleveland's director of player personnel at the time, Bob Nussbaumer, that the Browns' draft priorities were defensive end and wide receiver. Yet if a certain player was available, the needs of the team could be insignificant. Halas made the right call and the Bears landed Walter Payton as the fourth overall pick. After completing their remaining picks, Halas said, "We certainly did one thing. We helped our needs. I'm so enthused with the whole thing. I think it's the finest Bear draft in ten years."

The choice of Payton assured Halas's assessment was correct. Payton was dynamic from the start. Even though he wasn't the biggest runner, he played bigger than his size. He could run over tacklers with his nonstop leg action, which would often be on full display as he burst into the air—like "The Great Farini," a nineteenth-century human cannonball—and landing in the end zone.

Payton had great command of his running style, mixing up his pattern like a great baseball pitcher who can throw a hundred-mile-an hour fastball, an amazing slider, and a killer changeup. By shifting and changing speeds, Payton used his stutter-and-go move to lure the tackler into believing he might change direction laterally, but then charge ahead with his head down, making tacklers miss or fall off him. His stiff arm was as lethal as a Mike Tyson jab. He was able to make tacklers pay a price for getting too close.

During his fourteen-year career, Payton carried the ball over three hundred times for all but three seasons: his first, last, and one in the middle (1982). Since 2017, the NFL has only had eight runners who have carried the ball over three hundred carries in one season, and only two have done it twice—Derrick Henry of the Titans and Zeke Elliott of the Cowboys. It was routine for Payton to carry the load of the Bears' offense, and because of his conditioning habits and dedication, he never wore down, despite his size.

Payton pushed himself to become the best. He was a complete back, taking great pride in performing his best in running, blocking, and catching. Over the course of their 1985 season, the Bears outscored their opponents by 258 points and became the winners of Super Bowl XX. Payton was equally amazing that season. At the tender age of thirty-one, Payton averaged 4.8 yards per carry—the second best in his career—and gained 1,551 yards on the ground, carrying the ball 324 times.

Unlike "Papa Bear" Halas, Payton was never going to settle on a coin flip to decide the quality of his career. He did everything in his power to assure himself the odds were in his favor. And we all benefited from watching him play.

24
DICK "NIGHT TRAIN" LANE

2x NFL Interception Leader

7x First Team All-Pro • 3x Second Team All-Pro • 7x Pro Bowl

All-Decade Team: 1950s •
All-Time Team: 50th & 75th Anniversaries

14-Year Career • 157 Games Played; 143 Started

68 Interceptions; 5 Returned for Touchdowns

The 1963 Detroit Lions secondary, coached by Don Shula, consisted of four future Hall of Fame players, including Dick LeBeau, Yale Lary, Lem Barney, and perhaps the best of them all, defensive back Dick "Night Train" Lane. Lane was a terror, and played the game with an unorthodox style and physicality. Lane had an innate ability to theorize and strategize the game, often confronting Shula (in a nice way) about how to play the angles of the game and how the angles affected his coverage on the receivers in relation to his teammates. When Lane first entered the league, he was getting beat on deep passes and often playing out of control. He worked alone late into the night on his footwork and angles, talking and cussing to himself out for his poor body placement on the receiver, which created a problem in his coverage. Once Night Train determined how to solve his problem, he then became a nightmare for the receivers he covered and anyone he tackled.

When you walk into an NFL locker room today, there is a huge sign detailing the correct way to tackle, with an emphasis on seeing where you're headed, not lowering your head and using your helmet as a weapon. Lane often led with his head, trying to knock the runner out. When the NFL started to cover the faces of their players with plastic protecting their mouth and eyes, Lane used the plastic device as a way to bring down the runner. Since face masking wasn't a violation, it became one after Lane kept ripping helmets off heads. When he started to clothesline runners as a tackle, the NFL passed another rule outlawing the move. None of these rule changes made Lane slow down his aggressiveness. He played the game with no regard for his body. He would extend himself using the full force of his momentum to derail the runner in his tracks. There was no form tackling with Lane. He was relentless and fearless. His size and power proved effective when supporting the run, and his speed and hands were equally effective when playing the pass.

Lane was also an effective four-down player, helping in the kicking game. Most thought Lane took too many chances with his guessing. But great corners never guess; they anticipate, with a tactical reason for their decisions. Lane loved to bait quarterbacks into making a throw, pretending he was nowhere near the receiver, out of position, and then regain his coverage with the ball in the air. As soon as the quarterback let the ball leave his hand, he knew that Lane had duped him. Lane's long frame and wingspan served him well when attempting to block kicks or intercept passes. Had Lane played today, he might be the perfect safety, not because he lacked foot speed or the coverage skills for corner, but rather because of his ability to cover and support the run. Night Train and 49ers great Ronnie Lott had similar styles: both were physical players with the skills and instincts to play safety and corner. Lane would be a hard player to block in any run support, willing to take on bigger linemen. His physical toughness playing inside would allow the defense to use their nickel defenses regardless of the personnel group or the down and distance. The closer to the line of scrimmage he played, the more fear he placed in the offense. At safety, Lane would dominate all three levels of the defense, while highlighting his ball skills, instincts, and tackling.

Comparing Lane to corners today isn't easy as no one shares his willingness to throw his body around. Xavien Howard of the Dolphins is similar in his ability to win early in the route, be physical with the receiver, and make plays on the ball. Many might say that today's rules would prevent Lane from being as dominating as he was when he played in the 1950s and '60s, which has merit. However, the more you understand Lane, who overcame so many obstacles in his life—starting from the time he was abandoned as a baby by his mother—it's fair to conclude he would have adjusted. His dogged determination was one of his strongest traits. As the rules changed, he would have changed.

23
JONATHAN OGDEN

1x Super Bowl Champion

4x First All-Pro • 5x Second Team All-Pro • 11x Pro Bowl

All-Decade Team: 2000s • All-Time Team: 100th Anniversary

12-Year Career • 177 Games Played; 176 Started

American author Michael Lewis has covered many subjects in his career, ranging from bond sales to baseball. In his 2006 book *The Blind Side*, Lewis discussed the evolution of the left tackle position in the NFL, based on the arrival of great pass rushers like Lawrence Taylor of the New York Giants. The title of Lewis's book is a reference to the back of a right-handed quarterback. When a right-handed passer sets up to pass, his blind side is the spot the left tackle plays; thus he needs adequate protection to avoid unknowingly getting clobbered. Lewis argues that left tackle is the most important position outside of the quarterback in the game and that without a great tackle the quarterback will be prone to injuries. When Jonathan Ogden played for the Baltimore Ravens, he became the prototype of a great left tackle with his six-foot-eight perfect frame—long torso, shorter legs, and the athletic skills to handle any great pass rusher, including a player of Taylor's talent.

When Lewis wrote his book, Ogden had already completed his ascendency. In football, once the offense makes an adjustment, then the defense needs to react with an adjustment of their own. This constant maneuvering allows the game to grow intellectually. Because of Ogden's constant domination, the defense posed a simple question to themselves: why rush your best rusher against your opponent's best pass blocker? The one-for-one exchange makes little sense when few, if any, were ever going to beat Ogden pass rushing, unless the defensive player can only rush from one side. Ogden could block anyone at any time, and because of his size and athletic skills, he was hard to run around or through. Most players were taken out of the game when facing Ogden. Defensive players like Taylor could rush from either side. By aligning Taylor against the weaker tackle, the quarterback was helpless even though he was right handed and could see Taylor coming. Just because you can see Taylor attacking offers little help. Kind of like being in the jungle and knowing a lion is coming toward you—what can you do? Once rushers could rush from different sides, both offensive tackle positions became vital.

Defensive coaches wanted their best rushers on the right side of their defense, so they were willing to forsake size and power for speed and rush ability. As a result, many right ends were undersized, becoming vulnerable to defending the runs to the left. With a big power-blocking tackle like Ogden, the undersized right ends had a problem. When the left tackle can dominate in the run game—creating movement—and win the one-on-one matchup, the defense is forced to adjust. To help defend the run, the defense must align a defensive back near the right side of the line to help with run support. This limits their overall effectiveness in other areas. By the time the defensive ends were ready to pass rush, Ogden had worn them down considerably and their effectiveness vanished. Ogden was sensational at controlling the line of scrimmage, beating up on smaller, less physical ends. Many evaluators gushed openly over his skills when pass blocking, and yet it was his run blocking that changed the game for any team facing the Ravens. His toughness and movement in the run game made him elite. One maxim to always remember: when a great left tackle can dominate in run blocking, the offense becomes impossible to slow down.

Ogden was easy to spot on the playing field, even as a college player at UCLA. The first thing you'd notice was his incredible size, which lured your eyes immediately toward him. Once he started to move—dominating the defender in front of him—your eyes became glued only to him. Ogden's play made him an evaluator's best friend. Because he was so talented and gifted athletically, a player who was able to beat him, albeit even slightly, became a legitimate prospect. Once when I was still in Cleveland, preparing for the draft in 1996 and knowing we'd have a high selection because of the Ravens' sudden move to Baltimore, I watched Ogden play against the University of Arizona. When I saw Teddy Bruschi, a smaller rusher, giving Ogden fits, making him actually work and sweat to block him, I immediately became a huge Bruschi fan. Based on how he performed against Ogden, he became a surefire prospect the following season. It's no wonder Bruschi went on to have a successful career in the NFL.

In his book, Lewis gave the left tackle glamour and importance, allowing fans to see the position in a new light. He is still correct: the blind side matters when building a team. It now extends to the right tackle position as teams throw the ball more often with the edges open, requiring two great tackles to win a championship. Ogden gave the game the prototype for how an elite left tackle performs, in both run and pass.

22
RANDY MOSS

Offensive Rookie of the Year • 5x Receiving Yards Champion

4x First Team All-Pro • 6x Pro Bowl

All-Decade Team: 2000s • All-Time Team: 100th Anniversary

13-Year Career • 218 Games Played; 193 Started

982 Receptions • 15,292 Receiving Yards Gained • 156 Receiving Touchdowns

In 1997, during my one year outside of the NFL, I worked for CBS as their information man on *The NFL Today*. I spent a lot of time with former Notre Dame head coach Lou Holtz, who was handling the college show on Saturday, and we would watch games together in the green room during his breaks. Holtz, always with his trusty pipe in hand, excitedly told fascinating stories about his career, his philosophy of football, his horrible experience as the head coach of the New York Jets, and all the amazing players he coached. But when the conversation turned to Randy Moss one day, Holtz put his pipe down and became deadly serious. With his famous fast-talking lisp, Holtz proclaimed, "Randy Moss was the finest high school player I have ever watched play, and the finest athlete. He was smart, tough, and all this bullcrap about him being a bad kid is hogwash. He was coming to Notre Dame before the fight." Holtz was referring to a high school fight in which a white student used a racial slur against one of Moss's friends. The fight cost Moss his admission to Notre Dame. Florida State head coach Bobby Bowden, who believed Moss was as good as Deion Sanders, tried to enroll him. Bowden said, "Deion is my measuring stick for athletic ability, and this kid was just bigger than Deion." Bowden said Moss chose to stay near his home and attend Marshall University in Huntington, West Virginia, though this praise coming from two coaching legends cannot be ignored.

Watching Moss run, catch, and dominate on the football field, I feel that the praise of both men, while highly appreciative, is not strong enough to describe this once-in-a-lifetime athlete. Having seen Jerry Rice early in his career and Tim Brown later, I can say that when I finally watched Moss both live and in person, I knew he was an athlete a cut above. This statement of opinion is in no way a derogatory comment regarding Rice or Brown; it is simply recognizing the elite level of athletic talent Moss displayed.

With his long frame and wingspan, Moss had the quickness to separate at the line and the speed to outrun anyone. When the ball was in the air, his height, jumping ability, and hand-eye coordination dominated. Moss was impossible to double cover. If the defensive coordinator attempted to use a bracket technique, which aligns two defensive backs on each side of the wide receiver to protect the defense if he goes right or left, Moss would simply run straight, never turning. Then Moss would use those afterburners, leaving both players in the dust. If the coordinator chose to jam Moss at the line of scrimmage and have another defender over top, protecting against the deep ball, Moss would use his quickness to separate and then force the deep defender to retreat deeper and deeper, leaving a large chunk of the field open. Pick your poison: either way Moss was going to get open and the ball was heading into the end zone once every six catches. Take a moment and think about that ratio. Once every 6.1 catches, Moss was in the end zone. His hands were sensational, softly plucking the ball out of the air, at times only using one hand. Moss would toy with defenders, not showing his hands to make the catch until the last moment, often creating pass interference penalties as the defender was still running and not expecting the ball. Watching Moss play, it was clear he was at a different speed than most everyone he faced.

Moss fell one game short of being able to hoist the Lombardi trophy, which would have been a great ending to an amazing career. The Moss I watched every day in Oakland worked hard, wanted to hear the truth, and most of all, wanted to help the team win games. When he arrived New England, he did all those things, and then some. Bill Belichick, not one to throw around compliments, once referred to Moss as "one of the smartest players I've ever coached. Certainly, the smartest receiver. He taught me more about receiving and the passing game than by far anybody else."

And each time I think of Moss, I still think of how sad Holtz was that Moss never played for the Fighting Irish.

21
DEION SANDERS

2x Super Bowl Champion • 1x NFL Defensive Player of the Year

6x First Team All-Pro • 2x Second Team All-Pro • 8x Pro Bowl

All-Decade Team: 1990s • All-Time Team: 100th Anniversary

14-Year Career • 188 Games Played; 157 Started

53 Interceptions; 9 Returned for Touchdowns

212 Punt Returns • 2,199 Punt Yards Gains •
6 Punt Return Touchdowns

155 Kickoff Returns • 3523 Kickoff Yards Gained •
3 Kickoff Touchdowns

Al Davis loved the NFL Combine. He rarely attended All-Star games or went to college games across the country, but he never missed the Combine. He would stay at the Westin adjacent to the RCA Dome, which provided an indoor walkway to the Colts' stadium. The Combine was two events in one. The workouts on the field grabbed the headlines as the number-one item, which the fans and draftniks wanted to know about. Davis loved both events, with a slight lean toward watching the players run the forty. He would position himself in the seat directly along the start of the forty, where he could able to look each player in the eye, before they took off on their timed run. His signature cologne smell reached far, dominating the air for hours, so when each player returned for their second run, they recognized the aroma in the air. However, the most important part, the fuel that drove the engine of the NFL off-season, occurred in each hotel within a five-block radius, and that was the behind-the-scenes maneuvering of potential free agents with their representatives and the trade conversations between teams.

The 1989 NFL draft was loaded with top talent. Four of the first five picks in the draft now wear gold jackets. Florida State's Deion Sanders wasn't at the Combine to do anything but display his incredible speed. Sanders got to the starting point, set his hand down, and took off, running a 4.29 and 4.27. The second time he ran, he did another 4.27 and 4.33 (all times are from the NFL Combine). Once crossing the finish line, he didn't slow down and wasn't seen again. Like a puff of smoke, he vanished into the wind. No bench-press test or Wonderlic test. No interviews with any teams outside the top five. Sanders made his statement, loudly and fast.

During his NFL career, Sanders was a defensive player with offensive skills, able to turn one mistake into a touchdown. He was often ignored by the opposing offense as they designed their pass plays away from his coverage. Sanders was a three-meal cover corner: he could win at the line (the best breakfast corner); then slightly off in coverage, reading the depth of the quarterback's drops, and break on the ball (a rare lunch corner); and finally, he demonstrated that rare speed at the top of the routes (a sensational dinner). Even though he wasn't a physical tackler, often keeping himself away from the brutal contact, he was still capable of making the tackle when needed.

Deion was also an entertainer. He created Prime Time, an alter ego, who brought excitement to the game with dancing and celebrations. His play backed up every showman move he displayed on the field. His talent to entertain didn't distract from his talent to dominate on the field.

In 1995, when the NFL was operating under a hard salary cap, teams used a large signing bonus to lower the cap number and still provide players with adequate cash. The Cowboys signed Sanders to a seven-year contract worth $35 million. Sanders was to receive $12 million upon signing the contract, and then $1 million in base salaries over the first three years of the contract. By creating a seven-year contract with a low salary, the Cowboys were able to fit Sanders's overall compensation within their salary cap and still give him the cash he demanded over his first three seasons. Other NFL owners cried foul when they learned of this circumvention of the signing bonus rule. As a result, the NFL and the players' union, the National Football League Players Association, passed the "Deion Rule," which required the salary and the roster bonus of the first three years to be within equal portion of the total signing bonus.

Sanders also demonstrated his unusual ability to for high-level play well in two sports, playing for five NFL and five MLB teams. He had an amazing array of athletic skills, from his hand-eye coordination to his body control and ability to generate instant speed. Athletic talent like Sanders is rare, and as he now enters the coaching world as the head coach of Jackson State, he is becoming a talented leader of men. Perhaps one day he will coach someone with the same rare skills he possessed.

20
BRUCE SMITH

2x NFL Defensive Player of the Year •
2x NFL Force Fumble Leader

8x First Team All-Pro • 2x Second Team All-Pro • 11x Pro Bowl

All-Decade Team: 1980s & 1990s •
All-Time Team: 100th Anniversary

19-Year Career • 279 Games Played; 267 Started

200 Sacks

I can vividly recall when my father took me to my first professional baseball game. We saw the Phillies play the San Francisco Giants at Connie Mack Stadium in Philadelphia. Each time a ball was hit high into the air, I thought it was a home run. Whenever the ball soared, I reacted and jumped out of my seat. I was only ten years old, so everything was new to me. It took me some time to understand the visual difference between a well-hit ball and a not-so-well-hit one. Eventually, I learned.

Fourteen years later I had a similar learning experience while covering the Blue–Grey Game in Montgomery, Alabama, while preparing for the 1985 draft. I was up close to some of the most talented players in college football. On the field, everyone looked great, and I was mesmerized. Considering that only five years earlier I was playing football for Hofstra, it was powerful to see players near my age with far greater skills than I had witnessed before. On the field that day, I knew that for me to improve as a personnel evaluator and have a career in the profession, I was going to need to separate levels of good. When I walked over to watch the one-on-one pass-rush drills between the offensive line and defensive line, another revelation was thrust upon me. Evaluating rare talent wasn't going to be my problem. Seeing greatness was easy; all I had to do was watch Bruce Smith. Much like a diamond collector knows a rare stone without the need of a microscope, greatness shines differently, and Smith had a rare shine.

And yet Smith wasn't even interested in playing in the game. How anyone convinced him to play was remarkable, considering he was a surefire first over-all pick. Once he arrived in Buffalo, the Bills' fans had the same reaction I had that day in Montgomery; they saw the rareness of this athlete and his ability to dominate in all areas of the game, from rushing the passer to stacking the run. Smith often placed his right hand down—Al Davis's preference—and, with a perfect stance, got off the ball and worked the offensive tackle, inside or out. His spin move became legendary. To be an effective spin rusher, the defender has to engage the offensive tackle when he is spinning, which requires great balance and power. The power knocks the tackle back and the spin doesn't allow him to regain control. And Smith's burst, along with his great tackling ability, sent the quarterback to the ground.

After ballooning to 310 pounds during his rookie season, Smith became fa-natical about his weight and conditioning, lowering his weight to 290. Smith learned about the need to stay in shape at an early age, which is why he played nineteen seasons in the NFL. The only blemish on Smith's remarkable career was that he played in four Super Bowls, but was unable to win one. The Bills K-Gun offense allowed them to play with the lead and gave Smith the chance to rush the passer. They were just not good enough in three of those Super Bowl losses. The Giants' loss was the one they will always regret, and not because of Scott Norwood missing the kick wide right; rather, it was because they were the better team, but not better that day.

Before retiring at age forty, Smith only had six seasons when he did not re-cord double-digit sacks. Today, Myles Garrett of the Browns demonstrates the rare traits that Smith displayed over those nineteen seasons. He can take over any game and be equally effective in running or passing. And much like Smith, Garrett displays the athletic skills that go hand in hand with greatness. I can see Garrett's greatness thanks to Bruce Smith.

19
WILLIE LANIER

1x Super Bowl Champion

8x First Team All-Pro • 6x Pro Bowl •
2x AFL All-Star • 2x All-AFL

All-Time Team: 75th & 100th Anniversaries

11-Year Career • 149 Games Played; 145 Started

27 Interceptions; 2 Returned for Touchdowns

When Vince Lombardi arrived in Washington in 1969, I went over every draft choice, trying to learn as much as possible about each player by reading the *Washington Post* each morning, which always arrived two days late in Ocean City and cost me much of my allowance. I became fascinated with running back Larry Brown, who was an eighth-round pick in the 1969 draft and Lombardi's first pick. Like me, Brown was deaf in one ear. Seeing him play with a hearing loss gave me hope I could do the same. Watching him in a game one afternoon in 1971, I was surprised by Kansas City linebacker Willie Lanier (number 63), who made tackle after tackle and never allowed Brown to gain any yards. Lanier was all over the field, intercepting a pass in the first half and knocking down Washington quarterback Billy Kilmer when he attacked the pocket. He was not the biggest of linebackers in terms of height, but he was strong and sturdy, and when he made contact, Brown always fell backward. Watching Lanier play linebacker was an education. He was able to avoid the blocker, showed great burst and acceleration sideline to sideline, and had the ability to cover ground in the passing game. Although my beloved Brown and the Redskins lost for the first time that year (27–20), I found myself a Lanier fan.

Lanier was an unexpected draft pick for the Chiefs in 1967. He never talked to anyone from the team prior to being drafted from the tiny Morgan State, an all-Black university in Baltimore. Frank Barnes, a part-time scout and friend of Chiefs head coach Hank Stram, had pushed the coach to take Lanier, believing him to be the best backer in the draft. Even more astonishing, there were no Black players playing middle linebacker at the time. Much like the quarterback position, the middle linebacker was white only. For the Chiefs to select Lanier and allow him to become the starter demonstrated the progressive nature of the organization. As the first Black middle linebacker, Lanier was always under intense scrutiny, but it never affected his play. He was smart, intense, and team oriented, and he paved the way for future generations. Lanier personified the middle linebacker, playing the position the same way heavyweight champion Joe Frazier boxed. He could bob and weave, avoiding blockers, and when called upon to deliver a hit, he was explosive.

In only his second season, Lanier became the unquestioned leader of the defense. Playing the Jets in blustery Shea Stadium in the opening round of the 1969 playoffs, a day that Jets quarterback Joe Namath described as the worst day for passing in the history of football, Lanier was once again a tackling machine. The game was a defensive struggle. Early in the fourth, the Jets had the ball six inches from the Chiefs' goal line, trailing 6–3. Two runs into the heart of the Chiefs' defense proved futile, as Lanier and company knocked Jets running backs Matt Snell and Bill Mathis back, not gaining an inch. With backs split to either side of Namath in the backfield, Namath faked a handoff to Mathis and ran a bootleg, hoping to find Snell in the flat for the touchdown. With no one open, Namath decided to run, and took a hit from Bobby Bell, making him woozy, so the Jets had to settle for a game-tying field goal. That stand provided the motivation for the Chiefs' offense to score the go-ahead and eventual winning touchdown. From that goal line stand, forward Lanier became the unquestioned leader of a defense that would produce six future Hall of Fame players. Today, Lanier would be similar to Bobby Wagner of the Los Angeles Rams. Both are shorter in terms of height for the middle linebacker spot and are similar in weight. Lanier was more powerful on contact and would use his powerful lower body to knock runners back; Wagner is an effective open field tackler, without the same thump. Both players have great range and are able to attack the pocket, knocking over smaller blockers. It's safe to say that when I first watched Lanier, I knew few players had his skills, because few ever slowed down Larry Brown.

18
LANCE "BAMBI" ALWORTH

1x Super Bowl Champion • 1x AFL Champion •
1x AFL Player of the Year • 3x AFL Receiving Yards Leader •
3x AFL Reception Leader • 3x Receiving Touchdown Leader

7x AFL All-Star • 6x First Team All-Star •
1x Second Team All-Star

AFL All-Time Team • All-Time Team: 75th & 100th Anniversaries

11-Year Career • 110 Games Played; 109 Started

542 Receptions • 10,266 Receiving Yards Gained •
85 Receiving Touchdowns

Al Davis always loved discussing Lance Alworth. For Davis, the sheer mention of Alworth's name was like hearing a song on the radio and having it launch a memory of a wonderful time in your life. Davis dismissed any notion of a player being better than Lance. When I was working on a trade for Randy Moss, I made that comparison, which Davis challenged strongly and in his classic way: "Ah, you don't know what your f***ing talking about." (I heard that refrain at least a thousand times, if not more.)

During late November of 1961, with the AFL draft just days away, Davis, then an assistant coach for the Chargers, was planning on making a trip to Fayetteville, Arkansas, to check out Lance Alworth. When the phone rang late at night, Davis thought the airline was calling him.

Much to his surprise and disappointment, the call wasn't from the airline but from his mother, who informed him that his father, Louis, had suddenly died. Heartbroken and devastated, Davis headed east to his hometown of Brooklyn. During return trip to San Diego, he stopped off in Fayetteville, where he spent time with Alworth extolling the virtues of the Sid Gillman passing game and Chargers owner Barron Hilton. Alworth was reluctant to move from running back to wide receiver, wondering why he would have to change position and unsure of his hands. Davis, who had observed Alworth in pregame warmups displaying his spectacular hands, knew it would be a smooth transition. During this visit, Davis met Alworth's entire family, his wife's family, and his attorney, charming them with his famous Brooklyn accent. Years later, remembering the recruiting battle, Al LoCasale, a scout with the Chargers and eventual front-office executive with the Raiders, "Al spent a lot of time getting close to every-one, especially his attorney, a guy named Starr." (Sidenote: Everyone needs an attorney named Starr.)

Even though the Razorbacks didn't throw the ball to their running backs, Davis saw something that made him think Alworth was going to be the best receiver in the game. "Lance was one of maybe three athletes in my lifetime who had what I would call 'It,'" Davis often said. As with any love affair involving Davis, speed is always the starting point, and Alworth had speed, as verified by his track times. While attending Arkansas, besides playing football, Alworth competed in the long jump, the 100-meter dash, and the 220-meter dash, which gave Davis the comfort of knowing that what he was seeing on the football field was rare speed. For Davis, there was speed and then there was rare speed, his personal favorite. He never wanted players on his team to be fast; he wanted them to be the fastest.

Alworth was drafted in the first round by the San Francisco 49ers and by the Oakland Raiders, who then traded Alworth's rights to the Chargers for halfback Bo Robertson, quarterback Hunter Enis, and offensive tackle Gene Selawski. Now all Davis had to do was to get Alworth's name on the contract, which he did following the Sugar Bowl, in which the Razorbacks faced the University of Mississippi. With Red Hickey of the 49ers still in the stands, Davis ran onto the field, contract in hand, and Alworth became a Charger.

Davis was right about Alworth. His athletic talent fit perfectly into Gill-man's passing game, his hands were sensational, his speed carried the rare Davis stamp of approval, and from his first season, he was able to post one thousand yards in reception, which he would repeat for the next six years.

Alworth was like a smaller version of Randy Moss, able to take the top off the defense, and once the ball was in his hands, he was a great runner. When Alworth played, the defense could mug, harass, and almost tackle receivers at the line. It took hard work to escape, whereas Moss was helped by having rules preventing the initial assault. Having "It" for Davis meant Alworth was one player the opponent was incapable of taking out of the game. No double team or bracket coverage was going to work. And if a team played press coverage on

Alworth, they had to hope the defensive back would make contact at the line, or else Alworth would be running into the end zone. Any player attempting to press Alworth learned for himself that Alworth's initial quickness, combined with his speed, made it damn near impossible to jam at the line. Tyreek Hill, formerly of the Chiefs and now with the Dolphins, is much like Alworth—he is incredibly fast, with rare quickness, and he has "It." (For the record, Davis would have loved Hill, who would have been a Raider.)

In May of 1971, a three-team NBA-like trade occurred, involving the Dallas Cowboys, Los Angeles Rams, and San Diego Chargers. As part of the trade, the Cowboys dealt three players to San Diego for Alworth. Of the trade, Dallas coach Tom Landry said, "We were very reluctant to trade men the caliber of [Pettis] Norman, [Tony] Liscio and [Ron] East, but when the chance for Alworth came we couldn't pass it up." Alworth went on to help the Cowboys win Super Bowl VI against the Dolphins, catching a touchdown pass from Roger Staubach for the team's first score of the day.

In the Raiders' offices in Alameda, California, Davis installed a conference room called the Hall of Fame room, where rookie or free agent players would sign their contracts on a large table facing a wall that was lined with framed photos of former Raiders in gold jackets standing next to Davis and holding their busts. And then there was a photo of Alworth. His spectacular and dominating play on the field was a part of Davis's vision of the embodiment of offensive football. From the day he signed Alworth on the field at Tulane stadium after the Sugar Bowl, Davis made Alworth the standard for which any great receiver had to reach.

When you had "It," you were the best.

17
OTTO GRAHAM

4x AAFC Champion • 3x NFL Champion •
2x AAFC MVP • 3x NFL MVP • 2x Passing Leader •
1x Passing Touchdown Leader • 2x NFL Passing Rating Leader •
4x NFL Completion Percentage Leader

4x First Team All-Pro • 3x AAFC First Team •
2x Second Team All-Pro • 1x AAFC Second Team • 5x Pro Bowl

All-Decade Team: 1950s •
All-Time Team: 75th & 100th Anniversaries

10-Year Career • 126 Games Played; 114 Started

1,464 Passing Completions • 2,626 Passing Attempts •
23,584 Passing Yards • 174 Passing Touchdowns •
135 Interceptions

In 1936, Bill DeCorrevont, a running back from tiny Austin High School in Chicago, was the greatest high school star of the era. Every football fan within a hundred miles of Chicago wanted to see him play. An Associated Press report describing how DeCorrevont was drawing fans stated, "The spectators leave the field with the looks of amazement in their eyes, convinced what they have read is true." Meanwhile, just north of Chicago in the city Waukegan, Otto Graham, a two-sport, all-state player was not garnering much attention, though he accepted a basketball scholarship to Northwestern.

More than 120,000 fans turned out to watch DeCorrevont play his final high school game, in which he rushed for three touchdowns and passed for another, leading his team to a 26–0 win, all while playing with a broken collarbone. DeCorrevont and four other star teammates chose to play for head coach Pappy Waldorf at Northwestern, as the school was primed to compete in the Big Ten. But what made Northwestern a great team resulted from a serendipitous moment and an entirely different athlete. While casually observing an intermural football game on campus, Coach Waldorf noticed a freshman Graham throwing the ball with velocity and accuracy and wondered if he could convince this basketball player to give football a try. Otto Graham said yes, and by the time he was a senior, he earned first-team All-American honors in basketball *and* finished third in the Heisman Trophy voting in football. During their senior year, everyone was talking about Graham, not DeCorrevont.

Graham had the great skill of Michael Jordan, able to play any sport at the highest of level, and the winning pedigree of Tom Brady, as all of his teams, regardless of sport, competed for a title.

In the four years he played in the AAFC for the Browns, Graham displayed pinpoint accuracy down the field and won games, including all four AAFC Championship games. Because he was such a marvelous hand-eye-control athlete, Graham could anticipate the route, throwing the ball with great rhythm and timing. Unlike many quarterbacks, Graham became more accurate the farther he threw the ball, making him and Dante Lavelli a deadly, deep-ball combination. Some thumb their noses at the AAFC, believing the records Graham accumulated were against lesser competition, which is unfair and untrue. When the leagues merged in 1950, Graham's winning and stellar play remained constant. Others claim he never called his own plays (Brady, Joe Montana, Peyton Manning, and others didn't either), but that was considered a shortcoming in the 1950s.

During his career, Graham led his team to the equivalent of ten straight Super Bowls, winning seven and finishing with a 9–3 playoff record. Paul Brown, who recruited Graham, wrote in his autobiography, "As far as I am concerned, Otto Graham was the greatest player in the game's history, playing the most important position." Powerful words coming from a man who watched all the game's greats.

As for our high school phenom DeCorrevont, he was drafted in the fourteenth round by Washington in 1942, but did not play until 1945, after he finished serving in WWII. He retired in 1949 after two seasons with the Bears.

16
BARRY SANDERS

1x NFL MVP • 2x Offensive Player of the Year •
4x NFL Rushing Leader • 1x NFL Rushing Touchdown Leader

6x First Team All-Pro • 4x Second Team All-Pro • 10x Pro Bowl

All-Decade Team: 1990s • All-Time Team: 100th Anniversary

10-Year Career • 153 Games Played; 151 Started

3,062 Rushing Attempts • 15,269 Rushing Yards Gained •
99 Rushing Touchdowns

352 Receptions • 2,921 Receiving Yards Gained •
10 Receiving Touchdowns

In 1948, Norman A. Sas succeeded his father as the president of Tudor Metal Products. The company was struggling and Sas needed to find a new product for the company. With table games becoming popular at the time, Sas later recalled, "I thought, 'Gee! If we could come up with some football figures and get them running against each other, we'd have a football game." That's just what they did, and before long, Tudor Metal became Tudor Games. From the game's conception in 1948, to 1967, when Tudor acquired the NFL license allowing the game to feature players in team helmets and colors, Electric Football became a staple of every young football fan's Christmas list. "For the first ten years, we generated more money for NFL properties than anyone else," Mr. Sas once shared. Forty million games were sold, and people "grew up with the game imprinted on their psyches," said Jerry McGhee, a member of the board of directors of the Miniature Football Coaches Association.

When Barry Sanders joined his ten siblings in the living room of their three-bedroom home in Wichita, Kansas, in 1977, he discovered a copy of Electric Football wrapped under the tree. As Sanders watched these little figurines move in all different directions, he knew at that moment the position he was destined to play: "I identified with the running back," he would later say. The game sparked an interest that led Sanders to sign up for the Beech Red Barons, a Wichita youth team. During his first game for the Red Barons, Sanders behaved like the running back on the electronic field—going east, then west, and then running faster than anyone to the end zone. It was the first time Barry Sanders put on pads, and he scored three touchdowns. Sounds about right. After Oklahoma State football coaches George Walstad and Bill Shimek saw tape of his high school performance, they stole the game film so another Big 8 school wouldn't discover his rare talent and snatch him up.

In 1989, with the third pick overall in loaded draft, the Lions knew Sanders was their man. Sanders was not just a running back; he was a game changer. He could change the game on the carpet inside the Silverdome or on the grass at Lambeau Field. He played the game with all ten spikes in the ground and embarrassed any would-be tackler. The only athlete with better lateral quickness doesn't even play football—Allen Iverson of the Philadelphia 76ers, who could shake, rattle, and roll with elite quickness just as Sanders could. Sanders could stop on a dime, shake his hips like the players in Electric Football, and hit top speed instantly. His incredible hands and body control as a route runner often went unnoticed. His route tree was far more than a simple screen or run toward the flat. His shake-and-bake skills made him impossible to cover one-on-one. He was too hard to tackle for any defensive corner, too quick and fast for any safety, and too talented in all areas for any linebacker.

When Sanders entered the league, the single set back was in full swing. The formation required a special type of running back to make the offense effective. He didn't need anyone in front of him to make a penetrating tackler miss or clear a hole. Each time I watched Sanders play—marveling at his power and space talent—I felt that had he been utilized away from the formation, taking advantage of his rare open-field skills, he might have averaged over ten yards a catch. That would be a spectacular number for a running back. Sanders could make any offense effective. And the Lions were able to reach the playoffs five times during his career, even without a great quarterback under center.

15
ROGER STAUBACH

2x Super Bowl Champion • 1x Super Bowl MVP •
1x NFL Passing Leader • 4x Passing Rating Leader

1X Second Team All-Pro • 6x Pro Bowl

All-Decade Team: 1970s • All-Time Team: 100th Anniversary

11-Year Career • 131 Games Played; 114 Started

1,685 Passing Completions • 2,958 Passing Attempts •
22,700 Passing Yards • 153 Passing Touchdowns •
109 Interceptions

20 Rushing Touchdowns

13 Comebacks • 21 Game-Winning Drives

The Patriot Way in New England, conceived of by Patriots head coach Bill Belichick, consists of being a great teammate and always placing the team goals above individual achievements. It embodies the ideals of elite football: a high degree of discipline, attention to detail, commitment to the task at hand, speaking for yourself, never giving up, always competing, preparing for any situation, staying in the moment, and most of all, letting your actions on the field do all the talking. The "Way" has delivered six Super Bowl wins for the franchise. The "Way" also perfectly describes Tom Brady. But it originated with former Cowboys quarterback Roger Staubach. As a kid, Belichick watched Staubach and later wanted every player he coached to prepare and perform identically to how the quarterback prepared and performed. In essence, the Patriot Way would mean fielding a team full of Staubachs.

Now, that might be unrealistic to carry out, but it was a fabulous starting point. With Staubach as the model, Belichick looked for players who shared his DNA, an approach that shaped his overall team building. Belichick once said:

When I look back on it, one of the things I learned at Annapolis, when I grew up around the Navy football teams in the early sixties—Joe Bellino, Roger Staubach, Coach Wayne Hardin, and some of the great teams they had—I didn't know any differently. I just assumed that's what football was. Guys were very disciplined. They worked very hard. They did extra things. They were always on time, alert, ready to go, team-oriented, unselfish. I thought that's the way it all was. I wasn't aware of it at the time, but I can see how that molded me.

After winning the Heisman Trophy in 1963, Staubach was required to serve four years in the military. He spent one year in Da Nang, South Vietnam, serving as a naval lieutenant. During a thirty-day leave, he returned to the States, and while there he quietly met the Cowboys in Thousand Oaks, California, the home of their summer training camp. He worked out with them, and during those practices, it was clear to all watching that Staubach was special with his arm, his accuracy, his poise, and his ability to move. Head coach Tom Landry said, "If last week is any indication of what his future is, we think he's an excellent prospect."

Staubach returned to Dallas full time in 1969, starting four games his first two seasons. Then, in his third season, at the age of twenty-nine, he took over. He led the Cowboys to their dominating win over the Miami Dolphins in Super Bowl VI. It was the first Super Bowl win for the Cowboys, and despite his age, Staubach saw many more championship wins. From 1973 until he retired in 1979, Staubach was the best quarterback in the league, and no lead was safe with him under center.

Most will remember Staubach for all his amazing come-from-behind wins, or his two Super Bowl titles. His numbers may not garner as much attention as those of other top quarterbacks, but serving his country during his prime years contributed to lowering his career production. You never hear Staubach complain, or regret missing time in the league, because Staubach was a model for the Patriot Way: he was willing to do something for the team—in this case, his country—even if wasn't good for him.

THE BACKUP QUARTERBACK

In the course of writing this book, I found that evaluating Staubach during his career proved worthwhile, even for a Washington fan like myself. Lessons come in different ways, at different times, with different context—the only requirement is your memory. Having the ability to recall events in past games, much like Rams head coach Sean McVay does with amazing detail, can help a coach avoid a potential pitfall later in their career. Every game supplies a learning experience in some form.

On Thanksgiving Day of 1974, after Ocean City High School played against our rival, Pleasantville, my family went over to my uncle Charlie's house to enjoy the day and be thankful for life's blessings. No one other than me cared about the games on the television. My favorite team was playing my least favorite team, and the outcome of this Cowboys-Redskins skirmish would bring with it bragging rights at school on Monday. With everyone in the dining room cracking nuts, drinking wine, and telling stories—all things Italian families did after eating a big meal—I sat ten feet from the thirty-six-inch screen, watching running back Duane Thomas score a touchdown on a wheel route from quarterback Billy Kilmer. I jumped off the chair in excitement because Washington was now ahead 16–3. Knowing Staubach could overcome any lead, I wasn't feeling confident or cocky; there was still over a quarter and a half to play.

Then, in perhaps the most important play of the game, Washington defensive front Diron Talbert—one of my favorite players—ran a Tom game inside with Bill Brundige (i.e., when one of the defensive tackles penetrates inside and the other folds around him) and opened the middle of the defense, allowing Staubach to take off up the middle and then to his left for a first down. The tackle didn't look devasting, or overly physical, yet when Staubach got off the ground with no help, he was clearly wobbly. At this point, my excitement was high, hoping Staubach was okay, just not okay enough to return to the game. On the next play, rookie Clint Longley replaced Staubach, and as I heard my family laughing in the other room, I, too, was quietly celebrating.

My celebration ended...quickly. Longley's first pass looked awful. He seemed dazed and confused. The second pass was slightly better, finding running back Walt Garrison for a first down. But the third play was the beginning of the end. Longley faked a throw inside, then launched a perfect strike to tight end Billy Joe DuPree for a touchdown. Washington's offense went three and out, and now Longley appeared better than Staubach, carving up Washington's defense with pinpoint passes. When the quarter ended, Dallas was in the lead 17–16.

Washington showed resiliency, coming back to score and taking the lead, 23–16, which calmed my nerves. Dallas then fumbled and put the game squarely in Washington's control, as a two-score lead at this point might've ended the game. Washington sent Mark Moseley, one of the last straight-on kickers left in the NFL, to try a twenty-nine-yard field goal. Ed "Too Tall" Jones blocked the field goal attempt, and my heart sank. At this point, my nerves were rattled, and my shirt was filled with sweat, while my family was all still having a grand old time in the other room. They had no idea what I was going through just a few feet way.

With 1:45 left in the game, Dallas began their final drive, with their entire season on the line. A loss would end their playoff chances. Facing fourth and six, Longley completed a pass to Bob Hayes for the first down at midfield. Just thirty-five seconds remained as I was on my feet, pacing in front of the television. On the next play, my heart sank as I watched Longley backpedal straight back, turning his shoulders to the left and launching a deep pass. Drew Pearson streaked down the sideline and caught the perfect pass for the touchdown. Game over. It was one of the worst Thanksgivings of my life and one I would never forget. Meanwhile, no one in my family had ever stopped eating or laughing in the other room.

Before the game, Talbert claimed their game plan was to "knock out Staubach and get that rookie in the game." At least they achieved their goal. From that day forward, I was always concerned about a sudden change of quarterbacks and not knowing the details of what the backup was capable of.

Fast-forward nineteen years, on the shores of Lake Erie with the Browns as they faced the Miami Dolphins and the great Dan Marino. Late in the second quarter, after throwing an incomplete pass, Marino quickly lifted his leg off the ground, signaling for the bench to send in another quarterback. Enter Scott Mitchell. My mind went back to that awful Thanksgiving. Mitchell moved the ball to the Browns' five-yard line and then tried to throw an out route to his left. Browns defensive back Najee Mustafaa jumped the route for a touchdown, giving the team a 14–10 lead. In the second half, Mitchell became like Longley and won the game with his play. Even though I knew to never underestimate the backup and never forgot the Longley game, the results were the same.

Years later, when I worked for Al Davis, he would force the defensive coordinator to evaluate every quarterback in the draft. Clearly, he too was traumatized by the Longley game.

14
DICK BUTKUS

2x NFL Defensive Player of the Year

5x First Team All-Pro ● 3x Second Team All-Pro ● 8x Pro Bowl

All-Decade Team: 1960s & 1970s ●
All-Time Team: 75th & 100th Anniversaries

9-Year Career ● 119 Games Played; 119 Started

22 Interceptions

After the Bears won against the Lions 27–24 on Thanksgiving Day, 1964, against the Lions, 27–24, George Halas, defensive coordinator George Allen, and the rest of the Bears' front office headed to the Summit Hotel in New York City to take part in the 1965 draft. The war between the AFL and the NFL for college players was intensifying, and this early start date allowed NFL teams to get a jump on the competition. The Bears' draft board, assembled by Allen and Halas, featured Dick Butkus, a middle linebacker from Illinois, as the best player in the draft and the number-one college player in the country. Kansas running back Gale Sayers was a close second. When it came their time to select two picks in a row, it was an easy decision. Butkus became the third pick in the 1965 draft, and the Giants—with the first overall pick—considered Butkus before choosing Auburn's Tucker Frederickson "because," as Giants vice president Wellington Mara said at the time, "he is the best all-around fullback in the country." During his senior year, Fredrickson averaged 4.4 yards per carry, won the Jacobs award for the best blocker in college football, and finished eighth in the Heisman voting. The Bears then selected Gale Sayers with the fourth pick, which gave them future two Hall of Fame players from the draft. Halas, son of owner George Halas, said, "As far as we're concerned, we got the No. 1, 2, and 3 college football players in the country. We would have been happy if two of the three had been left for us." The third first-round pick of the Bears that year was defensive lineman Steve DeLong, who ended up signing with the AFL Chargers.

In recent years, the NFL draft has followed the universal law of supply and demand. When the supply is high, the cost comes down, thus lowering the importance of position. When the supply is low, the cost will increase and the need to satisfy the demand becomes greater as the competition increases. Rule changes impact the scheme adjustments, which then impacts the supply, affecting demand. Being creative with scheme can allow circumvention of the supply chain, and thus some teams can zig while others zag. A Bill Belichick specialty. As a result, positions are placed into two categories. The first involves what we can call "replaceable," meaning the supply of players for the position is large, so there is no need to draft those positions early. Or it might simply be that the overall talent in the available pool of players isn't at an elite level, regardless of position. The second includes "irreplaceable" players. In this situation, the supply of qualified players is low, and unless a team takes the position at the top of the draft (that is, the first five picks), they may never satisfy the demand. Because each draft pick equates to a certain dollar amount, there is an economic value to quantify the change that has occurred. Therefore, running backs, fullbacks, and run-stuffing big middle linebackers might be replaceable in today's draft, but not in 1965.

Currently, the running back is devalued, especially the fullback. Based on the analytics and the supply for the position, there is no chance three running backs will ever be consecutively selected in the top two picks again. Since 1965, the quarterback's value has increased. Therefore, today Joe Namath be wouldn't the twelfth player selected in the draft, as he was by the St. Louis Cardinals in 1965. Also, a middle linebacker who never leaves the field, based on the personnel groupings of the offense, has become irreplaceable. This puts a player like Dick Butkus—a man of great talent—back in vogue.

The fact is, the way middle linebacker Dick Butkus played will never really go out of fashion. Butkus was a turnover machine every time he hit a ball carrier or receiver coming across the middle. Though the NFL didn't keep statistics on forced fumbles when he played, Butkus had a reputation for being able to strip the ball upon tackling. He recovered twenty-nine fumbles during his career, along with twenty-two interceptions. Butkus showed great speed and could cover distance in the passing game, allowing him to make plays on the ball. He wasn't interested in taking on blocks; he was not a shed-and-throw linebacker. In fact, he played like an undersized backer, slipping and maneuvering around the blocker. He avoided contact until he dished the contact. He wasn't going to get bogged down on some guard when there was a running back to tackle or a quarterback to maul. At the start of the play, Butkus was a ballerina; at the end, a bulldozer.

Because of Butkus's size, his rugged style of play, and the emphasis on the passing game, many might think he would struggle in today's game. Hogwash; he would be even better. The middle linebacker has shrunk in terms of height and weight, and Butkus would appear as an anomaly, thus creating doubt regarding his impact. However, what has never changed over the course of the league's history is that size matters; football is a still a game for the big man. Butkus was big and fast, and when he hit the ball carrier, pain was inflicted. As defensive end Deacon Jones once said about Butkus, "He tried to put you in the cemetery, not the hospital." When Butkus played, no one wanted to get front of him, nor would they today.

Had Butkus played today, he would be a favorite of Bill Belichick, who loves big backers and wants to use them as fifth rushers. The offense would have to scheme in the week leading up to the game to account for Butkus. And any player who dictates coverage or an adjustment has value, and creative coaches like Belichick will use their strengths to create the mismatch they desire. If Butkus were playing today, Belichick would mess around with his opponent's protections schemes, forcing the offensive line to account for Butkus, and then design his blitzes accordingly. For Belichick, Butkus would be an integral part of the pass defense, either in coverage, blitzing, or creating an advantage for other players. Anyone who thinks Butkus wouldn't be on the field on every down doesn't understand the value of size and toughness.

The game might have changed (and fullbacks are almost as rare as the black rhino), but middle linebackers who can dominate on the first, second, and third level of the defense, and put fear into the opposing team, will never change. Butkus was great then and would be great today.

13
PEYTON MANNING

2x Super Bowl Champion • 1x Super Bowl MVP •
5x NFL MVP • 2x NFL Offensive Player of the Year •
4x Touchdown Passing Leader • 3x Passing Yards Leader •
3x Passing Rating Leader •
2x Completion Percentage Leader

7x First Team All-Pro • 3x Second Team All-Pro • 14x Pro Bowl

All-Decade Team: 2000s • All-Time Team: 100th Anniversary

17-Year Career • 266 Games Played; 265 Started

6,125 Passing Completions • 9,380 Passing Attempts •
71,940 Passing Yards • 539 Passing Touchdowns •
251 Interceptions

Whenever I watch *The Bourne Identity*, which is frequently on television, there is always one scene that reminds me of the great Peyton Manning. I know, what could Jason Bourne, a man with no recollection of who he is or what he is doing, and one of the greatest passers in NFL history have in common? Please let me explain. The movie begins with the amnesiac Bourne near death, being rescued from a ship. Once on land, he attempts to piece his life back together, while being pursued by unknown assailants. While lying low in a restaurant with a woman he has befriended, Bourne describes the little he knows about himself: "I can tell you the license plate numbers of all six cars outside. I can tell you that our waitress is left-handed and the guy sitting up at the counter weighs two hundred fifteen pounds and knows how to handle himself. I know the best place to look for a gun is the cab or the gray truck outside, and at this altitude, I can run flat out for a half mile before my hands start shaking. Now why would I know that? How can I know that and not know who I am?" Despite his lack of memories, he possesses a remarkable skill set, as he is able to take in everything around him.

Peyton Manning played football like he was Jason Bourne. When Manning broke from the huddle, his eyes would find offensive line coach Howard Mudd standing on the sideline, away from Manning in clear view. Mudd was like a third-base coach, giving Manning signals on what might be coming from the defense. Then, like Bourne, Manning would quickly survey the defense for their specific alignments. Manning was like a computer, collecting data and processing information at record speeds. When he played with the Colts, their offense never shifted; they remained static before each play. Why? Because Manning (and, to a degree, Mudd) wanted to survey the defense, anticipate the call, and then run the best play to attack. If anyone on offense moved or created confusion, the defense would move, forcing Manning to recalibrate as the play clock ran down.

Once the defensive coordinators throughout the league got wise to Manning's talent, they had to revise their strategy. Since Manning was looking for indicators from alignments, depths, and shifts, the defense decided to remain static. They aligned in the exact same spot every play—never cheating an inch in any direction, always maintaining the discipline in the alignment, and never, ever, ever moving until the play clock was under five seconds. Did this "statue" approach keep Manning from being successful? Not really, but it helped take away one of his many natural edges.

The Colts' offense relied on being simple to start, and then complex with their adjustments for each opponent. By having a foundation of simplicity, Manning could utilize his incredible talents and the Colts' offense would be impossible to slow down. Like all great quarterbacks, when Manning played, he was quick minded to make up for not being quick footed. He controlled the football with pinpoint accuracy and fit the ball into the tightest of windows. He could slide his feet, had a knack for feeling the rush, and never took his eye off the secondary. He understood the protections, could make the right adjustments at the line of scrimmage, and ensured he was protected.

There was a time in the league when safety blitzes from depth were popular. Teams would cheat their safety down toward the line of scrimmage, and then from ten yards after the ball was snapped attack the passer, hoping to catch him off guard because the protection scheme didn't account for him. Manning didn't need the line to block the safety—the ball left his hand before the safety was even within two yards of him. (Then, Manning being Manning, he would slap the safety on the backside as if he did something great and run the next play.)

The brilliance of Manning occurred before the game started. His preparation and attention to detail allowed him to have the answers before taking the test. He understood the opponent, the defensive coaches, and how they would think react and call the game. He was the poker player who could read the hands of his opponent by examining body language and facial expressions. And, other than his rookie season and the 2001 season, Manning's Colts always registered double-digit wins. He was never out of any game, regardless of the score, and was the man responsible for putting the middle eight—the last four minutes of the first half and the first four of the second—into everyone's football vocabulary. If a team defers the toss and can have the ball with four minutes or less at the end of the first half and then get the ball to start the second, they can extend a lead, or close down a deficit. What was the best defense against Manning? Have Manning on the sideline. And if a team could control the middle eight, they gave themselves a better chance to defeat Manning and the Colts.

Winning it all was another matter. With Tom Brady and Bill Belichick in New England, the rivalry between the Colts and the Patriots was intense. They met fourteen times during the 2000s, with the Patriots winning eight games and two Super Bowls. The Colts won six games and one Super Bowl. Each game was an epic chess match between two well-coached and in-game adjusted teams. Manning took the blame for playoff failures, even if they weren't all his fault. The Colts were never a big physical team, particularly on defense. When they had to play outdoors on grass, the lack of size and physicality became apparent, and without the benefit of the home crowd noise helping their smaller defensive line get off the ball, opposing teams found successes offensively. Only once did the Colts hold the Patriots to under twenty points during the Brady-Manning battles. As great as Manning was, his 14–13 playoff record falls short of his talent. Manning was fun to watch and learn from. From his pregame ritual with Marvin Harrison to his competitive fire on the field to his overall understanding of the game, he was a huge football resource. And you could learn from him—from the minute he entered the huddle, to what hash mark he wanted the ball to start the drive, and to how he coached the players after each play. Even when his arm or his movement wasn't the same because of a prior neck injury, Manning made two plays in an AFC Conference Championship game against the Patriots during my time with the team, which prevented us from going to another Super Bowl. Those two checks caught our linebacker Jamie Collins out of position and resulted in us losing a game and a chance at another title. *The Bourne Identity* had multiple sequels; we'd be lucky if we ever got another Peyton Manning.

12
JOE MONTANA

4x Super Bowl Champion • 3x Super Bowl MVP •
2x NFL MVP • 1x NFL Offensive Player of the Year •
2x NFL Passing Touchdown Leader • 2x Passing Rating Leader •
5x NFL Completion Percentage Leader

3x First Team All-Pro • 2x Second Team All-Pro • 8x Pro Bowl

All-Decade Team: 1980s •
All-Time Team: 75th & 100th Anniversaries

15-Year Career • 192 Games Played; 164 Started

3,409 Passing Completions • 5,391 Passing Attempts •
40,551 Passing Yards • 273 Passing Touchdowns •
139 Interceptions

It was the morning of Super Bowl XIX on January 20, 1985, and the 49ers' locker room was filled with players, coaches, and staff, all remaining completely silent for hours. No one said a word, and no one wanted to say anything. As I walked around the room, pacing and avoiding eye contact with everyone, a sense of gratitude came rushing over me. How could I be so lucky? How at twenty-five years old could I experience something so amazing? To me, a barber's son who had crossed Highway 9 to chase my dream, the locker room on this day seemed like the place where dreams did come true.

The 49ers' scarlet jerseys were neatly hung, perfectly pressed, cleaned, and ready to be placed over the shoulder pads that sat at the base of each player's locker before the team went off to battle the Miami Dolphins. The equipment men, led by Bronco Hinek, Chico Norton, and Teddy Walsh (relation to Bill) were there hours before the game, making sure that each player had everything he needed. Head coach Bill Walsh arrived early, dressed in his game-day attire of gold slacks, white sneakers, and a scarlet V-neck 49ers sweater with a white oxford shirt underneath, its perfectly pressed collar neatly showing. He looked like a five-star general in his uniform of the day, moving and weaving until finally lying down with both hands folded behind his head, as if he were ready to take a midday siesta. Walsh wanted everyone to relax, act cool, and not get overexcited. The one player Walsh wasn't worried about was the skinny kid from western Pennsylvania, Joe "Cool" Montana, nicknamed for always maintaining his cool under pressure.

As with any discovery of a great player, false stories are told enough times that people believe them as truth. With Montana, many believe Bill Walsh needed someone to throw while working out receiver James Owens at UCLA, and Montana happened to be available, ready to provide an arm. Once Walsh saw Montana's athletic talent, he instantly fell in love. But according to Walsh, this wasn't true. Montana was already on his radar, with Walsh impressed with his spectacular comeback under impossible conditions in the Cotton Bowl, when the quarterback led Notre Dame to victory after they were trailing 34–12 at the start of the third quarter. Walsh later shared this account: "We were coming off a 2–14 year. We were in dire straits everywhere. I investigated every viable college quarterback…Joe threw for an hour. The minute I saw him drop back—his quick movement, those quick, nimble, Joe Namath–type feet—I got very serious. As much as I wanted Steve Dils, who'd been my quarterback at Stanford, who knew my system, I knew I had to forgo that for Joe. Joe was bigger and quicker, and he threw better." I believe Walsh because he never did things by the seat of his pants. He was detail oriented, especially when considering a quarterback. He would openly tell me, "Michael, few can coach the position, and even fewer can evaluate the position." And Walsh could do both.

For Walsh's offense, the quarterback had to be like a great boxer with quickness and movement, throwing well-timed punches. Walsh didn't care about arm talent or size; the quarterback needed great feet that worked with his arm in complete harmony, and Montana was perfectly in alignment.

Walsh also didn't run pass plays; he ran perfectly timed pass plays. He needed detailed precision and rhythm to every throw, from an athlete who could hit the third, or fifth, step of the drop and then throw the ball to a perfect location. Montana was exceptional in this area, and with Walsh's detailed teaching, they formed the perfect duo. Montana said, "It was intimidating the first year, having to learn the volume of things he taught. I had to forget college and start over." Together, they succeeded.

When a great quarterback player meets a great coach who tailors the entire team around the strengths of the offense, then a dynasty is formed. We see it with Belichick and Brady, with Graham and Brown, and with Walsh and

Montana. In such partnerships, both the quarterback and the coach play equal parts in the success, but the coach's ability to know the talent of the player enhances the talent of the coach.

Montana remained true to his nickname and never became nervous in the locker room before the game against Miami. He walked around as if he were playing in a pickup game at the rec center. He never worried about the opponent, only about his play. Montana dominated the day, moving the ball up and down the field, throwing for 331 yards and three touchdown passes, and leading the 49ers to thirty-eight points and their second Super Bowl ring. It would be my first, and not a day that passes that I am not thankful for being able to watch Montana practice, play, and win.

11
DAVID "DEACON" JONES

2x NFL Defensive Player of the Year • 5x Sack Leader

5x First Team All-Pro • 3x Second Team All-Pro • 8x Pro Bowl

All-Decade Team: 1960s •
All-Time Team: 75th & 100th Anniversaries

14-Year Career • 191 Games Played; 168 Started

173.5 Sacks (unofficial)

"Who is that guy?" is a common refrain when watching tape and, instead of the player you're scouting, another jumps off the screen, commanding your attention. Perhaps the greatest "Who is that guy?" moment occurred in the Los Angeles Rams' offices in 1961. Scouts Eddie Kotal and Johnny Sanders were studying college tape with an eye on running back Eugene White from Florida A&M. As the tape rolled, Sanders told Kotal, "Never mind the halfback, what's this big kid's name? He looks like the best player on the field." Two weeks later, the Rams announced in the fourteenth round, the 186th pick overall, that they had selected defensive end David "Deacon" Jones from South Carolina State.

Jones had rare speed for a big man. He was explosive off the ball and could run with anyone on the field. Once during a game against the Washington Redskins, Jones had to close down on their star receiver—and perhaps one of the fastest players in the NFL—Bobby Mitchell, after he broke free along the sideline. Instead of pushing him out of bounds, Jones decided to run stride for stride with Mitchell, causing his head coach, Harland Svare, to ask Jones why he allowed Mitchell to gain a few more yards. Jones said, "Sorry about that, Coach. But I had to find out if I was as fast as Mitchell. And I was."

Jones would catch running backs from behind and remind them he was the fastest as he brought them to the ground. Jones also had great agility and power. He was famous for his head slap, which was later outlawed by the NFL, yet his game featured more than one move. Along with Lamar Lundy, Merlin Olsen, and Roosevelt Grier, Jones helped form the Rams' Fearsome Four. All tall, lean, and strong, these four players made life hell for the opposing quarterback.

The combination of the four made each of them special. A dominating defensive line can singlehandedly control the game when a team has more than one player who can win against one-on-one blocking. Coaches spend hours upon hours trying to isolate their best rusher on one lineman, trying to avoid the double teams, the slide protections, and the back from chipping. When a team has two players who are hard to handle alone, they become great; when they have four, as the Rams did, they take over the game.

Jones put fear in opposing quarterbacks with his relentless style of play. Once, Lions quarterback Karl Sweetan had a memorable encounter with Jones as they walked off the field at the Coliseum. Sweetan had taken a beating from Jones, as the Rams dominated the entire game, winning 24–3. Walking behind Jones, Sweetan made a funny face at him, which all the writers waiting to gain entrance to the locker room could observe. When a reporter asked Sweetan about the childish gesture, he said, "Sure, I did it. But I made sure his back was turned."

In 1963, Jones came to training camp weighing 290 pounds, which gave him more power but limited his quickness. Once he realized he didn't need more weight to play with power, he shed the weight and made sure he was always near the 250-pound mark, getting leaner and leaner with each season. Jones had speed, explosive quickness, toughness, length, and one of the greatest bursts to close of any defensive lineman. Had he played today, Jones could easily track down Patrick Mahomes of the Chiefs or Josh Allen of the Bills if they escaped the pocket. Speed in the defensive line limits the movement in the pocket, and Jones had all the speed he needed.

Jones had four seasons of nineteen or more sacks, and from 1964 until 1970, he registered 127.5 sacks. Those numbers are unofficial, and there is no telling how many quarterback hits or hurries he was able to produce during that time period. No one in today's game has his combination of speed and power. Myles Garrett and Bruce Smith are similar, but not as quick. Jones stands alone, below just one other defensive end in NFL history, and it will be a long time before a team has another "Who is that guy?" moment that produces a talent like Jones.

"WHO IS THAT GUY?" BEFORE THE AGE OF INFORMATION

Back in 1995, sitting in my hotel suite in Santa Clara, California, and hearing the rain hammering the windows with a steady force, I knew practice for the East-West Shrine game was not going to happen. It was another day lost watching players in person. Days like this occasionally happen in Northern California in January, when rain, not sunshine, dominates the landscape. Fortunately, whenever attending a bowl game, our scouting staff, which was led by Jim Schwartz, made sure we brought our video equipment and beta tapes to continue preparing for the draft. Schwartz, head coach Bill Belichick, scouting director Dom Anile, and I gathered in a large room with a projection screen, watching the LSU Tigers defense playing against the Alabama offense. Our focus was on number 88, Gabe Northern, an LSU defensive end projected to be a potential starter in the league. As we rolled the tape, we all had a "who is that guy?" moment. Belichick asked Anile about number 94, to which Anile answered honestly, "I have no clue. He must be an underclassman." In the days before cell phones and Google, we had to scramble; there was no instant information at our fingertips. We had to work hard for the information. I told Schwartz to call back to the office and ask our scouting department secretary, Ann Pershey, to fax us the bio of this mystery man. When Schwartz finally returned from the front desk with fax in hand, we learned that number 94 was Anthony McFarland, a freshman from Winnsboro, Louisiana. Four years later, McFarland was the first-round pick of the Tampa Bay Buccaneers.

10
DON HUTSON

3x NFL Champion • 2x MVP • 8x NFL Reception Leader •
7x Receiving Yards Leader • 9x Touchdown Leader •
5x Scoring Leader • 1x Interception Leader

8x First Team All-Pro • 4x NFL All-Star

All-Decade Team: 1930s •
All-Time Team: 50th, 75th & 100th Anniversaries

11-Year Career • 116 Games Played; 60 Started

488 Receptions • 7,991 Receiving Yards Gained •
99 Receiving Touchdowns

30 Interceptions

Don Hutson, playing wide receiver for the University of Alabama, was a star in every sport he attempted. From Pine Bluff Arkansas, Hutson walked onto the football team, helping them win a National Championship in 1934. Hutson was long and lean, with rare track-timed speed, so when he first began his career on the gridiron, he was thought to be too slender. That soon changed when no one could compete with his speed and the Alabama football team, with Dixie Howell as quarterback, became a passing team.

When Packers head coach and general manager Curly Lambeau traveled to Los Angeles in 1935 to watch Alabama prepare for the Rose Bowl against Stanford, he was smitten by Hutson's speed, catching ability, and overall athletic talent. Lambeau knew he needed that talent for his Packers. During the game, Hutson took the top off the defense, scoring on a fifty-four-yard touchdown pass and a fifty-nine yarder to help the Crimson Tide win 29–13. After the game, Lambeau offered Hutson $300 per game (roughly $6,300 today) to join the Packers. Hutson had to be willing to accept two checks—each for $150, from different banks—to keep his salary a secret from the other players.

Hutson signed with Lambeau, but he also signed with another NFL team, the Brooklyn Dodgers. Signing players in the 1930s was open warfare, as contracts meant nothing until approved by the league office. After each team learned of the other's contract, NFL president Joe Carr informed both that whichever letter arrived at his office with the earliest postmark would decide where Hutson would play. The Packers' letter arrived with a time stamp of 8:30 a.m., seventeen minutes before Brooklyn's, and Hutson became a Packer, causing Lambeau to joke, "It's lucky I sent my letter special delivery." American journalist Hunter S. Thompson once wrote, "Luck is a very thin wire between survival and disaster." I am sure Lambeau would agree.

Hutson instantly made the Packers' offense a deep-play attack. The first play of his NFL career was an eighty-three-yard touchdown pass against the Bears. Lambeau moved him to the flanker position, the first time anyone ever spread the formation. With his long stride and amazing lateral quickness, Hutson was catching deep passes from quarterback Arnie Herber. During this time, a football actually wasn't easy to throw or catch. Hutson's hands were soft and his hand-eye hand coordination was excellent. He made the game look easy, and there was no one on the field who could match his speed (measured at 9.7 in the 100 meters), or his ability to tackle and kick field goals. He also had lateral movement to avoid tacklers.

That quickness and speed allowed Hutson to run his routes using fakes, body shifts, and head motion to get his defender off balance. When you examine a passing game in any NFL team's playbook, there is always a straight line indicating the pass route. Hutson was the first to bring deception to the route, which is why he led the NFL in touchdown receptions for nine seasons. Watching Hutson run past players is startling, as he always had two to three steps on everyone. He wasn't just open; he was wide open.

Each time I watch him catch that round, watermelon-shaped brown ball, I think how much better he would have been in today's game. His soft hands and catch radius would shine so brightly that he would become a nightmare for any defensive back to cover. In today's game, there's no player who has skills comparable to Hutson's.

It has been seventy-seven years since Hutson caught his last pass, yet his skills and remarkable achievements still hold the test of time, and they will continue to be greater than most of those who come after him. He offered a glimpse into rare perfection, which should never be forgotten.

9
"MEAN" JOE GREENE

4x Super Bowl Champion • 2x NFL Defensive Player of the Year

5x First Team All-Pro • 3x Second Team All-Pro • 10x Pro Bowl

All-Decade Team: 1970s •
All-Time Team: 75th & 100th Anniversaries

13-Year Career • 181 Games Played; 172 Started

77.5 Sacks (unofficial)

In 1979, Bill Backer of the McCann Erickson advertising agency, the man who conceived the famous "I'd Like to Buy the World a Coke" campaign, launched another, this time with a young fan meeting Mean Joe Greene in the tunnel of the stadium. As the commercial begins, we hear the crowd roaring and see Greene holding onto the rail as he limps toward the locker room. The young boy is polite, calling to Mr. Greene and offering him help off the field. Greene shrugs and pivots away from the little boy, who then tells Greene that he is the best player ever. As though his best days are behind him, Greene shrugs and says, "Yeah." In a gesture of good will, the boy offers Greene his Coke, which Green after some hesitation accepts and then downs in one giant sip. In exchange, Greene gives the boy his jersey. Not only did the ad become a worldwide success and win a Clio award for the best advertisement, it helped fans see Greene in a different light and will always be a part of his life story.

There is a fine line between being tough and being competitive. When a great athlete possesses both, along with talent, many focus only on the "tough part," creating a narrative and labeling the person. Greene was tough from childhood, but hidden in that toughness was a will to win. He had a temper, but soon coaches redirected his temper and this man became unblockable. When Steelers coach Chuck Noll was given the authority to run the draft in his first season, he was amazed to evaluate a talent like Greene. For Noll, picking Greene was a sure thing. Everyone in the organization marveled at the size and speed of this young rookie. When Greene ran a 4.8 at 270 pounds, it prompted longtime trainer Ralph Berlin to say, "I've never seen a guy that big run that fast." And when Greene got angry, he'd play at an even higher level. With Greene being drafted, the Steel Curtain was established and became the most dominating front in football, following the Rams' Fearsome Foursome.

Some might compare Greene to current Cardinal J. J. Watt for his physical size and dominance. But Greene was different in the sense that he was always near the ball, working inside. He never ventured outside and forced teams to change their protection schemes. Watt played end, and in nickel situations would move inside. Greene also had more lateral and vertical quickness, making him harder to handle. When someone like Greene is playing, regardless of the era, it's hard to find comps.

RETHINKING THE WIDE RECEIVER

The football fan base has fallen in love with the wide receiver position. Teams are drafting wide receivers in the first round, believing these players will change their fortunes instantly. Bill Walsh, an offensive coach, said the wide receiver position was the last position that a team with an abundance of needs should address. He understood the value was finding serviceable receivers in the later rounds. Wide receivers are like going to a steakhouse. They are the side dish, the garlic fries, the sauteed mushrooms, and the onions; they add to the splendor of the meal. But the steak is the reason you're there, and the steak decides the meal, much like the defensive line determines the game.

With any extensive project there is usually a valuable learning lesson or a reinforcement of what might otherwise be overlooked during one's professional career. My love of defensive linemen has never wavered. I love them so much that my perfect draft would be taking one in every round. They are the key to winning football games and to being in position to win championships. It is strikingly obvious that the teams that build strength on strength—meaning adding to a strong defensive line—end up not only with a powerful nickname but a title as well. Why don't more teams behave in the manner of the Minnesota Vikings' Purple People Eaters, the Rams' Fearsome Foursome, the Cowboys' Doomsday Defense, the Dolphins' Killer Bees, or the Steelers' Steel Curtain? As much as the game has changed, how to win a title never changes. Strong quarterback play and domination in both lines are the ingredients to winning a title, and most receivers never live up to expectations.

The impact of the commercial was immense for Greene, as the Coke commercial story continued with a made-for-television movie advancing the story after his meeting in the tunnel. Greene played in Pittsburgh until 1981, when he retired and moved into a coaching and front office role. His impact on the game and the Steelers, like the commercial, was immeasurable.

8
JOHNNY UNITAS

1x Super Bowl Champion • 3x NFL Champion •
3x MVP • 4x NFL Passing Yards Leader •
4x Passing Touchdown Leader • 2x Passing Rating Leader •
1x Completion Percentage Leader • 3x Bert Bell Award

5x First Team All-Pro • 3x Second Team All-Pro • 10x Pro Bowl

All-Decade Team: 1960s •
All-Time Team: 50th, 75th & 100th Anniversaries

18-Year Career • 211 Games Played; 185 Started

2,830 Passing Completions • 5,186 Passing Attempts •
40,239 Passing Yards • 290 Passing Touchdowns •
253 Interceptions

Steelers head coach Walter "Keez" Kiesling was not buying Unitas. From the first day of practice, when he witnessed Unitas stammer and incorrectly answer a question, he believed Unitas was too dumb to play pro football. He banished Unitas to the bench and never gave him a chance to compete for a position on the team. In need of money—he had one child and another on the way—Unitas started looking elsewhere. He reached out to the Browns, but they had just talked Otto Graham into coming out of retirement and had no need for Unitas. With no other NFL options available for a paying football job, Unitas decided to play for the Bloomfield Rams of the Greater Pittsburgh League, a semipro team, for six dollars each game.

Unitas knew he never received a fair chance with his hometown team. So did his Bloomfield teammates, who would send letters to every NFL team extolling the talents of their quarterback. Their mail campaign rivaled that of any presidential candidate or spam email artist. The postcards came quickly and often, with a simple note: "There's a boy in sandlot ball here, playing for the Bloomfield Rams, who's worth looking at. His name is John Unitas."

Colts coach Weeb Ewbank was one of the recipients of the unsigned notes. He knew of Unitas from his relationship with Louisville coach Frank Camp and had a spot on the roster. Ewbank felt Unitas must love the game to risk playing on a dirt field in the semipro league and was not convinced about Unitas's reputation for not being smart. He felt Unitas would be good for the team.

Unitas became a member of the Colts and started seven games during his first season with the team. By his next season, he was the full-time starter and orchestrated the come-from-behind drive at Yankee Stadium against the New York Giants, sending the game into overtime and winning the 1958 NFL title.

As the captain of the visiting team, Unitas got to call the coin toss for overtime. He called heads, but when the coin settled onto the grass field, it came up tails. As far as the people in the press box felt, it was the only bad call he made all day. When quarterback Charlie Conerly scrambled on third down, he ended up six inches short of the first down. People in the stands pleaded for Giants head coach Jim Lee Howell to go for it on fourth down—nothing changes in football; everyone wants the coach to take enormous risks—but Howell sent Don Chandler onto the field to punt the ball away. The Colts offense took the field at their own twenty-yard line and began their drive. On the fifth play of the drive, Unitas got sacked and now faced third and fifteen. In the huddle, Unitas called for a formation the Colts hadn't run all day—a slot formation with explosive receiver Lenny Moore behind the right end. This drew two Giant defenders toward Moore, and he had a hard time separating. Facing heavy pressure from the Giants' defensive line, Unitas sidestepped the two defenders and waved for Raymond Berry to go deep. He connected with Berry to the Giants' forty-two-yard line and kept the chains moving.

On the next play, Unitas noticed Giants linebacker Sam Huff aligning near Berry and called for a trap play with fullback Alan Ameche, who took the ball twenty-three yards to the Giants nineteen-yard line. Unitas conferred with Ewbank on the sideline, who told his star quarterback to keep the ball on the ground for three plays and then kick the field goal. After Unitas broke the huddle, he observed Giants defender Cliff Livingston lined up man-to-man on his tight end Jim "Bucky" Mutscheller, who had run a tight corner route. Unitas's throw was deadly accurate and Mutscheller made the play at the one-yard line. With the next play, Ameche scored and the game was over. Thirteen plays in total, all called by Unitas himself, disproved any notion he lacked the mental ability to play in the NFL.

Many felt the game launched the NFL into the number-one sport in America, making football popular and Johnny U a legend. All he needed was a chance. Not a bad three-year turnaround. Unitas's story is inspirational considering how he went from not getting a rep to throwing for forty thousand yards and 290 touchdowns and becoming the second-greatest quarterback in the game.

7
ANTHONY MUÑOZ

9x First Team All-Pro • 2x Second Team All-Pro • 11x Pro Bowl

All-Decade Team: 1980s •

All-Time Team: 75th & 100th Anniversaries

13-Year Career • 185 Games Played; 182 Started

Working alongside of Bill Walsh, Sam Wyche understood the virtues of divergent thinking. As Walsh would tell his assistants, "If we are all thinking alike then no one is thinking," which motivated Wyche to think differently. Walsh's influence stayed with Wyche when he became the head coach of the University of Indiana in 1983. He knew beating the likes of Michigan or Ohio State wasn't going to happen unless he developed a new strategy, which he did with the Sugar Huddle. The strategy entailed exhausting the other team to gain an advantage. And after winning three games with this strategy, Wyche received a call from former boss Paul Brown, who offered to put Wyche in charge of the Cincinnati Bengals in 1984. Wyche brought the Sugar Huddle along with him.

He inherited a coaching staff, which three years earlier had played in the Super Bowl, and a roster that needed repair. Amazingly, the Bengals had three number-one picks in 1984, though none of them made as much of an impact as their second-round pick, quarterback Boomer Esiason; their eighth-round pick, guard Bruce Reimers; and their ninth-round pick, Bruce Kozerski. Those three players, along with the great left tackle Anthony Muñoz, created a powerful offensive line. They could block anyone. With their zone scheme and their fast pace of running plays, along with their skills and talent, by 1988 the Bengals' offense was impossible to slow down, when they reached the Super Bowl. Muñoz was the centerpiece of the offense, with his incredible athletic talent, balance, and power. He was impossible for any rusher to get around. He was incredibly agile his feet and never out of position. Muñoz was like mild-mannered Clark Kent, whom no one could imagine as Superman. He never had to act tough, but he played tough all the time in his quiet way. Muñoz made the game look easy, almost effortless. He played at the highest levels each and every Sunday. After each game, his grades were nearly perfect.

Muñoz made the game look easy. He never was on the ground, and was able to slide and punch with perfect timing. If there ever was a true dancing bear, Muñoz was that bear. He was light on his feet, never out of position, and never needed help blocking any rusher. Muñoz was like a machine, playing each and every Sunday at the highest of levels. It was impossible to remember him having a bad game.

While I was with the Browns, Muñoz made life miserable for our defensive line. As the director of pro scouting during this time, I was in charge of writing reports on each player—their background, strong points, and weak points, along with a summary—hoping to offer our defensive players a clue as to how to win against their opponent. Muñoz was one of the few players who never had a weak point. Even at the age of thirty-four, before he retired, Muñoz demonstrated no diminishing skills. His game looked perfect. There was nothing weak about his game, no faults or lack of consistent effort. It's no surprise Muñoz became the first Bengal to reach the Hall of Fame for his incredible play.

6
RONNIE LOTT

4x Super Bowl Champion • 2x NFL Interception Leader • 1x Co-Forced Fumble Leader

8x First Team All-Pro • 10x Pro Bowl

All-Decade Team: 1980s & 1990s •
All-Time Team: 75th & 100th Anniversaries

14-Year Career • 192 Games Played; 189 Started

63 Interceptions; 5 Returned for Touchdowns

After being soundly beaten 17–3 on the road in the Meadowlands in 1985 by the New York Football Giants, in Wildcard Weekend, Bill Walsh knew he had to overhaul his roster, starting with finding a defensive rusher and someone who could cover in the secondary. For the first time since accepting the job in 1978, Walsh needed to infuse the 49ers with young talent.

Before the plane landed back in the Bay area, Walsh had already called me up to the front with instructions for notebooks to assemble, college reports for him to view, and the schedule of the Senior Bowl practices. He wasn't messing around; he was going all in on the college draft, and so was his coaching staff. He knew there was a sense of urgency, and when Walsh felt urgency, it tended to multiply threefold.

Walsh came from the Paul Brown school of player personnel, which relied more on the coach's evaluation than the scouts'. Walsh would often remind me to never become a traditional scout—a former fired bad coach now telling a good coach whom to select. Walsh respected scouts—if they understood the plight of the coach, if they had a sense of appreciation for the craft of coaching and didn't blame every failure on the coach. He demanded that I understand the 49ers' scheme, ask what the player could do, and always place the player in the best light. So during this off-season, he wanted his coaches to be heavily involved in using the scouts for a sense of direction. Once the coach was assigned a player, he would write a report and grade the player, and then every Saturday that winter and into spring, we would have meetings to review the players.

In one of those Saturday meetings, we were discussing an incredibly talented and explosively fast defensive back named Tim McKyer from Texas Arlington University, the same place where we had drafted an offensive lineman, Bruce Collie, the year before. McKyer had rare talent, but he was frail and not physical, and he was never interested in run support. Had McKyer even attempted to be half interested in physical contact, he might have been a top ten pick. As it was, he was barely hanging on our draft board until our defensive backfield coach, Ray Rhodes, proclaimed, "Coach we can take McKyer. Ronnie will make him tackle." My head spun around as I looked at Rhodes and wondered, Who is Ronnie? Walsh heard Rhodes but didn't confirm one way or another until the draft, when we selected McKyer with the sixty-fourth pick overall.

Rhodes later informed me that even though he would demand McKyer play more physically, Lott would have far more impact. Lott would be able to make McKyer scared to death to return to the huddle if he gave it one of his signature turn downs on a tackle. And if you have even been on a football field and watched Ronnie Lott play, lead, demand, and compete, then you knew what Rhodes said was completely true.

Ronnie Lott possessed that Michael Jordan competitive gene that fuels others and demands more of himself. Former NBA coach Jeff Van Gundy once said, "Your best player must set the tone of intolerance for anything that gets in the way of winning." Those words describe Lott perfectly. Selected as the eighth pick overall in the 1981 draft by Bill Walsh, Lott came to define, control, and drive the 49ers. When Lott first arrived in San Francisco, he had Jack Reynolds, a crusty old linebacker, to help him navigate the path toward leading from within. By the 1986 season, after Walsh had recorded one of the greatest drafts in modern times, Lott had a bunch of young players to shape, mold, and develop into stars, most notably Charles Haley, the great pass rusher from James Madison and a fourth-round steal for Walsh. The defense never got the credit or national popularity like the offense did, yet it was Lott's competitive drive that moved the dynasty forward. Inside that locker room only one voice carried; it was Ronnie's. The birth of the 49ers' dynasty was as much about Lott as about anyone else in that building.

Lott had many hard hits, which some may say would be outlawed today, though upon close review, many of them were shoulder tackles. Lott was great at being in position and using his shoulder to knock down the ball carrier or the receiver. His power came from his instincts. He was always in the right place at the right time, which allowed him to play with more physicality. He was always under control and, like a great boxer, in balance to deliver his knockout blow. He studied the game and his opponents, knowing that working hard Wednesday to Saturday would help ensure he was always in the most perfect position. Then his instincts would take over. Lott wasn't a dirty player or an out-of-control hitter. He was composed and tactical, and he understood how to get to the junction point of the ball and the runner better than the defender. Whether he was playing safety or corner, Lott saw the game in slow motion. He was equally effective playing either position, and he made it to the Pro Bowl for each. Today, he would be best served to play in the middle of the defense, creating havoc.

Lott would excel on all three levels and force the offense to account for him in their protection scheme if he played today. He would run over any running back attempting to block him, and unless the offense had a lineman accounting for him, he would harass the quarterback the entire game. He would be a weapon on defense to neutralize the run or the pass, depending on how he was deployed. If used in the run game, Lott would play like a Will linebacker, roaming from sideline to sideline, making every tackle. In the passing game, he would roam center field and then make sure the receiver never wanted to cross the middle of the field again. The rules might have limited his impactful hits, but nothing would eliminate his toughness or ability to intimidate.

Part of the scout's job is to observe players and understand how they prepare for the task at hand—how serious they are in understanding the details of the game, how to take the practice field to the game field, and how to show others how to become great players. Watching Lott every day was an incredible experience for a young scouting professional, and that experience was unmatched until I watched Tom Brady in New England. Lott was more than a hard hitter, more than a tough guy who played through an amputated pinky finger, more than a coverage man, and more than a football player. He was the foundation piece that built something bigger than himself, a football dynasty.

5
JERRY RICE

3x Super Bowl Champion • 1x Super Bowl MVP •
2x Offensive Player of the Year • 6x Receiving Yards Leader •
2x NFL Reception Leader • 6x NFL Touchdown Leader •
1x NFL Scoring Leader

10x First Team All-Pro • 1x Second Team All-Pro • 13x Pro Bowl

All-Decade Team: 1990s •
All-Time Team: 75th & 100th Anniversaries

20-Year Career • 303 Games Played; 284 Started

1,549 Receptions • 22,895 Receiving Yards Gained •
197 Receiving Touchdowns

Six weeks before the 1985 NFL draft began, one specific line on the phone was glowing on my desk, which meant only one thing—Nicole wanted something. Nicole was Bill Walsh's secretary and served as the conduit through which Coach conveyed what he needed. This call was different. No instructions, no pleasantries—all that was mentioned was, "He wants to see you." It didn't sound good. I was a gofer, not someone at a level to be seen or heard. Walking down the long corridor, I felt everyone knew I was heading to the back room, where my "judgment day cometh," and the verdict couldn't be good. Once before, I had peeked my head inside this small, well-appointed office, and it was like visiting the Batcave. Gofers don't get to go inside the Batcave. This time, Walsh called me in...by name.

"Michael, I want you to do a special project for me, and I don't want anyone to know what you are doing, and that includes Razzano," was his opening line. (Tony Razzano was my main boss, the 49ers' director of college scouting, and the man who gave me my start in the NFL.) Walsh asked for a large-scale book report on three specific players. He didn't want any scouting jargon or a repetition of what the coaches had said, but a deep dive into each player's personality, his character, and his love of the game, and he wanted the report to convey an understanding of what made each player tick. He wanted structure to the report, not bullet points or random notes. I had to present a flow of comprehensive thoughts that would tie everything together, but offer no conclusion. He didn't want my opinion; he wanted to read what others thought—from grade school to high school, anyone who had interactions with the players and could offer a unbiased point of view. Walsh then gave me the list—Al Toon of Wisconsin, Eddie Brown of Miami, and Jerry Rice of Mississippi Valley State—and he told me he needed the report finished in one month.

Each player was unique and filled with many examples that would provide Walsh with the information he needed, but one player was distinctive in his background, the obstacles he had faced, and the inner will of his character. The remarkable trait of perseverance was evident in every part of Jerry Rice's life.

The words "hard work" and "determination" came up with each person I talked to from his high school. When I asked for an example of his hard work, they would mention Jerry working with his father, loading heavy, hot bricks in the deep summer with heat and humidity strong enough to send a resting man indoors. I can vividly remember hearing Rice's senior year numbers and not believing they could be true. Eighty receptions and thirty-five touchdowns seemed so far-fetched. And Rice only lost two games his junior and senior seasons. And yet no school had recruited him. How could no one want a talent like this on their team? His brother Tom was on scholarship at Jackson State, though they didn't seem interested. With no one calling, Rice took his only offer, which came from Archie Cooley, the head coach of Mississippi Valley State.

Soon most of America came to know about Rice and the Mississippi Valley offense, with Rice's speed and incredible hands bolstering an offense that threw the ball on average 55.8 times per game, along with running the no-huddle. Using a formation that looked like an inbound play in basketball, with four receivers stacked one after another, the offense game became unstoppable, averaging 640 yards per game, with a 496.8 passing-yard average. By the time Rice was done, he amassed eighteen Division I records and had every NFL team scout visiting him.

Later, Walsh thanked me for the report, but never indicated what direction he was thinking of taking come draft day. I can't say my report altered anything about the '85 draft or made me more important in the role of drafting Rice. But it demonstrated Walsh's eagerness to understand each prospective player and to dig deeper than most to find answers. He wasn't happy until he had all the data, and from that day forward I believed Walsh could never make a mistake; I could only give him bad data. Did Walsh think Rice would become the best receiver ever in football? No, but he knew that with his ability to develop Rice and Rice's willingness to learn, great things were on the horizon. Walsh called Rice an "absolutely majestic football player." And "majestic" is the right word. Rice was able to do everything Walsh wanted, and then some.

Walsh loved calling the "Colorado route" near the goal line as part of his offense. It begins as though the receiver is going to run a slant, and then suddenly he turns his body quickly, using flexibility in his hips to burst in the opposite direction of the slant. Not all receivers can run the Colorado route. It takes smoothness, no wasted motion, and the flexibility in the hips to pivot suddenly. Rice had all of those moves, and then some. The Colorado route was one of the main factors contributing to his 197 touchdowns.

Another component critical to understanding Rice's greatness was his conditioning and stamina. He never got tired, never needed a break, and always was better in the fourth quarter than in the first. As the game went along, Rice got stronger, grew more powerful, and broke tackles with more regularity. When the ball was in his hands, he was one of the best runners on the field, with vision and change of speeds that deceived opponents. Rice always played at the same speed, from start to finish; there never was a slow route. Every route was at full speed, and his playing speed was faster than most players' timed forty speed. With cleats and the ball in his hands, Rice became faster and faster.

What separates good from great is God-given talent. What separates great from elite is a willingness to keep improving and keep working, and being driven. Rice wasn't good or great; he was elite because of his incredible willingness to drive himself beyond. He wasn't trying to prove his doubters wrong; he was proving to himself he was capable of something bigger, something better. Rice never needed outside motivation; his constant internal battle became his source of drive. Most never understand the difference between motivation and drive. Motivation is a desire, something we want to achieve; drive is how far we are willing to tax our bodies and minds to conquer what lies ahead. Rice had incredible drive—and that drive manifested itself on the field in college and in the pros.

Today, a picture of Jerry Rice holding the 2002 AFC Championship trophy high above his head hangs in my office. He was the first player I ever played a part in drafting and one of the finest I've ever seen perform.

4
REGGIE WHITE

1x Super Bowl Champion • 2x Defensive Player of the Year •
2x NFL Sack Leader

8x First Team All-Pro • 5x Second Team All-Pro • 13x Pro Bowl

All-Decade Team: 1980s & 1990s •
All-Time Team: 75th & 100th Anniversaries

15-Year Career • 232 Games Played; 228 Started

198 Sacks

Coming off a 5–11 record in 1992, the Lions still had hope for the future and, with the Ford family resources, could afford a prize free agent like defensive end Reggie White of the Philadelphia Eagles. It was the first year of NFL free agency; nothing was normal, and for the first time since the AFL/NFL Wars, recruiting talent became important. The spring of 1993 in the NFL was the Wild, Wild West, and White was going to be the sheriff of the new frontier, which included adding the Lions to his list of team visits.

Teams were informed of the strict rules when it came to recruiting, and there would be no backroom promises or side deals, as every dollar a player would receive was going to be attached to the salary cap. Agents like Jimmy Sexton—who represented Reggie White—were now in the driver's seat, setting up scout visits and openly holding competitions for their players.

Sexton became White's agent in 1989 after White had a huge-falling out with his former agent, Patrick Forte, who was hired by the Eagles' front office and added an option year to White's contract without his approval. Sexton's first order of business representing White was hiring respected Philadelphia attorney John Langel to assist his case and filing a civil suit against Forte and the Eagles, stating, "White will not play under terms of the option, which the player did not even know about until the Eagles announced its existence last year." White was only twenty-eight at the time, entering the prime of his career. In his first four years in Philadelphia, he recorded seventy sacks—yes, seventy—and won Defensive Player of the Year in both 1987 and 1988. But before the case made it to court, Sexton agreed to a new four-year deal with the Eagles for White. But Sexton never could have anticipated that 1993 would become the first year of unrestricted free agency, and even at the tender age of thirty-one, White was still the most unblockable player in all of football.

While White was in Detroit, listening to head coach Wayne Fontes and others in the Lions organization telling him all the wonderful things they could do for his ministry, Sexton's beeper kept going off (this was still the era before cell phones). The Packers were calling, desperately wanting to be included in the White sweepstakes. General manager Ron Wolf, head coach Mike Holmgren, contract man Mike Reinfeldt, and recruiter Ray Rhodes all called before Sexton finally agreed to have White fly out and have a face-to-face with the Packers' brass.

White and Sexton boarded the Packers' private plane and went to Green Bay for a one-day trip. The Packers were ready with their sales pitch, led by their star quarterback Brett Favre. White had two priorities, one off the field and one on. He wanted to hear from all teams how could he advance his ministry in his new town and he wanted to know if the team could win a title. White knew the money was going to flow no matter what; he wasn't sure how much because Sexton was too smart to put a cap on a number. Sexton never said to any team, "It will take X amount," because he wasn't going to negotiate against himself. White loved his visit in Green Bay, telling everyone he would go home and pray, and listen to what God wanted him to do. By the time he returned to Knoxville, Tennessee, there were several messages on his answering machine, all in a hushed, quiet voice that sounded like it was Holmgren, telling him God was calling and wanted him to sign with the Packers.

Ron Wolf knew what White would mean to his team. Green Bay was no longer a destination spot for veterans, especially Black players. With free agency finally operational in the NFL, Wolf needed a major salesman, at any cost. During negotiations, each time Sexton increased the dollar amount in the total package he was negotiating for, Wolf would say yes. Finally, Sexton asked Wolf, "There isn't a number you won't go to, is there?" Wolf honestly replied, "No." By the start of April, White was down to three choices—the 49ers, Washington, and the Packers. Many felt the Packers were the odd team in the three-team race and were being used by Sexton to increase the offers from the other two. But White genuinely liked the Packers, and Sexton knew they would always have the best offer. In the end, the Packers offered White $17 million for four years, and on Tuesday, April 6, he joined Green Bay.

In an instant, the Packers became a team to fear. White made grown men look small with his signature hump move, stolen from watching the Raiders' Howie Long, a move that was impossible to anchor once White made contact. These large men went flying in the air when White hit them. White wasn't a speed rusher nor did he play with any finesse, but he was power, power, power all the time. He could stop the run, shed the blocker, and burst to the ball with ease, at times appearing as though he was the biggest kid playing peewee football. He had Herman Munster–like qualities of size, power, and kindness; he played hard, was competitive, and would always help the man he knocked down up off the ground.

Because the game was sheer power for White, he was hard to chip with the back or double team with the tight end. White was instinctive, and once he felt the protection sliding toward him, he would power one of the two men assigned to block him back into the quarterback. He never ran an edge or around a block, just always through the blocker. No one was able to stand in front of him for very long. Nothing could stop him from dishing out punishment.

Wolf and the Packers delivered on the promise of winning a title, and along with Favre, White was a driving force in making Green Bay a destination spot. There is never going to be another player like White. At times, J.J. Watt has demonstrated the same dominance and power, but not for as long. White left us too early, dying in 2004 at the tender age of forty-three. His impact on the game and the lives he touched will never be forgotten.

3
JIM BROWN

1x NFL Champion • 3x MVP • 8x Rushing Champion •
5x Rushing Touchdown Leader • 1x NFL Scoring Champion

8x First Team All-Pro • 1x Second Team All-Pro • 9x Pro Bowl

All-Decade Team: 1960s •
All-Time Team: 50th, 75th & 100th Anniversaries

9-Year Career • 118 Games Played; 118 Started

2,359 Rushing Attempts • 12,312 Rushing Yards Gained •
106 Rushing Touchdowns

262 Receptions • 2,499 Receiving Yards Gained •
20 Receiving Touchdowns

Jim Brown became part of the Browns again after Bill Belichick joined as head coach in 1991. To properly install a culture, Belichick firmly believed the players of the present must know and fully understand the past. Any great culture that grows, develops, and operates successfully must pay homage to those who have come before, and because he was now the head coach of this sacred franchise, Belichick was determined to mend any fences that the might have been broken in the past. Brown was never going to hold his tongue, and friendship between the two men grew in part because Belichick respected and wanted the hard truth from Brown.

So when Belichick would begin the Browns' rookie orientation, before the rookie mini-camp started, he would introduce Jim Brown along with many other great Browns players of the past, with video and a history lesson about the league and the team. Belichick wanted each new player to understand what it meant to wear the uniform, what the men before them had done, and why it was a great achievement for them to be part of this wonderful history. And Jim Brown's lesson was always jaw-dropping. Belichick would remind his new players that however good they believed they were in college or high school, no one—and he highlighted the words—*no one* could compare to Brown. Belichick explained that at Manhasset High School in Long Island Brown averaged fifteen yards rushing each time he carried the ball. He then averaged thirty-eight points a game on the hardwood playing basketball. Belichick's eyes would sparkle with glee as he launched into a description of Brown's remarkable achievements with the lacrosse stick and how no one in that sport ever saw anyone that big and fast with such amazing hand-eye coordination.

The rookies learned about Brown's four-sport career at Syracuse, how even though he was the best player on the basketball team he wasn't allowed to start because Syracuse only allowed two Black players on the court at the same time. Belichick took the players inside the 1957 NFL draft, which saw two halfbacks, Paul Hornung of Notre Dame and Jim Arnett of USC, go before Brown. Brown was the sixth pick of the draft, not the first.

Belichick would then turned his attention to Brown's NFL career. In week nine of his rookie season, Brown set an NFL record for rushing in one game, 237 yards on thirty-one carries and four touchdowns, beating the Rams. Then during another game in 1961, Brown beat his own record—242 yards rushing with thirty-four carries, only to watch the official scorekeeper remove five yards, thus tying his record in a win against Philadelphia. He ran faster than anyone on the field and never ran out of bounds, always dishing punishment. He caught short passes and turned them into long touchdowns. His talent spoke for itself. Belichick would then emphasize Brown's durability, and how he never missed a game. By the time the meeting was over, each new player knew Brown, respected him, and understood he was considered the best to ever play the game.

In one of his greatest speeches, Robert Kennedy said, "Few men are willing to brave the disapproval of their fellows, the censure of their colleagues, the wrath of their society. Moral courage is a rarer commodity than bravery in battle or great intelligence. Yet it is the one essential, vital quality for those who seek to change the world which yields most painfully to change." Jim Brown also had that quality. He wanted to change the world. Brown used his incredible talents to become a voice for progress in our nation's never-ending struggle with racism. Brown would say, "I have fought all my life for freedom, equality, and justice. I have always been an outspoken independent individual." Not everyone understood or appreciated Brown's voice in the NFL community, in part because it created discomfort and uneasiness. But all Brown wanted was the same seat at the table as everyone else, and he was willing to become the lightning rod for his sport, just as Muhammad Ali did for boxing and Bill Russell for the

NBA. Those men never shied away from the danger or the uncertainty, knowing their talents gave them a powerful voice to bring about change. When Brown announced his retirement from football on the set of the 1969 film *100 Rifles*, he explained, "I want more mental stimulation, I wanna have a hand at the struggle that is taken place in our country." And he did.

The NFL has struggled to advance minority candidates, which in my view has been because of a lack of training and development of leaders. The head coaching position requires a complete understanding of how to lead, which most NFL coaching candidates lack. Most of these candidates do not have foundational leadership, which is why almost one-third of the work force is removed every single year. If the NFL were truly serious about the advancement of minority candidates, they would create a leadership academy, honoring Brown, and teach leadership courses to young coaches. The Jim Brown Center for Leadership would be a nonprofit academy that operates year-round to develop leadership skills in coaches at all levels, showing participants how to be better leaders with knowledge of the game, and providing them with a greater likelihood of success.

Even after Belichick started his destiny in New England, he continued his teachings of Brown's qualities and talent. In 2016, after the Patriots beat the Browns in Cleveland, he took the players to view the statue of Brown on display and reminded them of the Cleveland Browns' greatness and how much history had occurred on the field they just left. Belichick put it best when he said, "My concern with Jim is that, as time goes by people, will forgot about how important he was to sports and society. I just hope people don't forget his legacy...He is without question one of the top two or three human beings I have every met and I am proud to be his friend."

REMEMBERING JIM BROWN

I loved that he even knew my name. Well, at least my last name.

Once, Bill Belichick, Jim Brown, and I visited the Riverfront State Prison, overlooking the Delaware River in Camden, New Jersey, to help with his Amer-I-Can program. In his heavy, authoritative voice, Brown leaned toward me and said, "*Luumbardi*, they have a no-hostage rule in this prison."

"What's that, Jim?" I replied.

"If a prisoner takes you, you're on your own," he answered. I gulped and acted like I hadn't heard the greatest running back of all time.

2
LAWRENCE "L. T." TAYLOR

2x Super Bowl Champion • 1x NFL MVP • 2x Defensive Player
of the Year • 1x NFL Sack Leader

8x First Team All-Pro • 2x Second Team All-Pro • 10x Pro Bowl

All-Decade Team: 1990 •
All-Time Team: 75th & 100th Anniversaries

13-Year Career • 184 Games Played; 180 Started

142 Sacks • 9 Interceptions; 2 Returned for Touchdowns

A Million Quarterback Hurries

In the spring of 1981, twenty-six of the twenty-eight general managers polled before the draft believed Lawrence Taylor was the best player. It wasn't a hard decision. Taylor was sensational playing for the Tarheels, as most of his tackles his senior season were behind the line of scrimmage, disrupting every offensive team he faced in the ACC.

Giants general manager George Young loved Taylor because he was the perfect combination of everything—his height, weight, and speed chart. He was "clean," meaning he had no flaws in his overall game. Over my years of working within the system, I have only one encountered one A player. According to the Giants' scouts, Taylor's final grade on their board, the highest for 1981, was a B8.0. That's still sensational. (Their system was based on standards starting with A and ending with K; other the years there was only one A player—running back Billy Sims from Oklahoma.)

In the first intersquad scrimmage, Taylor dominated with four sacks and a forced fumble. He was clearly the best player on the field. In the preseason, Taylor created more problems when facing the Steelers, causing quarterback Terry Bradshaw to ask his teammates, "Who is this guy? He keeps coming from my blind side and ripping my ribs apart." By week five of the regular season,

Vikings offensive coordinator Bob Schnelker, a former two-time Pro Bowl tight end, told his team, "Guys, let me tell you, I've seen Butkus, I've seen Nitschke, I've seen the best. Taylor is better than all of them."

Taylor's play on special teams made everyone notice. When special team coach Bill Belichick aligned Taylor at gunner, away from the interior line, much like a receiver, using his speed and power, Taylor was unblockable at the line, and then would find the returner, just like a fighter pilot locks his target in the air. The collisions caused fumbles and also forced other teams to use their big, fast players in the same manner, only without the same results.

Taylor's dominating play, his relentless competitive spirit, and his athletic talent changed the game offensively in both the run game and pass. For example, every team has a running play, tagged with the letters BOB, which stand for "back on backer." Now, what running back can block Taylor one-on-one? Short and long answer: no one. Every BOB had to go opposite of Taylor. There was only problem with that concept: who would block Taylor from running down the line and making the tackle from behind? Again, no one. Washington Redskins head coach Joe Gibbs developed his big one-back running game, using tight ends the size of linemen to help neutralize Taylor. 49ers' Bill Walsh and his great line coach Bobb McKittrick had to develop a dual-read guard-pass protection system in which John Ayers, an athletic left guard, would pull out from his position and attempt to handle Taylor coming off the edge. This protection scheme allowed a big man to block Taylor instead of blocking a running back, which was the norm before Taylor entered the league in 1981. How many players in NFL history can claim they changed schemes because of their dominating play? Not many.

When Taylor first arrived in New York, Bill Parcells was his defensive coordinator. He never backed away from confrontation with any player, he was clear with his rules. Parcells was honest and forthcoming with Taylor, telling him, "Lookit, I'm going to say what's on my mind and I won't bullshit you. So don't bullshit me." Taylor respected the honesty and, from that moment forward, allowed Parcells to coach him, which made him even more dangerous.

Belichick often told me that Taylor could have played anywhere, perhaps even corner in a Cover 2 scheme. He had football instincts all over the field, which is rare—and even rarer for a kid who wanted to become an MLB catcher, not a football star. He was hard to fool, hard to block, and hard to wear down, as his passion for the game and for competing fueled his play. His burst from the blocker to the ball carrier, either runner or quarterback, often went unnoticed. In scouting, we always measure forty times, and for pass rushers, their ten-yard dash. We never measure the ability to accelerate off the block point to the runner, which separates the good players from the great players. None of the defensive players in my top 100 have Taylor's burst. His burst was rare. No one who played the game before, or since, has come close.

Taylor played a game that was foreign to most football fans. He wasn't a linebacker or a defensive end; he was a dominating force who changed not only how teams played, but also how fans watched. We expected him to have superpowers—and he did. He played hurt, he played with a shoulder harness, and he played hard every single time he wore his uniform. His unyielding passion was obvious, and if he could love the game that much, anyone watching needed to feel the same. Taylor was unstoppable, and in every game he proved it.

THE GREATEST OF MISSES

Can you believe a team bypassed Taylor and five teams bypassed Jim Brown? Revisionist history is always easy, yet in both cases, it's still hard to comprehend, as both men dominated college football unlike any other. Rare greatness, which both men possessed and displayed at every level at which they competed, can be overlooked when our minds are not open to all the evidence. And now on to number one.

1
TOM BRADY

7x Super Bowl Champion • 5x Super Bowl MVP •
3x NFL MVP • 2x NFL Offensive Player of the Year •
5x NFL Touchdown Passing Leader • 4x NFL Passing Yards Leader •
2x NFL Passing Rating Leader •
1x NFL Completion Percentage Leader

3x First Team All-Pro • 3x Second Team All-Pro • 15x Pro Bowl

All-Decade Team: 2000s & 2010s •
All-Time Team: 100th Anniversary

23-Year Career • 335 Games Played; 333 started

Most Career Wins: 251

To become the best NFL player of all time, certain criteria must be met, showing without a doubt that this player rises above and beyond the competition. Much like the Brandt-Gilroy grading system, utilized in Dallas, in New England, and now with other NFL teams, there has to be a lettering system and a formal grade. For much the same reason that there was only one A-graded player—Billy Sims—in that system, there can be only one GOAT.

Tom Brady is that GOAT. Not because I type this wearing two Super Bowl rings that he helped me earn, but rather because he was still playing at a high level in his forties. He is the GOAT because he is the first athlete to stare Father Time in the face and laugh him away. When I joined the Patriots in 2014, Brady had just turned thirty-six, and it appeared that Father Time was taking over. He wasn't making all the same throws and wasn't looking down the field, and three games into the 2014 season, after he had been humiliated in Kansas City on Monday night, some local and national media questioned whether Brady was still able to play. The next twelve games, the playoff wins, and the Super

Bowl victory ended the speculation of his pending demise. He had a resurgence, as if he were cast in the 1985 movie *Cocoon*, about an elderly group of men who trespass into a neighbor's pool to swim without realizing the pool is filled with alien lifeforms, making them feel and act younger. Brady was rejuvenated and continued to perform at the best of his career.

One of the many GOAT traits Brady possesses is his remarkable ability to play through pain and injury. In the 2014 preseason, Brady tore his calf muscle during his usual Thursday resistance training dropbacks—it wasn't slightly sprained or pulled, but torn, and he went on the injury report. Most players with a torn calf, young or old, would have zero chance to play three days later. Not Brady. He played and kept playing all season. In 2016, after he was suspended for four games as a result of the "Deflategate" controversy, which included more inaccurate misinformation than the Warren Report, Brady took an awful hit from Seattle strong safety Kam Chancellor, which caused internal bleeding, and yet he still never missed a snap and he threw for over three hundred yards. By the way, 2016 was the only time in Brady's career that he missed a game, outside of the 2008 season, when he tore his ACL in game one.

So what makes Brady the best of the best? Here are the five criteria for being the GOAT that he has not only met, but that has established as a result of his own achievements. Perhaps in the next hundred years some other player will surpass these achievements, but it's highly doubtful.

Number One: Possess Supreme Dedication

There is no one more dedicated to his craft, from his conditioning and nutrition to his film study and understanding of the game and his opponents. Don't call Brady after eight o'clock at night, because the lights are already out and he is getting the rest he needs to attack the next day. He never stops working, and more remarkably, he never gets bored. How many out routes or slants has Brady thrown in his life? It's impossible to count, but he continues to throw them every single day, as if he were some high school freshman getting called up to the varsity. There is nothing left to chance; he does the same thing each day, from how he eats and sleeps to his work on flexibility and massage therapy.

Number Two: Win Title Championships

In only one season during his twenty-two-year career has Brady not won more than ten games, and we must go back twenty years to find it—his only 9–7 season. His career regular-season record is 242–73. Otto Graham won seven titles with the Browns, but he left the game when he was thirty-four years old. Brady was just getting started at thirty-four. Brady has played in forty-seven playoff games, winning thirty-five and losing just twelve. Besides his seven Super Bowl wins, he has also played in ten Super Bowls, losing two to the New York Giants in 2007 and 2011. Getting to the final four is a mark of excellence, and Brady has done that thirteen times over his NFL career. Who will ever make that claim again? No one wins more than Brady, and it's hard to imagine anyone will ever break his playoff record. His ability to win games, regular or postseason, is unmatched.

Number Three: Build Passion
with Rare Competitiveness

When I hear Bruce Springsteen discuss how his challenging relationship with his father fueled his passion for his career and created the voice he shared with his audience, it reminds me of how Brady uses the neglect he faced, from college recruiters to the NFL draft, to fuel his competitive spirit each day. He never has forgotten that professional evaluators failed to understand his play and his excellence, and he uses the oversight to fire up his engine. All great players on this top 100 list share have the competitive drive, and those in the top ten seem to have a little more of it. And Brady, like GOATs from other sports, has it the most.

Number Four: Rewrite History

When Nolan Ryan was forty-four years old and pitching for the Texas Rangers, he went 12–6, had a 2.91 ERA, and threw 173 innings, striking out 203 batters, which is amazing and hard to imagine, except when you look at Brady. At forty-four, Brady has attempted the most passes in his career (719), completed the most (485), and thrown for forty-three touchdowns, the second most in a single season in his career. He continues to destroy the record books for passing because of his incredible ability to execute. Brady is deadly accurate, with pinpoint precision. He isn't the point guard who will turn the ball over; he is only going to throw the ball to receivers he trusts to run the correct route and to be in the exact spot of the pass. A lack of trust is the reason that some players don't sync with Brady on the field and fail to achieve the numbers and break the records he has broken. Brady needs perfect timing and details in the route running, which isn't always the case for some younger receivers. They feel they can ad lib or run a half-assed route. When they do, two things happen—they get their assed ripped in the huddle and they never see another pass.

Number Five: Score Points

Brady's 624 touchdown passes are currently fifty-three ahead of the closest competition, and he will add more in the 2022 season. From 2001 until he left in 2020 (with the exception of 2008), Brady scored 8,037 points with the Patriots, averaging a shade under twenty-eight points per game. The Patriots scored over four hundred points ten times; over five hundred four times, and under four hundred just five times. While he was the Patriots, the only time the offense scored fewer than four hundred points was in 2006.

Brady walked away for forty days after the 2021 season, only to return to attend to his unfinished business, although it is hard to imagine what has been left undone. He has shown no signs of aging when playing in 2021, as Michael Jordan did when with the Wizards, or Hank Aaron when with the Brewers. He looks and appears as if he could play ten more years, and none of us are laughing at the suggestion. Brady is the GOAT, graded a A9.9—above everyone else.

ACKNOWLEDGMENTS

This book would never have been written without the love and support from my wife Millie and our two sons, Mick and Matthew, along with their wives, Michelle and Julie, and their fabulous five children, Dominic, Leo, Michael, Dean, and our only girl Sienna. Millie's love and devotion reflects in those she touches and—for more than half my life—she's touched and tremendously improved mine.

My mother passed down her love of writing to me and even though she never was able to read either of my books, her presence shines brightly on every page—thirteen years after she closed her eyes for the last time, her voice still rings loudly in my ear. As Jim Nantz eloquently wrote, my father Mike isn't cutting hair any longer, but he still wishes he was. His work ethic and love of his craft were the greatest gifts any father can give a son. For that I am forever grateful. And since he and my Uncle Fred Palermo are still moving along at 96, they both deserve praise and each week on my podcast, The GM Shuffle, Uncle Fred's wisdom makes an appearance. My second mother, Marie Barry, deserves special thanks as well; her existence in my life over the last 30 years has been a godsend and, at 96, she continues to keep charging. And to my Aunt Gloria Gordan, my mother's best friend and the kindest woman ever, I am thankful.

Life never slows down. Along the way we lose those near and dear to our hearts, causing us to look back with fondness and love. From my wonderful in-laws Stosh and Lucille Kluzinski, their sons Michael and Stanley, my cousin-in law Nina Lombardi, my Uncle Mike Palermo, his wife Betty, my Uncle Charley (who almost made that 100-year milestone), to my friends and mentors who helped shaped my football career, Frank Sciro, John Cervino, and John McVay—I miss you all each day.

I extend special thanks to the rest of my family: my sister Marie and her husband Tom; my cousin Big Daddy Vince (as he has become famously known on The GM Shuffle) and his partner Susan; my nieces and nephews—Dr. Alyssa Lombardi and her husband Jeff, Dr. Nick Lombardi and his partner Dr. Hannah, and Sgt. Joe Lombardi and his wife Veronica; my wonderful niece Michelle Kluzinski and her mother Yeimy; my cousin MaryAnne Coggins and her husband

Tom, who are loyal Eagles fan and the best dog/house sitters ever; and the self-proclaimed Mayor of Ocean City, Sal Deldoe and his wife Barbara, who passed away, but made the best chocolate cookies this fat boy has ever eaten.

To my second family, the Nolan's—Pat (the most interesting man in the world) and Bernadette (my second wife), along with their children Patrick, Justin and his wife Melissa, and Katie and her husband Mike (the biggest Giant fan ever), along with their children Michael and Lilly—thank you.

I'm truly blessed to have found Bill Berman, my "almost brother," who I met strolling down the alley one day near my home in Ocean City. Since then, my family has extended to entire Berman clan. Bill offered advice and counsel with each page. I am forever thankful. By finding Bill, I've added three very special woman to my life—his wife Anissa, the nicest of the nice, and their daughters, Abby and Anna, both of whom have allowed me to enjoy life with teenage daughters, thankfully part time.

Lifelong friends are the greatest gifts we can receive during our journey in this world. Brilliant wordsmith Jim Nantz was generous with his time and thoughts and I appreciate his willingness to be a part of this book. Marc Badian, persistent with his original idea for the book, was a constant source of comments, ideas, and *Seinfeld* references. I cherished his review of each chapter

I am deeply thankful for all my friends who have always helped along the way: the Daily Coach team comprised of George Raveling, Alex Cervasio, and Kimati Ramsey; my entire VSiN family, starting with the legend Brent Musburger and his brother Todd and son Brian, who had the original idea for VSiN, along with Bill Adee (a wordsmith in his own right), my cohost Patrick Meagher, Mike Palm, Femi Abebefe, Elliott Bauman, and the many others who help make my job at VSiN wonderful; Paul Brady; Don Martindale; Gil Brandt; Sean Sweeney; Adnan Virk; Tom Crean; Eric Musselman; Buzz Williams; Chris Ballard; Ed Dodds; Tony Galante; Dr. Anthony Alfieri; Dr. Stephen; Peter Abate; Will Hill; Ken Scigulinsky; Jay Kelleher; Dr. Sam Vainisi and his late brother Jerry; and Thomas Gable.

Rick Gosselin was an enormous help providing research and suggestions for the book. His knowledge of the game and his love of the history are Hall of Fame worthy. Ron Wolf doesn't need another gold jacket—he is already in the Hall—but his assistance in shaping this book was incredibly valuable. So was the help and support of my agents Jim Levine and Courtney Paganelli and the crafting and shaping support from my wonderful editor Randall Lotowycz and the faith provided by Jess Riordan and the rest of the Running Press team. I am forever grateful to everyone else who lent a hand with the book, starting with the great Joel Solomon, who offered sage advice, and my first editor and reader Trevor Kapp, as well as others who shared their wisdom—Bill Parcells, Jimmy Johnson, Ernie Accorsi, Bill Keenist, Bob McGinn, Peter King, Rick Venturi, Alex Gracini, John McClain, Harvey Hyde, Ryan Holiday, Shane Parish, Jim Dixon and the great Peter Kaufman, who devotes his life to helping others.

I owe an enormous debt of gratitude to Bill Belichick and his willingness to share his wisdom and thoughts on the game he loves and has studied for over six decades. His friendship is one of my life's most treasured gifts and, without his willingness to teach and share, I would have not been able to write a single sentence. Many of the pages of this book are filled with the wisdom passed down to me from the greatest of the greats—Bill Walsh and Al Davis. Both men shaped my career and there isn't a day that passes when I am not thankful for their kindness.

I am a faithful lifelong member of the Church of Bruce Springsteen. I never would have embarked on my football journey had I not heard Bruce preaching to cross Highway 9, to "show a little faith, there's magic in the night." His words changed my life and gave me the inspiration needed to chase a dream, which I am still chasing. As a practicing partitioner, I read the gospel according to Saint Bruce daily and hang on his every word.

And going along with the lovely proverb, "If the kindest souls were rewarded with the longest lives, dogs would outlive us all," Bella and Lana are the kindest of all. They both shared my writing room every day without complaining or judging. A few cookies always helped their boredom.